Criminal Litigation and Legal Issues in Criminal Procedure

Readings and Hypothetical Exercises

Fifth Edition

Criminal Litigation and Legal Issues in Criminal Procedure

Readings and Hypothetical Exercises

Fifth Edition

Brent E. Newton

Attorney at Law

NITA®

National Institute for Trial Advocacy

Address inquiries to:
Reprint Permission
National Institute for Trial Advocacy
325 West South Boulder Road, Suite 1
Louisville, CO 80027
Phone: (800) 225-6482
Email: permissions@nita.org

ISBN: 979-8-88669-000-2
FBA 2000
eISBN: 979-8-88669-001-9
eFBA 2001

Library of Congress Cataloging-in-Publication Data
Names: Newton, Brent E., 1967- author.
Title: Criminal litigation and legal issues in criminal procedure: readings and hypothetical exercises / Brent E. Newton, of Counsel, Gerger, Hennessy & Martin.
Description: Fifth edition. | Boulder, CO : NITA, National Institute for Trial Advocacy, [2022]
Identifiers: LCCN 2022035640 (print) | LCCN 2022035641 (ebook) | ISBN 9798886690002 (paperback) | ISBN 9798886690019 (ebook)
Subjects: LCSH: Criminal procedure--United States--Problems, exercises, etc. | Trial practice--United States--Problems, exercises, etc. | LCGFT: Problems and exercises.
Classification: LCC KF9619.85 .N49 2022 (print) | LCC KF9619.85 (ebook) | DDC 345.73/05--dc23/eng/20221031
LC record available at https://lccn.loc.gov/2022035640
LC ebook record available at https://lccn.loc.gov/2022035641

Printed in the United States.

Wolters Kluwer

Official co-publisher of NITA.
WKLegaledu.com/NITA

SUSTAINABLE FORESTRY INITIATIVE
Certified Chain of Custody
Promoting Sustainable Forestry
www.sfiprogram.org

Dedicated to my wife, Tirza Bartels, and my daughters,
Anna and Georgia Bartels-Newton

CONTENTS

Class One

Introduction

1.1 Introduction and Course Overview

Criminal Litigation and Legal Issues in Criminal Procedure incorporates the substantive law of criminal procedure into a trial advocacy course. The traditional trial advocacy course focuses exclusively on "skills training" (e.g., learning techniques for cross-examining a witness), but incorporates little, if any, substantive law. Conversely, a traditional substantive criminal law or criminal procedure course focuses exclusively on legal principles and doctrine, ignoring the courtroom advocacy skills that encompass substantive law. *Criminal Litigation and Legal Issues in Criminal Procedure* merges elements from both course types into one to bridge the gap between them.

Organized into a fourteen-class structure, this book covers virtually all of the stages of a criminal case—from the probable cause hearing through the sentencing hearing and hearing on a motion for a new trial. The substantive and procedural law covered is national in scope and is not limited to any particular jurisdiction. Most of the issues addressed in this course implicate federal constitutional law principles that apply to all criminal prosecutions, whether they occur in state or federal court; occasionally, the exercises will involve nonconstitutional federal law (e.g., the United States Sentencing Guidelines).

Each class includes a brief lecture about the substantive law applicable to the stage at issue. The remainder of each class consists of oral advocacy exercises involving factual hypotheticals that implicate the relevant substantive law principles. The exercises require each student to play the role of either defense counsel or prosecutor.[1] The hypotheticals involve fully developed factual scenarios. No additional factual development is required.

Unlike a traditional criminal law or criminal procedure course where students are expected to finish the course having mastered a wide breadth of knowledge about substantive law issues, *Criminal Litigation and Legal Issues in Criminal Procedure* seeks to provide students with the basic skills to use substantive law in the courtroom. Writing a masterful exam answer in a substantive course, while an

---

1. Each week, the students alternate roles. Some students may have predilections towards one side or the other, but during this course each student must play both roles in a zealous manner.

important part of legal education, is one thing. Standing on your feet and orally advocating a legal point in a precise and persuasive manner is another. The latter involves speech and debate skills in the context of legal advocacy; it will be the focus of this course.[2]

Unlike a traditional trial advocacy course or a mock trial competition, this course uses no "live" witnesses. Rather, students make legal arguments or otherwise use substantive law based solely on the factual hypotheticals provided. The exercises seek to hone students' *advocacy* skills and, in particular, students' ability to marshal the relevant legal principles as applied to the factual hypotheticals. Effective legal advocacy on substantive law issues is a skill that all litigators, including criminal law litigators, need to master. Researching legal issues and effectively arguing a legal position in written form is, of course, an important arrow in a litigator's quiver. All too many attorneys, including many criminal law practitioners, lack the skills to effectively advocate legal issues orally.

Most of the oral advocacy exercises involve legal arguments to a trial court (a role played by the instructor). On two occasions—voir dire and closing arguments—students advocate to a jury (played by fellow students). The two types of legal advocacy—one to a judge, the other to a lay jury—involve different approaches, which will be addressed during the course.

In this course, students are assigned their factual hypotheticals and role-playing assignments one week before each class. In addition to the hypotheticals, students should read the assigned materials for each class and prepare oral presentations. No additional legal research is necessary. In fact, to ensure that both sides' arguments are premised on a discrete body of law, students should not engage in additional research.

Except for the first class, every student will make a short oral presentation each week. Depending on the number of students in the course, each student's presentation will be approximately five to ten minutes in length. The instructor—and eventually fellow students, as the semester progresses—will play the role of trial judge during exercises. The instructor and fellow students will critique each student after their presentation. As this course progresses and students get more practice, each student's comfort level and proficiency in legal speech and debate skills should improve.

1.2 The Stages of a Criminal Prosecution

Understanding the rules of criminal procedure and applying them in practice requires a basic understanding of the process in a typical noncapital felony prosecution. What follows is a brief "flowchart" of a typical case:

2. This course is designed either to be taken concurrently with (or after) a traditional criminal procedure course or to be taken as a "stand-alone" course. Criminal Procedure is not a prerequisite for Criminal Litigation.

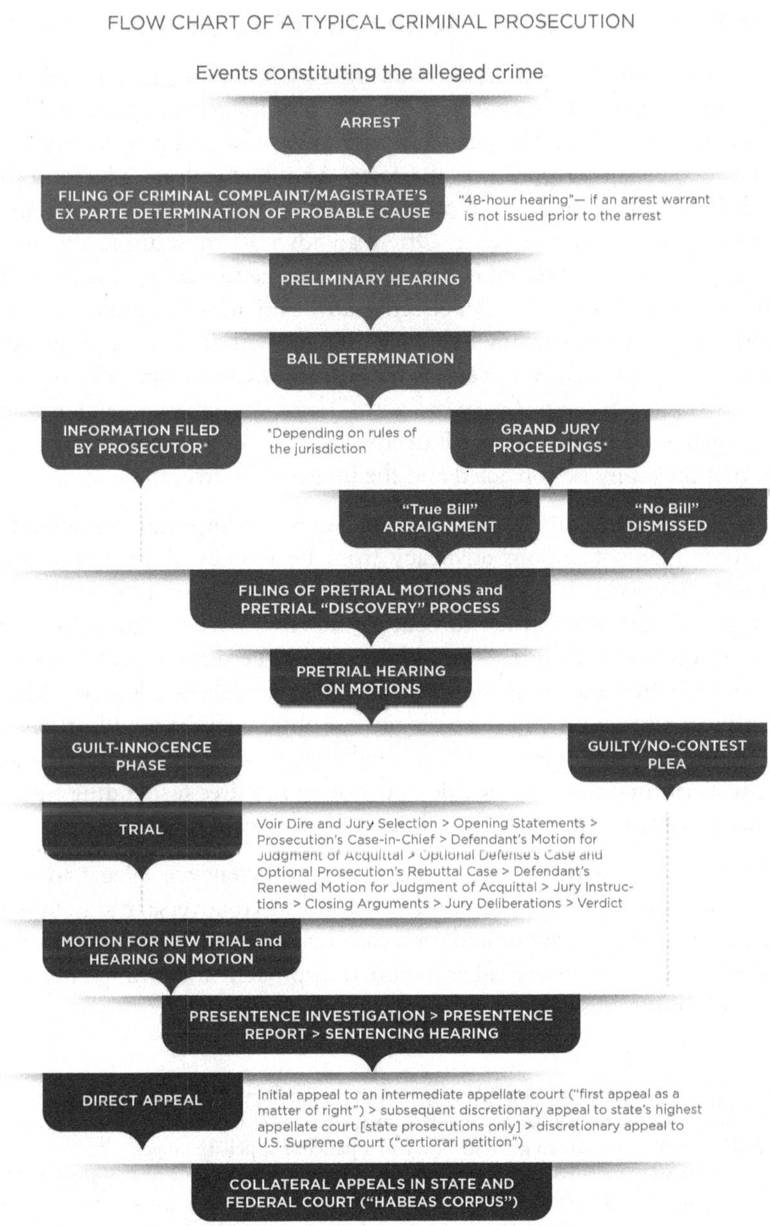

There are variations in the stages of a criminal prosecution, depending on the jurisdiction. However, criminal prosecutions in most jurisdictions, at least in felony cases, include these different stages. We will assume, for purposes of this course, that a criminal prosecution in the hypothetical jurisdiction of Nita—in which our factual hypotheticals occur—includes these different stages.

1.3 A Brief Introduction to the Art of Legal Advocacy

There are two main types of legal advocacy—advocacy to a judge[3] and advocacy to a jury. The former involves a partisan discussion of the relevant facts and law, typically emphasizing the law. The latter likewise involves a partisan discussion of the facts and law, typically emphasizing the facts. An effective legal advocate, whether making their pitch to a judge or to jurors, is part actor, part legal scholar, and part sagacious conveyer of common sense. Often, an advocate must argue a position that may be contrary to their personal beliefs about some factual or legal issue—which is where the "part actor" comes in. An effective advocate must champion that position enthusiastically, even if personally they may disagree with it. The role of an advocate necessarily is to be partisan for their client, at least where the advocate's position is nonfrivolous.[4] As the Supreme Court has said, "The very premise of our adversary system of criminal justice . . . is that partisan advocacy . . . will best promote the ultimate objective that the guilty be convicted and the innocent go free."[5]

Our adversarial criminal justice system includes one important exception to the general requirement of zealous advocacy from both sides. A prosecutor, while a lawyer and legal advocate, is also a public servant whose first and foremost duty is to do justice.[6] Occasionally, the prosecutor's role as a partisan advocate and their obligation to do justice collide. When that occurs, the duty to seek justice is paramount, even if that means forsaking the role as a zealous advocate. Many law students (like many lawyers) have ideological or philosophical predilections toward either the prosecution or defense in a criminal case. Learning to be an effective legal advocate in a criminal case for one side or the other requires suspending such beliefs and learning to argue effectively from both perspectives.

The ability to argue both sides enhances your proficiency as a legal advocate. In the English criminal justice system, on which our own adversary system is based, a private barrister may be appointed on a case-by-case basis to prosecute or defend in criminal cases.[7] This course takes a similar approach to learning effective legal advocacy in criminal cases.

---

3. You may engage in advocacy to multiple judges in the case of appellate advocacy. This course does not address the specialized legal advocacy involved in appeals, although legal advocacy to a single trial judge is similar in many respects to legal advocacy to a panel of appellate judges.
4. Even the most passionate advocates should not make frivolous legal or factual arguments. A legal frivolity is an argument "squarely foreclosed by statute, rule, or authoritative court decision"; such binding legal authority is not subject to being reconsidered or overruled. Barefoot v. Estelle, 463 U.S. 880, 894 (1983). A factual frivolity "is lacking any factual basis in the record of the case." *Id.*
5. Herring v. New York, 422 U.S. 853, 862 (1975).
6. *See* Berger v. United States, 295 U.S. 78, 88 (1935) (explaining that a prosecutor is "the representative not of an ordinary party to a controversy, but of a sovereignty whose obligation to govern impartially is as compelling as its obligation to govern at all; and whose interest, therefore, in a criminal prosecution is not that it shall win a case, but that justice shall be done").
7. *See* Peter W. Teague, *Guilty Pleas and Barristers' Incentives: Lessons from England*, 20 Geo. J. Legal Ethics 287, 289 & n. 9 (2007).

Mastering the art of effective legal advocacy comes only from repeated practice, which is why this course involves weekly exercises. Some people are better at advocating in writing; others are better advocating orally. The two skills draw on related talents—in particular, analytical ability and a facility with language. Effective oral advocacy, however, requires a certain dramatic ability, channeled passion, self-confidence, and comfort with interpersonal interaction that written advocacy does not.

Every aspiring litigator has a "natural advocate" inside—their own personal style that cannot be taught. For every one of you, that natural advocate has appeared throughout your life in contexts other than the legal arena—anytime you have felt passionately about some matter and, using reason and logic, have genuinely expressed that passion when seeking to convince another person of the merit of your position. Such natural advocacy is not contrived or artificial; it reflects your genuine personality and emotions. This course will help you discover the natural advocate inside yourself and harness it in the special context of legal advocacy.

1.4 The Factual Hypotheticals and Corresponding Case Law

With a few exceptions (noted in the hypotheticals), the factual scenarios in this course occur in or around the fictional Nita City, located in the fictional State of Nita. Nita is located in the fictional Twelfth United States Circuit. Some of the hypothetical cases occur in state trial court in Nita; others occur in federal district court in Nita.

In the vast majority of hypotheticals, the relevant dates do not include the years (only the months and days). Do not assume that such dates occurred on any particular days of the week (unless specific days of the week are mentioned in a particular hypothetical). In a small number of hypotheticals, specific years are mentioned because those years are relevant to the hypothetical exercises.

Each hypothetical assigns case law and occasionally also a statute, sentencing guideline, or pattern jury instruction. Most of the assigned cases to be read in conjunction with the hypotheticals are actual decisions of federal circuit courts or state supreme courts. Treat these lower court appellate decisions as nonbinding, persuasive precedent in state and federal trial courts located in Nita. The remainder of the assigned cases are actual decisions of the Supreme Court of the United States, which, of course, must be treated as *binding* precedent[8] in a state or federal trial court in Nita (just as they would be in a state or federal trial court located in a real state). We have assigned persuasive case law from another jurisdiction's appellate courts to invite legal arguments based on persuasive authority when no applicable binding case law exists. *When case law from other jurisdictions has been assigned, assume the legal issues in the hypothetical exercises present issues of first impression for*

8. Assigned statutes or sentencing guidelines are binding (as opposed to persuasive) authority.

the state or federal trial court in Nita. The assigned cases from other jurisdictions often include majority, concurring, and dissenting opinions. Rely on concurring or dissenting opinions if they best support the position you advocate during the hypothetical exercises.

Time permitting, familiarize yourself with all five of the hypotheticals and the corresponding legal authorities assigned each week. Each student will be required to make a weekly presentation on only one of the five assigned hypotheticals. Some level of familiarity with the other four hypotheticals and the legal issues implicated by them will enhance your knowledge of the substantive law and foster meaningful critiques of fellow students' presentations. In addition, as the course progresses, students increasingly will be assigned the role of the trial judge in some of the exercises—meaning that during at least some weeks of the course, you will be required to prepare not only for your presentation as an advocate, but also for the role of trial judge in different hypothetical exercises.

Class Two

Preliminary Hearings

After a defendant is arrested (with or without a warrant), they may be entitled to a preliminary hearing, which also is commonly referred to as a "preliminary examination" or a "probable cause hearing."[1] In most jurisdictions, the right to a preliminary hearing expires once a grand jury has returned an indictment.[2] A preliminary hearing is not required by the United States Constitution, although the right is generally afforded by statute or court rule in every jurisdiction.[3] In federal court, defendants charged with felonies and nonpetty misdemeanors have a statutory right to a preliminary hearing; in many state courts, only defendants charged with felonies have a statutory right to a preliminary hearing.[4] Although not required by the Constitution, a preliminary hearing is nonetheless a "critical stage" of the proceedings at which a defendant is entitled to the assistance of counsel and other procedural protections.[5]

In some jurisdictions, preliminary hearings rarely occur—most defendants waive them or are indicted by a grand jury before a preliminary hearing can be conducted. In other jurisdictions, such as California and the federal system, preliminary hearings are much more commonplace.

A preliminary hearing is an adversarial proceeding in which the prosecution has the burden to establish "probable cause" that the defendant committed the charged offense. If the magistrate or judge who conducts a preliminary hearing determines that probable cause exists, the charges remain and the defendant is "bound over" (i.e., detained without bond or released on bond) pending the grand jury's hearing of the case or disposition of the charges by a guilty plea (in the event the defendant waives their right to a grand jury).[6]

A preliminary hearing should be distinguished from the ex parte proceeding at which a magistrate or judge determines whether probable cause exists after a

---

1. *See, e.g.*, Fed. R. Crim. P. 5.1; Cal. Pen. Code § 872; Tex. Code Crim. Proc. Art. 16.01.
2. *See, e.g.*, Jaben v. United States, 381 U.S. 214, 220 (1965); Bowens v. Superior Court, 820 P.2d 600 (Cal. 1991).
3. United States v. Coley, 441 F.2d 1299, 1301 (5th Cir. 1971).
4. *See, e.g.*, Fed. R. Crim. P. 5.1(a); People v. Reno, 272 N.W.2d 144 (Mich. App. 1978).
5. *See, e.g.*, Coleman v. Alabama, 399 U.S. 1 (1970) (providing for right to counsel at preliminary hearing).
6. *See generally* Yale Kamisar et al., Modern Criminal Procedure 1007–37 (12th ed. 2008).

defendant has been arrested without a warrant. The latter is sometimes referred to as a "forty-eight-hour hearing" or a "*Gerstein* hearing" and is required by the Fourth Amendment of the United States Constitution.[7] Such an ex parte proceeding is not an adversary hearing—the defendant is not represented by counsel at such a hearing and the "proceeding" is typically nothing more than a magistrate's or judge's review of an affidavit of an arresting officer to determine whether probable cause exists to support the warrantless arrest.

Even to a greater degree than the ex parte "forty-eight-hour hearing," the preliminary hearing serves a "screening" function. That is, its primary function is "to discover whether or not there are substantial grounds upon which a prosecution may be based."[8] The preliminary hearing has secondary purposes as well, including the preservation of testimony (to impeach the witness at trial or to allow the testimony to be admitted as substantive evidence at trial if the witness later becomes unavailable) and pretrial discovery of the prosecution's evidence by the defense.[9]

As noted, at a preliminary hearing, a magistrate or judge must find that "probable cause" exists to "bind over" a defendant. The U.S. Supreme Court has elusively defined that quantum of proof in the following manner:

> The substance of all the definitions of probable cause is a reasonable ground for belief of guilt. And this means less than evidence which would justify . . . conviction. . . . [I]t mean[s] more than bare suspicion[.] Probable cause exists where the facts and circumstances within [a person's] knowledge and of which [he or she] had reasonably trustworthy information [are] sufficient in themselves to warrant a man of reasonable caution in the belief that an offense has been . . . committed [and that the defendant committed it].[10]

Probable cause is thus a lesser quantum of proof than a "preponderance" of the evidence, "clear and convincing" evidence, and "proof beyond a reasonable doubt." It is, however, greater than the quantum of "reasonable suspicion" required for *Terry* stops and similar law enforcement encounters governed by less than probable cause.[11]

---

7. Gerstein v. Pugh, 420 U.S. 103 (1975) (holding that such an ex parte determination of probable cause is required by the Fourth Amendment). It is called a "forty-eight-hour" hearing because the Supreme Court has held that, under the Fourth Amendment, such an ex parte proceeding generally must occur within forty-eight hours of the defendant's arrest in order to be constitutional. *See* County of Riverside v. McLaughlin, 500 U.S. 44 (1991).
8. Thies v. State, 189 N.W. 539, 541 (Wis. 1922).
9. Kamisar et al., supra n. 6, at 1014–18.
10. Brinegar v. United States, 338 U.S. 160, 175–76 (1949) (citations and internal quotation marks omitted).
11. *See* Terry v. Ohio, 392 U.S. 1 (1968). *See also* infra Class 5.

In criminal law, "probable cause" is used in at least four contexts: 1) the quantum of proof required for a police officer to arrest a person for an offense without an arrest warrant or to engage in a warrantless search for or seizure of contraband or incriminating evidence (which is the same standard governing a magistrate or judge who issues an arrest warrant or search warrant);[12] 2) the quantum of proof required for a magistrate or judge to sustain a warrantless arrest at an ex parte "*Gerstein* hearing"; 3) the quantum of proof required for a magistrate or judge to "bind over" a defendant at the conclusion of a preliminary hearing; and 4) the quantum of proof required for a grand jury to return an indictment. Although theoretically the four types of probable cause mean the same thing, in reality they each mean something slightly different.

The most demanding variant of probable cause appears to be the quantum of proof that magistrates or judges require to bind over defendants at the conclusion of preliminary hearings.[13] Logically, the quantum of proof governing a grand jury should be the most demanding, considering that dismissal of charges at a preliminary hearing does not bar a subsequent indictment by a grand jury. However, it is widely believed that many grand juries do not actually apply the probable cause standard in any meaningful way—thus the adage, "a grand jury will indict a ham sandwich."[14]

In the vast majority of jurisdictions, when determining probable cause at a preliminary hearing, a magistrate or judge is not constrained by the Fourth or Fifth Amendment's exclusionary rules concerning physical evidence and confessions.[15] That is, illegally seized evidence or an illegally obtained confession (e.g., one obtained without *Miranda* warnings) is admissible at a preliminary hearing. However, the jurisdictions are divided over whether the rules of evidence (including the general rule against hearsay) apply at a preliminary hearing, although most jurisdictions permit probable cause determinations to be based on hearsay.[16] In virtually all jurisdictions, a defendant is not permitted to defeat a finding of probable cause by presenting evidence of an affirmative defense to the charges (such as insanity or entrapment) and, instead, is only permitted to offer truly "exculpatory" evidence that negates an essential element of the charged offense.[17]

---

12. *See* Whiteley v. Warden, 401 U.S. 560, 566 (1971) (probable cause standard governing police officers who engage in a warrantless search or seizure is the same as the standard governing a judicial official who issues a search or arrest warrant).
13. *See* Williams v. Kobel, 789 F.2d 463, 468–69 (7th Cir. 1986); Hunter v. District Court, 543 P.2d 1265, 1270–71 (Colo. 1975) (Erickson, J., dissenting) (citing cases and Model Code of Pre-Arraignment Procedure 596–97); Myers v. Commonwealth, 298 N.E.2d 819, 823–24 (Mass. 1973).
14. *See* People v. Carter, 566 N.E.2d 119, 124 (N.Y. 1990) (Titone, J., dissenting).
15. *See* Fed. R. Crim. P. 5.1(e); *see also* State v. Kane, 588 A.2d 179, 184 (Conn. 1991).
16. *Compare* Fed. R. Evid. 1101(d)(3) (rules of evidence inapplicable at federal preliminary hearing), *with* Tex. Code Crim. Proc. art. 16.07 (rules of evidence applicable at Texas preliminary hearing).
17. Kamisar et al., supra n. 6, at 1037.

In most jurisdictions, magistrates or judges who preside over preliminary hearings are generally permitted to make only limited credibility determinations about evidence, even when the defense has introduced competing evidence to rebut the prosecution's evidence.[18] Generally, the court should not make credibility determinations or weigh competing evidence when determining whether there is probable cause; the charges may be dismissed based on credibility determinations only if the magistrate or judge reasonably concludes that the prosecution's evidence or witnesses are incredible as a matter of law.[19] Furthermore, many courts have stressed that a preliminary hearing is not a "mini-trial" and thus a magistrate or judge presiding over the proceeding should not permit the defense a full-fledged opportunity to rebut the prosecution's case—an opportunity that is afforded to the defendant at a subsequent trial.[20] Therefore, if, after a reasonable yet limited opportunity for the defense to cross-examine the prosecution's witnesses and offer exculpatory evidence in rebuttal, the evidence *viewed in a light most favorable to the prosecution* establishes probable cause, then the defendant will be bound over.[21]

Hypothetical One: Preliminary Hearings

State v. Smith

On Friday, January 7, around 11:30 p.m., Nita City police officer **Samuel Jones** was patrolling Richmond Avenue in Nita City in his police cruiser when he noticed two young men, who appeared to be in their late teens, standing in a dimly lit parking lot outside of the Rave Dance Club. The Rave Dance Club is an "18–20 club" that caters to persons eighteen to twenty years old (persons old enough to stay out past Nita City's 11:00 p.m. curfew for minors, but not old enough to legally go to a club that serves alcohol). Officer Jones was aware of the Rave Dance Club's reputation for illegal "rave parties," where some persons who come to the club buy, sell, and use illegal drugs, in particular "ecstasy" (chemically known as MDMA). Nita City Police Department records show that, during the past two years, officers made four separate arrests at or very near the club for ecstasy possession. All four arrests resulted in convictions.

Officer Jones noticed that the two young men—later identified as **Rob Smith** and **Peter Brown**, each nineteen years old—appeared to be exchanging a small object hand-to-hand. At the subsequent preliminary hearing, when questioned about what he had seen, Officer Jones testified that he did not see what the object

18. *See, e.g.*, Desper v. State, 318 S.E.2d 437 (W. Va. 1984); Myers v. Commonwealth, 298 N.E.2d 819 (Mass. 1973).

19. *See, e.g.*, Hunter v. District Court, 543 P.2d 1265 (Colo. 1975).

20. *See, e.g.*, Coleman v. Burnett, 477 F.2d 1187, 1201 (D.C. Cir. 1973).

21. *See* Williams v. Kobel, 789 F.2d 463, 468–69 (7th Cir. 1986); *see also* People v. Hall, 999 P.2d 207 (Colo. 2000).

was nor could he say which of the two men passed the unknown object to the other man.

Officer Jones drove his car around the block and returned to the Rave Dance Club approximately fifteen minutes after first seeing Smith and Brown. This time, he noticed Smith and Brown entering a Yellow Taxi cab in the club's parking lot. Suspicious that they possessed illegal contraband, Officer Jones pulled over the cab by activating his patrol car's lights and siren.

As he approached the cab, Officer Jones saw both Smith and Brown sitting in the backseat of the cab. Officer Jones asked the cab driver if he could search inside the cab, including in the backseat, and the cab driver consented to such a search. Officer Jones found no incriminating evidence inside the cab.

At that point, Officer Jones asked Smith and Brown if he could search their pockets and wallets. Without hesitation, Smith consented to such a search. Inside Smith's pockets were house keys, a package of condoms, and a pack of chewing gum. Smith had $124 in cash in his wallet (six $20 bills and four $1 bills). No drugs or other contraband were found on Smith. Brown refused to consent to a search of his person and stated, "I want a lawyer. I know my rights." Officer Jones nevertheless searched Brown and discovered a glow stick, a baby's pacifier, and a small baggie containing six pink pills of ecstasy in Brown's pocket.[22] Brown had $80 in his wallet (all in $20 bills). Officer Jones arrested both Smith and Brown for possession of ecstasy.[23] Without reading the teens their *Miranda* warnings, Officer Jones asked them what object they had exchanged in the parking lot. At virtually the same time, Brown said, "Nothing" and Smith said, "A pack of rubbers, man." Neither man said anything further.

At the subsequent preliminary hearing, Officer Jones testified about the foregoing events and also testified that he had over ten years of experience in working on many dozens of drug cases, including those involving ecstasy. He testified that glow sticks and pacifiers are commonly used by persons using ecstasy during illegal rave parties. He further testified that ecstasy pills ordinarily sell for between $10 and $20 per pill at the retail level. He opined that six pills—the amount that Brown possessed—is "a quantity that is consistent with either personal use or small-scale distribution, such as would occur at a rave club."

When cross-examined by defense counsel, Officer Jones testified that when he took Smith and Brown into custody, no blood or urine tests were performed to determine whether either man had illegal drugs in his system. Officer Jones stated that a fingerprint test had not been performed on the plastic baggie containing the

---

22. Officer Jones performed a field test on one of the pills and determined that, in fact, it was MDMA.

23. The elements of this offense are 1) knowingly 2) possessing (either alone or jointly with another person) 3) a controlled substance. Ecstasy is a controlled substance.

ecstasy tablets and that the baggie had been thrown away (but the pills had been preserved). Officer Jones testified that neither Smith nor Brown had a prior criminal record.

Prosecutor: Argue that there is probable cause to bind over Smith.

Defense Counsel: Argue that there is not probable cause to bind over Smith.

To prepare for this hypothetical exercise, read *Maryland v. Pringle*, 540 U.S. 366 (2003), and *State v. Bockert*, 893 P.2d 832 (Kan. 1995) (majority and dissenting opinions).

Hypothetical Two: Preliminary Hearings

State v. Baker

At 10:30 a.m. on March 23, **Maria Gonzalez** was walking down Main Street in Nita City when a young man ran up behind her and stole her purse from her arm. Gonzalez did not get a good look at the young man's face, but she was able to describe him as being a white male in his "late teens, early twenties" and being "medium build" and "approximately 5'10" to 6'1" tall." No other eyewitnesses were available when police officers arrived.

Gonzalez's purse contained a wallet (with a $20 bill in it, but no other money) and a checkbook with a new book of checks in the name of Gonzalez and her husband, **Martin Gonzalez**. The checks, numbered 2001–2040, were on a Bank of Nita account. Gonzalez immediately contacted her bank and placed a hold on her checking account.

At 1:30 p.m. on the same day, **Calvin Baker**, a forty-nine-year-old Black man, appeared at the teller's line inside a branch of Bank of Nita in Nita City that was approximately five miles from the scene of the crime. Baker was 5'7" tall and weighed 230 pounds.

Baker presented check number 2001 in the amount of $200 purportedly signed by Martin Gonzalez[24] and made out to "Calvin Baker." The "memo" section of the check stated "tools." The check was wrinkled, and the handwriting and signature on it were not neatly written. The date was misspelled "Merch 24." Baker presented his valid driver's license when he approached the teller to cash the check.

The teller who initially waited on Baker discovered that there was a hold on the account (based on the theft of the checkbook that morning) and took the check to her manager. The manager called the police. A video recording of the bank's teller line showed Baker reading a magazine article as he waited for approximately

24. At the preliminary hearing, the arresting officer testified that Martin Gonzalez had denied being the one who wrote the check purportedly signed by him.

five minutes before the manager approached him. The bank's manager told him that "there is a problem with the check" and that "we need to verify funds." Baker responded in a firm, but polite manner: "That check is good. The man who bought my tools is a rich lawyer. I sold him my tools. Call the man, you'll see." Baker did not attempt to leave the teller's line.

A few moments later, the police arrived at the bank and approached Baker. Without arresting him and without reading him *Miranda* warnings, the police asked Baker where he got the check. Baker, who came across as unsophisticated and undereducated, responded:

> I got the check from a rich lawyer. A man who cuts his grass and takes care of his house asked to buy some tools from me. You know—an edger, a blower, and things like that. I sell that stuff from my truck. I buy them from pawn shops and yard sales and then sell them to the guys who cut grass and do landscape. This young dude, who I've seen before, came up to me at lunchtime and said this rich lawyer he works for would buy some of my tools for him to work on the lawyer's yard. The guy pointed to where the lawyer's house was. He said the lawyer had to write me a check so he could write it off on his taxes.

Baker admitted that he never actually saw the supposed lawyer,[25] but claimed to the police officers that he honestly believed that the lawyer was the one who wrote the check.

When the police asked the name of the man who claimed to work for the lawyer, Baker said, "I don't know his name. I've just seen him before." When asked for a physical description, Baker described him as "kinda thin." The police then arrested Baker on charges of possessing stolen property.[26] When he was searched after being arrested, the police found a $20 bill (and no other money) in his wallet. Maria Gonzalez was shown the $20 bill recovered from Baker's wallet, but she was unable to say whether it was the same $20 bill that was inside her purse.

At the subsequent preliminary hearing, the prosecution presented proof of the foregoing facts and also presented evidence that Baker had two prior misdemeanor marijuana possession convictions during the past decade and one 20-year-old misdemeanor shoplifting conviction. The defense presented testimony of **Roy McMillian**, owner and operator of Roy's Landscape Company in Nita City. McMillian testified that Baker used to work for him two years ago and that, since he stopped

25. Martin Gonzalez is not a lawyer.

26. The elements of this offense are 1) knowingly 2) possessing 3) property that was stolen from another person with either a) specific knowledge that the property was stolen or b) deliberate ignorance about whether the property was stolen. Merely being objectively negligent about whether the property was stolen does not qualify as "deliberate ignorance." To be guilty of this offense, a defendant at least must have been subjectively aware of a high probability that the property was stolen at the time that he took possession of the property.

working for McMillian, Baker regularly bought and sold tools. McMillian opined that in his prior dealings with Baker, the latter was "honest," but "very naïve and childlike at times."

Prosecutor: Argue that there is probable cause to bind over Baker.

Defense Counsel: Argue that there is not probable cause to bind over Baker.

To prepare for this hypothetical exercise, read *Maryland v. Pringle*, 540 U.S. 366 (2003), and *State v. Clark*, 20 P.3d 300 (Utah 2001).

Hypothetical Three: Preliminary Hearings

United States v. Meyers

On June 2, DEA agent **Ronald Green** was watching passengers deplane from an international flight from Bangkok, Thailand, to Nita City's international airport. Agent Green noticed two female passengers—later identified as **Ursula Morse** and **Janet Meyers**—get off the plane together and walk toward the Customs area for inspection. Agent Green became suspicious because the two women were wearing unusually tall "platform" high-heeled shoes (five-inch heels). During the past year, DEA agents around the country had discovered an increase in heroin smuggling from South America and Asia by women wearing hollowed-out platform shoes. Agent Green also noticed that Morse and Meyers repeatedly looked around the gate area and the customs inspection area—as if they were looking for law enforcement agents. Agent Green called for backup, and he and another DEA agent, a female, approached Morse and Meyers.

Agent Green identified himself and his associate as agents with the DEA and asked to see the two women's tickets and identification. Both Morse and Meyers handed over their tickets and identification. The women's IDs showed that they were residents of the states of Florida and Nita, respectively. Their tickets showed round-trip travel from Nita City to Bangkok. The tickets had been purchased with cash from a travel agent only two days before the flight had left from Nita City. The women had spent only two days in Bangkok before returning to Nita City. They each had only one small suitcase.

Agent Green then asked if he and his female partner could inspect the women's platform shoes. Both women, who appeared nervous, refused to consent to the search of their shoes. At that point, Agent Green asked the women to walk over to a private room in the customs inspection area. Inside that room, a trained narcotics dog sniffed the women's shoes. The dog reacted to Morse's shoes in a manner that indicated the presence of a controlled substance, but did not react to Meyers' shoes.

At that point, Agent Green demanded that both women remove their shoes. Both women removed their shoes, which were then x-rayed. The x-ray machine revealed that Morse's shoes were hollowed out and contained a dense substance inside the secret compartment. The x-ray revealed nothing abnormal about Meyers's shoes. Agent Green then drilled a hole in Morse's shoes and found a whitish-brown powder inside. A field test of the substance showed it to be heroin. All the powder was removed from Morse's shoes. It weighed approximately 500 grams.

Agent Green then arrested both Meyers and Morse for aiding and abetting each other in the possession of heroin.[27] Immediately after the arrests, Agent Green read the women their *Miranda* warnings and sought to interrogate them about the heroin. Each woman asked to speak to an attorney and refused to make a statement. Agent Green terminated the interview.

At the subsequent preliminary hearing, Agent Green testified about the foregoing facts. He also testified that it is extremely uncommon for travelers to purchase round-trip international flights with cash shortly before the flight leaves. Agent Green also testified that neither woman had a criminal record.

Prosecutor: Argue that there is probable cause to bind over Meyers.

Defense Counsel: Argue that there is not probable cause to bind over Meyers.

To prepare for this hypothetical exercise, read *Maryland v. Pringle*, 540 U.S. 366 (2003), and *State v. Bockert*, 893 P.2d 832 (Kan. 1995) (majority and dissenting opinions).

Hypothetical Four: Preliminary Hearings

United States v. Boyle

Herbert Boyle, a forty-five-year-old single man with no criminal record who lives alone in an apartment in Nita City, took his laptop computer to a local computer repair store for a repair. Boyle told the computer technician at the store that the computer inexplicably "locked up" when he was searching the Internet and required him to reboot. Boyle is a junior-high math teacher at a public school. He has never been married and has no children.

During the repair process, the computer technician noted that Boyle's hard drive was over 90 percent full of data, which was causing it to lock up. In examining the hard drive, the technician noticed many hundreds of images that had been downloaded from the Internet and were located in the web browser's "cache" of Boyle's computer.[28] Many of these images were sexually explicit photographs. The technician opened several files that appeared to depict young females; one of the images

27. The elements of this offense are 1) knowingly 2) possessing (either alone or jointly with another person) 3) a controlled substance. Heroin is a controlled substance.
28. The "cache" holds copies of recently accessed data such as a web page and pictures on web pages. When a computer user visits a website, the images on the web page are automatically placed in the cache without any specific action by the user.

appeared to depict nude prepubescent girls. The technician immediately contacted FBI agents, who came to the store, examined the images, and eventually seized the computer after obtaining a search warrant. Boyle was unaware that the technician had contacted the FBI. Boyle simply assumed the repair was taking longer than initially expected.

An FBI computer analyst examined the hard drive of Boyle's computer and located 4,457 sexually explicit files that had been downloaded from the Internet. Hundreds of such files contained images of young females, although an FBI medical expert determined that all but four such files contained images of females who were eighteen years old or older. Those hundreds of files had been downloaded from sexually explicit website that advertised "teen" pornography, but that contained the express disclaimer that the persons depicted were "eighteen years old or older at the time that the photographs were taken." Four of the files, including the one first discovered by the computer repair technician, contained pornographic images of prepubescent females (clearly below the age of eighteen). The computer analyst traced all four files to a single illegal website from Holland that unabashedly advertised illegal child pornography. A forensic analysis of Boyle's hard drive showed that his computer had been used to access that website, although it was not clear whether Boyle had intentionally accessed the website or, instead, whether he was unintentionally redirected to that website from a different website.

Based on the four child pornography images on Boyle's hard drive, the FBI obtained a search warrant for Boyle's apartment. Without any advance notice to Boyle that he was the subject of the FBI's investigation, the agents went to Boyle's apartment and executed the search warrant. After thoroughly searching Boyle's home, including computer disks that were found in his bedroom, the agents found no additional child pornography. The only sexually explicit materials found were legal adult pornographic magazines—with the models all being at least eighteen years old— although all of those magazines depicted "teen sex." Some of the images depicted models wearing school uniforms and their hair in pigtails. All such models clearly were intended to conjure up images of females below the age of eighteen years of age.[29] The agents also found several "family nudism" magazines that included nude yet legal photographs of prepubescent children. Such images were legal because they did not depict the nude children in a sexual context and, instead, depicted them in ordinary activities (e.g., playing volleyball).

Based solely on the four child pornography images found on Boyle's computer, the agents arrested and charged Boyle with possession of child pornography.[30]

---

29. Assume that pornography depicting persons eighteen years old or older who appear to be less than eighteen years old is legal.

30. The elements of that offense are 1) knowingly or intentionally 2) possessing or "accessing" 3) a photograph or computer image of 4) a person under eighteen years of age 5) who is engaged in sexual conduct or is in a sexually explicit position. There is no dispute in this case that the four

After being read his *Miranda* warnings and told what he was charged with, Boyle adamantly proclaimed his innocence. The agents then asked why there were four images of child pornography on his computer and why his computer had been used to access a website explicitly advertising child pornography. Boyle responded that he only looked at pornography of females who were eighteen years old or over, but that one time when he was looking at a legal "teen" sexual website, a "child porn site popped up on my screen without my even doing anything." Boyle further stated: "I immediately hit the 'close' button on my computer, but my computer screen kept showing child porn images. I eventually closed all the screens and turned off my computer." Boyle stated: "I like young women, but only 'legal' girls, not that child porn stuff. That's for sickos. I did not intentionally download any of those child porn images that appeared on my computer's screen. I swear to God I didn't." When asked about the family nudism magazines (which, the agents acknowledged were legal to possess), Boyle said, "That's different. Those photos aren't child pornography."

At the subsequent preliminary hearing, FBI agents testified about the foregoing facts. On cross-examination, defense counsel asked the FBI computer analyst whether it is possible that when a person is looking at one website, another linked website can pop up on the screen without the person having done anything intentionally to access the other website. The analyst testified that such linked websites automatically can pop up on the computer screen if they are programmed to do so by a webmaster. The analyst also admitted on cross-examination that photographic images from a website will be downloaded into the web browser's cache of a computer automatically when such images appear on the computer screen. In other words, such images, once they appear on the screen, will appear on the hard drive even if the person did not do anything affirmatively to download them.

Prosecutor: Argue that there is probable cause to bind over Boyle.

Defense Counsel: Argue that there is not probable cause to bind over Boyle.

To prepare for this hypothetical exercise, read *Maryland v. Pringle*, 540 U.S. 366 (2003); and *Hunter v. District Court*, 543 P.2d 1265 (Colo. 1975) (majority and dissenting opinions).

Hypothetical Five: Preliminary Hearings

State v. Payton

On December 26, **Roland Payton**, a twenty-year-old college sophomore on winter break, took a three-day domestic "holiday cruise" on Festival Cruise Lines with

---

images of child pornography on Boyle's hard drive qualify as computer images of persons under eighteen years of age who were engaged in sexual conduct.

two fraternity brothers. The cruise stopped overnight at Nita City's port on the evening of December 27. At the midnight buffet (which began at 11:30 p.m. on December 27), Payton met eighteen-year-old **Stella Lacey**, a college freshman on the cruise with her cousin, **Paige Bartles**. Payton and Lacey, who each had drunk numerous beers during the course of the evening and who each appeared mildly intoxicated, "immediately hit it off" according to Bartles. The two were seen leaving the buffet area around 1:00 a.m. on December 28.

According to Bartles's testimony at the subsequent preliminary hearing, around 4:00 a.m. on December 28, Lacey appeared at the door of the room shared by Lacey and Bartles. She was crying and said: "That guy Roland raped me. I told him to stop, but he kept going. God, I hope I'm not pregnant or have an STI." Bartles immediately called the ship's security officers, who in turn contacted the Nita City Police Department, which has jurisdiction because the ship was within Nita's territorial waters. Officer **Maria Stevens** interviewed Lacey later that morning and took her to the hospital for a "rape kit" to be performed. Doctors at the hospital examined Lacey and took a semen sample from her vagina. The doctors' report stated that Lacey's vaginal area was "consistent with recent sexual intercourse," but showed no "unusual tears or bruising beyond what would be expected from normal sexual intercourse."

That same morning, Nita City police officers arrested Payton based on Lacey's claim of sexual assault. When informed of the reason for his arrest, Payton invoked his right to talk to an attorney and did not give the police any statement. A criminal complaint was filed with the court later that day, and a magistrate conducted a preliminary hearing in early January (prior to the grand jury's hearing of the case).

Officer Stevens's police report, which she adopted as "100 percent accurate in terms of what Ms. Lacey told me on December 28," was introduced during her testimony at the preliminary hearing. The report stated that at approximately 7:00 a.m. on December 28, Lacey had given Officer Stevens the following account of the alleged rape:

> Complainant says that she and suspect [Roland Payton] met at midnight buffet and started flirting. The two later went for a walk around ship after leaving buffet area. After approximately one hour, the two went to suspect's room on ship and started "making out." Complainant and suspect were alone in room. Complainant says that after about five minutes suspect groped her breasts and she said, "No. Let's just kiss. I barely know you." Thereafter, suspect stated, "You know you want it," and then engaged in nonconsensual, unprotected sexual intercourse against complainant's will. Complainant said that she cried and asked suspect to stop, but he did not do so. After suspect finished, complainant got dressed and left for her room. Complainant's cousin then called the police. Complainant says that she was a virgin at time

of sexual assault and that it was very painful to her. Complainant said that she was not on birth control and fears pregnancy or STI.

The only prosecution witnesses called at the preliminary hearing were Officer Stevens, who discussed the contents of her police report and also testified about the results of Lacey's medical examination, and Lacey's cousin Bartles (whose testimony was recounted above).

The defense called two witnesses at the preliminary hearing. The first defense witness was Lacey's cousin, Bartles, who was recalled as a hostile defense witness (after being interviewed in the courtroom hallway by a defense investigator following her testimony for the prosecution). Bartles reluctantly admitted that prior to and during the cruise Lacey "repeatedly" had told her that she (Lacey) had engaged in sexual intercourse with her former boyfriend from high school and, thus, that she was not a virgin at the beginning of the cruise. Bartles also testified that Lacey's parents were "very conservative Catholics" and, according to what Lacey had told her, "would disown" Lacey if she engaged in consensual premarital sex, particularly if she became pregnant.

The second defense witness was **Rosemary Johannson**, who was a passenger on the same cruise as Payton and Lacey and who had occupied the room immediately to the left of Payton's room. Johannson, a retired schoolteacher who did not know either Payton or Lacey, testified that she was awakened "around 3:00 a.m." on December 28, by the "obvious sounds of a man and woman having sex" in the "room next door—the one to the right of my room."[31] Johannson, a widow and mother of three grown children, testified that in her opinion, "the woman sounded like she was having a good time during the sex, to say the least." According to Johannson, she also heard the unidentified female voice say "oh, baby" in an "endearing manner" at least twice. Johannson said that the "sex noises" continued "on and off" for around fifteen minutes, when the noises finally stopped, and she went back to sleep. She testified, "I remember looking at my clock when I went back to sleep; it said 3:16 a.m." When asked if she ever heard the female voice say "no" or "stop" at any point, Johannson said, "Absolutely not."

Payton did not testify on his own behalf. The prosecutor called no rebuttal witnesses.

Prosecutor: Argue that there is probable cause to bind over Payton.

Defense Counsel: Argue that there is not probable cause to bind over Payton.

To prepare for this hypothetical exercise, read *Maryland v. Pringle*, 540 U.S. 366 (2003), and *Hunter v. District Court*, 543 P.2d 1265 (Colo. 1975) (majority and dissenting opinions).

31. It was undisputed that she was referring to Payton's room, which was to the immediate right of Johannson's room.

Class Three

Bail Hearings

3.1 Bail Practices Generally

Bail practices vary widely in the many different jurisdictions in the United States. In most states, bail theoretically is available in the vast majority of noncapital cases (with exceptions for defendants with serious prior criminal records and defendants already released on bail in a prior case). In reality, though, while bail is set in the vast majority of state cases, defendants often do not secure release because they are unable to make bail even when it has been set.[1] Bail is typically granted or denied at the same time as the preliminary hearing in most jurisdictions.

Bail determinations in many states are informal and often involve prosecutors and defense counsel negotiating over the amount of bail and other conditions of release. Although many state courts are permitted to consider a defendant's general "dangerousness" in setting the bail amount and restrictive conditions of release (e.g., home detention with an ankle monitor), they usually cannot deny bail outright based on a finding that a defendant is a danger to the community.[2] Bail practices in many states rely heavily on bail bondsmen (also referred to as "corporate sureties"). Defendants typically secure release by paying a private bondsman a nonrefundable percentage of the bail amount (usually 10 percent) in exchange for

1. *See generally* John A. Chamberlin, Note, *Bounty Hunters: Can the Justice System Live Without Them?*, 1998 U. Ill. L. Rev. 1175 (1998) (discussing bail practices in the United States). In both state and federal criminal cases, there is no constitutional right to bail under the Eighth Amendment. Carlson v. Landon, 342 U.S. 524, 546 (1952). However, the Eighth Amendment does provide that if bail is authorized by statute or court rule, it cannot be set in an "excessive" amount. As the Supreme Court has stated:

> [Since] the passage of the Judiciary Act of 1789 . . . federal law has [provided for] bail. This traditional right to freedom before conviction permits the unhampered preparation of a defense, and serves to prevent the infliction of punishment prior to conviction . . . Unless this right to bail before trial is preserved, the presumption of innocence, secured only after centuries of struggle, would lose its meaning. The right to release before trial is conditioned upon the accused's giving adequate assurance that he will stand trial and submit to sentence if found guilty . . . Bail set at a figure higher than an amount reasonably calculated to fulfill his purpose is "excessive" under the Eighth Amendment.

Stack v. Boyle, 342 U.S. 1, 4–5 (1951).

2. *See, e.g.,* Ex parte Colbert, 805 So. 2d 687 (Ala. 2001).

the bondsman's posting the bail. In situations where the defendant and prosecutor do not agree to a particular bail amount, bail amounts are often determined by a schedule for particular offenses.[3]

Bail practices in federal court are dramatically different from traditional state court bail practices. In federal court, bail is not essentially granted automatically in noncapital cases, as it is in many state courts. Furthermore, a federal court's ruling on whether bail should be granted often occurs only after a formal adversary hearing referred to as a detention hearing. In federal cases involving defendants without serious prior criminal records and not involving alleged crimes of violence or drug-trafficking offenses, bail in federal court usually is set at a defendant's initial appearance in court without a detention hearing. But in many types of federal cases—especially those involving crimes of violence and federal drug-trafficking offenses—bail is granted or denied only after a formal, adversarial detention hearing.[4]

3.2 The Federal Bail Reform Act of 1984

Congress enacted the Bail Reform Act of 1984, 18 U.S.C. §§ 3141, *et seq.*, to rectify the widespread problem of federal defendants who commit a crime while on bond.[5] The passage of the Bail Reform Act marked "a significant departure from the basic philosophy of [previous federal law], which [was] that the sole purpose of bail laws must be to assure the appearance of the defendant at judicial proceedings" and that the granting of bail should be essentially automatic in noncapital cases.[6] The new act for the first time authorized federal courts to detain defendants without any bond prior to trial to assure either the appearance of the defendant or the safety of the community. The latter basis for detention commonly has been referred to as "preventive detention." In *United States v. Salerno*,[7] a majority of the U.S. Supreme Court, over a vigorous dissent, held that it is constitutional to detain a criminal defendant prior to his trial solely based on his dangerousness, even if the danger he poses does not relate to the crime charged in his case.

Under the Bail Reform Act, in theory at least, only a small fraction of federal defendants should be detained without bond. In the early days of the act, courts held that "[t]he wide range of restrictions available [i.e., the conditions of release] ensures, as Congress intended, that very few defendants will be subject to pretrial detention."[8] Another court held that "[t]his Act clearly favors nondetention."[9]

---

3. *See Chamberlin*, supra n. 1.
4. *See generally* David N. Adair, Jr., *The Bail Reform Act of 1984* (Fed. Jud. Center 2006, 3d ed.).
5. *See* United States v. Salerno, 481 U.S. 739, 741–42 (1987).
6. *See* S. Rep. No. 98-225, at 1, 3 (1983), as reprinted in 1984 U.S.C.C.A.N. 3182, 3185–86.
7. *Salerno*, 481 U.S. 739.
8. United States v. Orta, 760 F.2d 887, 891 (8th Cir. 1985).
9. United States v. Byrd, 969 F.2d 106, 109 (5th Cir. 1992); *see also* United States v. Holloway, 781 F.2d 124, 125 (8th Cir. 1986) (pretrial detention "is to be the exception rather than the rule").

The reality, however, is that a significant percentage of federal defendants actually are denied release on bail.[10] The reason for the difference between theory and reality is the large number of blue-collar crimes prosecuted in the federal system today (e.g., bank robberies, drug trafficking, and possession of illegal firearms), and the large percentage of noncitizen defendants who are subject to immigration detention even if they were released on bond in their criminal cases.[11] White-collar federal defendants—whose alleged crimes are nonviolent, who typically have very strong ties to the community, and who typically have no criminal record—are generally released on bail.

Under 18 U.S.C. § 3142, a federal district court—meaning a federal magistrate judge in the first instance—must order the least restrictive conditions appropriate for a defendant. There are three primary options available: 1) release on personal recognizance; 2) release with conditions, including a secured or unsecured bond; or 3) detention after a hearing.[12]

Assuming that release on personal recognizance without conditions does not occur, § 3142(c)(1)(B) lists conditions that the judicial officer must consider for release. The statute directs that the least restrictive conditions must be imposed. Two of the most common are 1) a financial condition, such as depositing a specific amount of money into the registry of the court or obtaining a surety, and 2) requiring a third-party "custodian," such as a defendant's boss or a close family member.

With respect to a financial condition, a federal court usually sets a large bond (e.g., $50,000), but either requires no money to be posted or requires a refundable deposit of only a small fraction (1 percent to 10 percent) of the bond amount, depending on a particular defendant's resources. Occasionally, a defendant with substantial holdings but few liquid assets will be required to put up real estate as security for the bond. Rarely, a defendant will be required to have a corporate surety or a bail bondsman secure the bond; however, bail bondsmen are generally disfavored in the federal system. Usually, private parties serve as noncorporate sureties.

In the vast majority of cases not involving a bail bondsman, a third-party custodian also signs the bond paperwork as a surety and is responsible for reporting any violations of the bond conditions to the court. Other typical conditions of release may include travel and residence restrictions (including a curfew and

---

10. *See* Sandra G. Mayson, *Dangerous Defendants*, 127 Yale L. J. 490, 506 (2018) (noting around two-thirds of federal defendants are detained without bond).
11. Lena Graber & Amy Schnitzer, *The Bail Reform Act and Release from Criminal and Immigration Custody for Federal Criminal Defendants* (National Lawyers Guild 2013). Available at https://nipnlg.org/PDFs/practitioners/practice_advisories/crim/2013_Jun_federal-bail.pdf (last visited June 21, 2022).
12. 18 U.S.C. § 3142(a).

electronic monitoring with an ankle bracelet), restrictions on personal associations (such as no contact with any prosecution witnesses in the case), restrictions on employment (e.g., no fiduciary positions for a white-collar defendant), regular reporting to the United States Pretrial Services Agency (an arm of the court that supervises defendants released on bail), prohibiting excessive use of alcohol or any use of drugs, and undergoing mental health or substance abuse treatment if deemed appropriate.

Congress has restricted the circumstances under which pretrial detention can be ordered,[13] and those circumstances are contained in 18 U.S.C. § 3142(f). The cases where bail can be denied outright (after a detention hearing) include 1) most drug-trafficking offenses; 2) most crimes of violence; 3) most firearms offenses; 4) any offense (whether violent or nonviolent in nature) involving minor victims; and 5) offenses for which the maximum sentence is life imprisonment or the death penalty (whether the offense is violent or nonviolent in nature).[14]

In such cases, pretrial detention is likely, but not automatic. Before detaining a defendant, the court must 1) find by a preponderance of the evidence that there are no conditions under which the defendant may be released on bail that will reasonably assure the appearance of the defendant for their court appearances (i.e., the defendant is a serious risk of flight), or 2) find by clear and convincing evidence that there are no conditions under which the defendant may be released that would assure the safety of the community (i.e., the defendant is a danger to the community).[15] In certain types of serious drug cases and in certain situations where a defendant previously was convicted of an offense listed in § 3142(f)(1), there is a rebuttable presumption that the defendant is a flight risk and a danger to the community.[16]

In all other types of federal cases (e.g., white-collar cases), the prosecutor may move for detention only if there is a serious risk that the defendant will flee or that the defendant will obstruct justice (such as by threatening a prospective witness).[17]

Although a court may consider the danger to the community that a white-collar defendant (or other type of defendant charged with a nonviolent or nondrug offense) poses in setting conditions of release, a finding that such a defendant poses a danger to the community is *not* by itself a basis to deny release on bond.[18] Only cases involving the specific types of offenses listed in § 3142(f) permit a court to deny bond outright based on a defendant's dangerousness.

---

13. *See* United States v. Ploof, 851 F.2d 7 (1st Cir. 1988).
14. 18 U.S.C. § 3142(f)(1)(A)–(E).
15. *Id.* at 3142(f).
16. *Id.* at 3142(e).
17. *Id.* at 3142(f)(2).
18. *See* United States v. Gibson, 384 F. Supp.3d 955 (N.D. Ind. 2019).

Hypothetical One: Bail Hearings

United States v. Mahmoudi

Fred Mahmoudi, who is forty-six years old, is an Iranian-born naturalized U.S. citizen. His parents brought him to this country from Iran when he was six years old. He became a naturalized U.S. citizen when he was fourteen years old. He completed school all the way through college in the United States. He graduated from the University of Nita *magna cum laude* with a BS degree in chemistry and a minor in Islamic studies.

All of Mahmoudi's immediate family, including his parents and two siblings, live in the United States. All became naturalized U.S. citizens. He has uncles, aunts, and cousins who still live in Iran. After he graduated from college, he married **Kimberly Gathmann**, a U.S. citizen not of Middle Eastern descent. They have two children, aged eight and ten. They have lived in Nita City since their marriage ten years ago. They have lived in the same home, on which they have a mortgage, since their marriage. It is valued at $485,000, according to the latest tax assessor's appraisal. Mr. Mahmoudi has been employed as a chemist for Nita Oil Company for twenty years. He earns $125,000 per year at that job. His wife is a stay-at-home mom who works part-time as a substitute teacher. Neither has ever been arrested before. Mr. Mahmoudi is a self-proclaimed secular Muslim who attends religious services on special occasions, but otherwise is not actively involved with the religion. His wife is an agnostic who does not attend any church or mosque.

On January 9, a federal grand jury returned a sealed indictment charging Mr. Mahmoudi with operating an "illegal money-transmitting" business in violation of 18 U.S.C. § 1960, a felony offense.[19] Section 1960 provides that a person commits an offense if he or she sends money abroad on behalf of a third party (1) without first obtaining a license to do so by the state in which the defendant operated the business if such a license is required[20] *or* (2) if the money was knowingly being transmitted abroad for the purpose of its being used to promote or support unlawful activity, whether or not the business is properly licensed. The indictment charged Mahmoudi with violating clause (1) of the statute, i.e., operating a money-transmitting business without a license as required by state law. The indictment did not charge him with knowingly sending money abroad to support any illegal activity.

Early in the morning on January 12, FBI agents arrested Mr. Mahmoudi at his home. He was taken in handcuffs to the federal courthouse, where he appeared before a federal magistrate judge. The assistant U.S. attorney announced that the government was seeking to detain Mahmoudi without bond. The magistrate judge ordered that Mahmoudi be held without bond pending a detention hearing.

---

19. The maximum prison term under 18 U.S.C. § 1960 is five years.
20. Such a license is required under state law in Nita.

At the detention hearing conducted the following day, the prosecution called FBI agent **Mary Jones** as the government's primary witness. Agent Jones testified that a confidential source (CS) had informed the FBI that during the past few years, Mr. Mahmoudi knowingly had served as a financial conduit for Islamic terrorists in various places in the Middle East. According to the CS, Mahmoudi ran a money-transmitting business, whereby he knowingly wired large amounts of money to Islamic charities, and at least one of these "charities" was a known cover for terrorist operations. According to Agent Jones, that charity, the Islamic Charitable Foundation of Egypt (ICFE), has been directly linked to multiple terrorist attacks in Europe. However, Agent Jones admitted on cross-examination that no evidence directly linked Mr. Mahmoudi to any terrorists, but only that he had twice wired $7,500 to ICFE on behalf of an unidentified third party.

Agent Jones further testified that the FBI had subpoenaed Mr. Mahmoudi's bank records, which showed that he had made 152 wire transfers to various Middle Eastern countries during the past decade. Most of the wire transfers were between $5,000 and $10,000. Most of those wire transfers went to Egypt, Iran, and Saudi Arabia, all of which have been identified as countries containing terrorist operations. Agent Jones testified that Mahmoudi had obtained a license from the State of Nita to operate a money-transmitting business ten years ago (prior to any of his wire transfers) and that he renewed that license on an annual basis until it expired one year ago. Only three wire transfers occurred after his license had expired. Those three illegal transfers were the sole basis of the federal indictment in this case.

Agent Jones also testified that State Department records show that Mr. Mahmoudi traveled to Cairo, Egypt, for a semester abroad in college over two decades ago. His passport shows two subsequent trips to Egypt—each for two weeks in duration— since he graduated from college. His last trip abroad was a year ago, when he traveled to Germany, another country in which large numbers of Middle Eastern terrorists are known to reside.

Agent Jones testified that after FBI agents arrested Mahmoudi, he agreed to give a statement. After being read *Miranda* warnings, he informed agents that he had operated a licensed money-transmitting business out of his residence as a means of supplementing his salary from his full-time job. He charged a 5 percent fee to persons who wished to wire money to other countries. He provided the agents with tax returns that showed that he had reported all of his profits from his money-transmitting business. Mahmoudi explained that money-transmitting businesses are common in the Muslim community in the United States and that "Americanized" Muslims, such as himself, have operated such businesses because "religious" Muslims are uncomfortable dealing with U.S. banks. Mahmoudi explained that he believed all of the money transferred by him had gone to legitimate Islamic charities in Middle Eastern countries. He adamantly denied being a "terrorist" and stated that he was a "proud American." He admitted that he let his state license lapse last year and that he had done three wire transfers without a license since that time. He stated that he intended to renew his license but never got around to doing it.

Defense counsel called two witnesses at the detention hearing—Mahmoudi's wife, Kimberly, and **George Gonzalez**, his supervisor at Nita Oil Company. Both witnesses testified that Mahmoudi was a hardworking employee and a family man. Gonzalez further testified that he has known Mr. Mahmoudi well for twenty years and that Mahmoudi had never said anything to indicate that he supported Middle Eastern terrorists. "He has always appeared to be a patriotic American, just like me," Gonzalez testified. On cross-examination by the prosecutor, Gonzalez admitted that he had been unaware that Mahmoudi had operated a money-transmitting business out of his home until he was arrested.

Both Kimberly Gathmann and George Gonzalez agreed to sign a bond in any amount of money as sureties for Mr. Mahmoudi. Kimberly testified that she and her husband had approximately $200,000 in IRA accounts and a 401(k) retirement account, which she would withdraw and deposit with the court to secure the bond. She also stated that she would surrender both her and her husband's passports to the court as a condition of bond.

Prosecutor: Move to detain Mahmoudi without bond.

Defense Counsel: Argue that Mahmoudi should be released on bond; suggest reasonable conditions for such a bond.

To prepare for this hypothetical exercise, read 18 U.S.C. § 3142 (the federal Bail Reform Act), as well as *United States v. Gibson*, 384 F. Supp.3d 955 (N. D. Ind. 2019).

Hypothetical Two: Bail Hearings

United States v. Newman

Michael Newman, a thirty-nine-year-old U.S. citizen, has been charged by federal indictment with being a felon in possession of a firearm, an alleged violation of 18 U.S.C. § 922(g)(1). The assistant U.S. attorney (AUSA) prosecuting the case has filed a motion to detain Newman under the Bail Reform Act, 18 U.S.C. § 3142(f)(1)(E), on the ground that Newman poses a danger to the community.

Newman's criminal record is limited to a single prior felony conviction for automobile theft committed when he was nineteen years old. He was sentenced to six months in jail for that conviction and thereafter successfully completed eighteen months of parole. Since he discharged his parole nearly two decades ago, he has worked sporadically as a construction worker. He has been arrested—but not convicted—for the misdemeanor charge of driving under the influence of alcohol ("DUI") on two occasions in the past ten years. Each DUI charge was ultimately dismissed for reasons that are not clear. Newman, an admitted recovering alcoholic, has entered in-patient rehabilitation programs for alcoholism on several occasions during the past ten years—most recently last year. Newman and **Crystal Brown** were married for six years but divorced last year. During the divorce proceedings last year, Brown claimed under oath that Newman physically abused her during intoxicated rages. Brown was the person who notified the police that Newman, a convicted felon, possessed a firearm. Her complaint to the police—that Newman had "stalked her" after the divorce (by repeatedly driving by her house)—resulted in Newman's car being searched, which revealed that he possessed a loaded .38 caliber pistol. All of the foregoing facts were established at the detention hearing conducted by the U.S. magistrate judge.

At the conclusion of the detention hearing, the AUSA presented—ex parte—to the U.S. magistrate judge an affidavit from an unnamed confidential source (CS) claiming that Newman had threatened to commit an unspecified "serious act of violence" if he were to be released on bond. Newman and his defense attorney were not told of the specific contents of the ex parte affidavit other than it alleged that Newman had made "a credible threat of serious violence." The AUSA requested that the magistrate judge interview the CS under oath at an in camera, ex parte hearing (i.e., a hearing closed to the public and from which Newman and his attorney would be excluded). The magistrate judge agreed to do so and, over the objection of Newman's attorney, conducted an in camera, ex parte hearing at which the CS testified under oath about Newman's alleged threat. At the end of this in camera, ex parte hearing, the magistrate called Newman and his attorney into court and stated:

> Although it was a close case, I was going to grant Mr. Newman release on bond until I had a chance to hear from the confidential source under oath in my chambers. What I heard was extremely disturbing and pushed me over to the side of denying bond. The CS provided credible testimony that Mr. Newman, if released on bond, would commit a serious act of violence. To protect the CS's safety, I will not reveal any more information about either the CS or the alleged threat made by Mr. Newman. Although I believe that Mr. Newman knows exactly what the threat is, I doubt he knows who the CS is. I want to keep it that way, for everyone's safety—in particular, the victim of the threat as well as the CS, who gave me good reason to believe that Mr. Newman would retaliate against the CS if Mr. Newman were to be released on bond. Therefore, I grant the prosecutor's motion to detain Mr. Newman and deny his request for bond on the ground that there is clear and convincing evidence that he poses a danger to the safety of persons in the community.

Pursuant to 18 U.S.C. § 3145, Newman's attorney immediately appealed the magistrate judge's order denying bond to the U.S. district judge assigned to hear Newman's case. Newman's attorney has argued that the magistrate judge committed legal error by considering the CS's testimony in an ex parte, in camera proceeding. Defense counsel contends that either the CS must be required to testify in open court and be subject to cross-examination by defense counsel or, instead, the magistrate judge must consider only the evidence offered at the original detention hearing in ruling on the prosecutor's motion to detain Newman. The AUSA has responded that, under the circumstances, the magistrate judge did not err.

Defense Counsel: Argue that the district judge should reverse the order of the magistrate judge.

Prosecutor: Argue that the district court should affirm the order of the magistrate judge.

To prepare for this hypothetical exercise, read 18 U.S.C. §§ 3142, 3145, as well as *United States v. Terrones*, 712 F. Supp. 786 (S.D. Cal. 1989), and *United States v. Eischeid*, 315 F. Supp. 2d 1033 (D. Ariz. 2003).

Hypothetical Three: Bail Hearings

United States v. Johnson

Dora Johnson is a forty-four-year-old accountant employed by the national accounting firm of Peters & Dahlin. She has no prior criminal record except an arrest in college for public intoxication. She is currently separated from her husband, **Marvin Johnson**. Ms. Johnson lives in Nita City with her two teenaged sons. A federal grand jury has returned an indictment charging Ms. Johnson with conspiracy and solicitation of murder using interstate facilities in violation of 18 U.S.C. §§ 371 and 1958, both felony offenses.[21] Ms. Johnson was charged along with a codefendant, **Harry Burns**.

Ms. Johnson was arrested and taken before a federal magistrate judge in Nita City, where an assistant U.S. attorney sought to detain her without bond. At the detention hearing, FBI Agent **Susan McCord** testified that Johnson and codefendant Burns had carried on an extramarital affair during the past two years. Both Johnson and Burns are employed as accountants by Peters & Dahlin. Johnson works in the firm's Nita City office, and Burns works in the firm's New York office.

According to Agent McCord, Johnson and Burns conspired to solicit a hit man, **Robert Brown**, to murder Marvin Johnson. McCord testified that Brown had been arrested on unrelated federal drug charges and, after being arrested, he cooperated with the authorities concerning the murder solicitation to reduce his sentence in the drug case. Brown stated that Burns had contacted him and agreed to pay him $50,000 to travel from New York to Nita City and murder Marvin

21. 18 U.S.C. § 371 carries a maximum prison sentence of five years, and 18 U.S.C. § 1958 carries a maximum prison sentence of ten years (assuming that no one is injured or killed).

Johnson. According to Brown, Burns told him that Dora Johnson was the one who would supply the $50,000 and that they were arranging for the "hit" because Marvin Johnson had told Dora Johnson that he planned on removing her as the beneficiary of his $2 million life insurance policy and Dora Johnson wanted him murdered before that occurred.

Agent McCord further testified that she had wired Brown with a recording device and also placed a recording device on his cell phone. While wearing the wire and using the monitored cell phone, Brown engaged in three different conversations with Burns. In each of the three conversations, Burns made incriminating statements about the murder conspiracy, including twice referring to "Dora" as being the one who would pay the $50,000 for the hit. At McCord's direction, Brown also telephoned Dora Johnson at her home, identified himself as "the guy who will be helping you and Harry Burns," and then stated that "I cannot reach Harry" and that "I need to reach him so we can get this thing over with." According to Agent McCord, in response to Brown's statements during this recorded call, Johnson angrily stated: "You are not supposed to call me. How did you get my number? Don't call me again." She then hung up the phone. After this recorded telephone call, the U.S. attorney obtained the indictment and arrest warrant for Ms. Johnson and Burns.

At the detention hearing, Ms. Johnson's attorney called four witnesses on her behalf—her father, her brother, and her oldest son (who is eighteen years old), as well as her supervisor at the accounting firm. Her father and brother, who each have good jobs and no criminal record, agreed to sign a bond in any amount set by the court. Each man testified that Ms. Johnson had suffered from long-term physical and emotional abuse at the hands of Marvin Johnson and that the couple's marriage had existed only for the children's sake during the past two years. Johnson's brother testified that he was aware of his sister's extramarital affair with Harry Burns, but Dora Johnson recently had told him that she intended to break it off.

Johnson's brother and her son testified that she had suffered from serious depression during the past few years and that she had become addicted to prescription pain relievers and alcohol. According to her son, she was intoxicated during most of her waking hours. Her boss testified that she had used up almost all of her accrued sick leave and vacation time and that she was planning to take unpaid leave soon to check herself into a rehab clinic. All four defense witnesses testified that Ms. Johnson would not flee if released on bond.

Johnson's attorney informed the court that she would agree to be placed in an inpatient clinic and/or mental health facility as a condition of her bond and also that she would surrender her passport to the court as a condition of her bond.

Prosecutor: Move to detain Johnson without bond.

Defense Counsel: Argue that Johnson should be released on bond; suggest reasonable conditions for such a bond.

To prepare for this hypothetical exercise, read 18 U.S.C. § 3142 (the federal Bail Reform Act), as well as *United States v. Barnett*, 986 F. Supp. 385 (W.D. La. 1997) (motions for pretrial detention) and 986 F. Supp. 405 (W.D. La. 1997) (motion for stay and revocation of magistrate's order of release).

Hypothetical Four: Bail Hearings

United States v. Duff

On January 12, **Eddie Duff** wrote a letter to the editor of the *Nita Times* newspaper in Nita City, in which Duff stated: "A bomb has been placed somewhere in your newspaper's building. It will go off sometime in the next week. Stop printing your garbage and get out before you die!" Duff, who has a long history of mental illness, placed his correct name and address on the top left of the envelope in which the letter was mailed (via first-class U.S. mail). On January 13, the editor received Duff's letter, called the police, and evacuated the building. A police bomb squad determined that no bomb was in the building, and the newspaper's operations resumed.

A federal grand jury proceeded to charge Duff with violating 18 U.S.C. § 876(c), which makes it a federal felony offense (carrying a maximum sentence of five years in prison) to mail a letter through the U.S. mail that threatens to injure or kill the addressee or any other person. Duff was arrested, and the assistant U.S. attorney moved to detain Duff without bond.

In addition to the facts concerning Duff's alleged crime, the following facts were established at the detention hearing. Duff, who is fifty-eight years old, was first diagnosed with paranoid schizophrenia at the age of twenty-one. Since that time, he has been in and out of psychiatric hospitals. However, he has gone for lengthy periods of time (up to three years) without engaging in any illegal behavior. He has held a variety of low-paying jobs, including most recently as a bagger at a grocery store, but primarily has depended on governmental assistance. He has no significant assets and lives in public housing.

During the past two decades, he has been arrested on six different occasions for making threats to kill or injure various people, including doctors treating him, the mayor of Nita City, and neighbors. Two of those threats—one to a neighbor and the other to the mayor (both incidents over a decade ago)—resulted in misdemeanor convictions for threatening to assault. He has no prior felony convictions. All of his threats occurred during periods when his mental illness was at its worst. With the exception of a two-decade-old incident when he punched a nurse at a psychiatric hospital, there is no evidence that he actually carried out any of his threats or otherwise engaged in physically violent behavior.

When he was arrested, Duff told FBI agents that he wrote the letter to the editor of the *Nita Times* because the newspaper recently had run an editorial that supported the reelection of Nita's governor. "I hate that son of a bitch [the governor]," Duff told the agents. "He deserves to die just like the King of England deserved it in 1776. I'll get a medal for shooting him just like Thomas Jefferson did."

FBI Agent **Cheryl Magness** testified for the prosecution that when the agents searched Duff's apartment pursuant to a search warrant, they found an unloaded .22 caliber rifle, but no bullets. Agent Magness testified that Duff claimed that he had inherited the rifle from his recently deceased older brother. Agent Magness said she had no proof—one way or the other—whether in fact Duff inherited the rifle as he claimed.

At the detention hearing, Duff's attorney called Duff's long-time psychologist, **Dr. Sharon Henderson**, who has treated Duff on and off for the past twelve years at the county's Mental Health and Intellectual Disability Center (MHIDC). Dr. Henderson testified that Duff had been taking his antipsychotic medication consistently during the time that she had treated him, but that "sometimes he still flies off the handle and gets extremely paranoid and angry" for "totally irrational reasons." Nevertheless, she opined, with the exception of the incident when he punched a psychiatric nurse, "he has never actually carried out his threats and does not appear to pose a real risk of actual violence." Dr. Henderson testified that she did not know that Duff had possession of a .22 rifle, but she said that Duff told her six months ago that his brother had died. She also testified that she had met with Duff at the jail after his arrest in this case and that he "seemed to have stabilized" since his irrational state at the time of his arrest. Finally, Dr. Henderson testified that Duff likely would deteriorate mentally if he remained in jail for any lengthy period of time. "He needs appropriate counseling and treatment, which he is not getting in the jail."

Duff has no immediate family still alive. He has some cousins who live out of state but has had no contact with them for many years. Dr. Henderson informed the court that she would be able to see Duff on an "an extremely regular basis" if he were to be released on bond and, if necessary, would see that Duff moved from his public housing unit into a publicly funded residential psychiatric facility.

Prosecutor: Move to detain Duff without bond.

Defense Counsel: Argue that Duff should be released on bond; suggest reasonable conditions for such a bond.

To prepare for this hypothetical exercise, read 18 U.S.C. § 3142 (the federal Bail Reform Act), as well as *United States v. Traitz*, 807 F.2d 322 (3d Cir. 1986) (majority and dissenting opinions).

Hypothetical Five: Bail Hearings

United States v. Marquez

Marco Marquez is a nineteen-year-old man who has lived in Nita City since he was six months old. He is a Mexican citizen (born in Mexico) but he is a permanent resident alien in the United States and possesses a valid U.S. green card. His entire immediate family lives in the United States; he has no close relatives in Mexico. His parents are permanent resident aliens, and his four younger siblings are all U.S. citizens (all having been born in Nita City). Marquez is the father of a one-year-old daughter, who was born out of wedlock to his girlfriend. Marquez applied for U.S. citizenship two months ago, but his application will not be processed for another few months. Marquez has no prior criminal record. He dropped out of high school in the eleventh grade and has had sporadic employment since that time. He lives on and off with his parents and his girlfriend. Marquez has not returned to Mexico since he was brought here as a baby. His primary language is English, and he speaks only some Spanish.

Marquez was arrested by DEA agents and was charged with conspiracy and aiding and abetting the possession of more than five kilograms of cocaine with the intent to distribute it, in violation of 21 U.S.C. §§ 841, 846.[22] At the time of his arrest, Marquez was sitting in the passenger seat of a truck and the cocaine was hidden in the truck's bed underneath boxes of produce. The driver of the truck, **Rick Stevens**, was being watched by DEA agents because a confidential source (CS) had told the agents that Stevens would be driving a load of cocaine from Nita City to New York. DEA agents, accompanied by state troopers, followed the truck on an interstate highway outside of Nita City until they observed Stevens commit a traffic violation (driving sixty-one miles per hour in a fifty-five-mile-per-hour zone). At that point, the troopers pulled over the truck. DEA agents then asked for consent to search the truck, and Stevens consented. After discovering the cocaine hidden in the back of the truck, agents arrested both Stevens and Marquez.

After being read *Miranda* warnings, both Stevens and Marquez admitted that there was cocaine hidden inside the truck and that they were traveling from Nita City to New York, where Stevens would deliver the cocaine to another person. Both Stevens and Marquez stated that the latter was "only going along for the ride," but that he knew that cocaine was inside the truck and that Stevens was planning on delivering it to someone in New York. When asked whether Marquez would be paid anything for coming along for the ride, Stevens said, "We never really talked about it," and Marquez said, "Maybe a hundred bucks or something like that. I don't know for sure." When agents searched the cab of the truck, they found a loaded handgun under the driver's seat. Both Marquez and Stevens denied

22. If convicted of the drug charges, Marquez faces a mandatory minimum prison sentence of ten years and a maximum sentence of life imprisonment. *See* 21 U.S.C. § 841(b).

knowledge of the firearm. The truck was registered in a third party's name. Stevens said the truck belonged to a man in New York who was part of the drug conspiracy.

At the detention hearing, DEA Agent **Lupita Rubio** testified about the foregoing facts, including Marquez's ties to the United States. On cross-examination by defense counsel, she admitted that the DEA had no prior knowledge that Marquez would be in the truck with Stevens. Agent Rubio testified that the Bureau of Immigration and Customs Enforcement would deport Marquez to Mexico if he were convicted of federal drug charges and that he would be legally barred from ever returning to the United States.

Defense counsel called Marquez's parents and his uncle, **Robert Marquez**, as witnesses. His parents testified that Marquez has no ties to Mexico (other than some distant relatives whom he has never even met) and that "all of his life is here in the U.S." His parents testified that they had no significant assets, but nonetheless would be willing to sign a bond for their son. Marquez's uncle, Robert Marquez, who is a naturalized U.S. citizen, testified that he owns a $250,000 home and that he also owns two Subway sandwich franchise stores. He testified that he would be willing to sign a bond for his nephew, that he would put his home up as collateral for the bond, and that he would allow his nephew to work at one of his stores while he was released on bond. He opined that Marco Marquez would not flee if released on bond and agreed to "watch him like a hawk" if he were to be released on bond. When asked by the prosecutor whether he believed that his nephew would run to Mexico if released on bond, Robert Marquez responded: "Of course not. He has no family there. He has no place to live there. He barely speaks Spanish. All of his people are here in the United States, including his baby, who he adores."

Prosecutor: Move to detain Marquez without bond.

Defense Counsel: Argue that Marquez should be released on bond; suggest reasonable conditions for such a bond.

Assume that the magistrate judge has found probable cause and the only issue before the court is whether Marquez should be detained without bond.

To prepare for this hypothetical exercise, read 18 U.S.C. § 3142 (the federal Bail Reform Act), as well as *United States v. Rueben*, 974 F.2d 580 (5th Cir. 1992), and *United States v. Bustamonte-Conchas*, 557 F. App'x 803 (10th Cir. 2014).

Class Four

Pretrial Motions

4.1 Pretrial Motions Generally

There are countless types of pretrial motions that the prosecution or defense can file in a criminal case.[1] For purposes of this course, we will divide pretrial motions into two primary classes: "suppression" motions (e.g., a motion to suppress evidence based on an unconstitutional search or seizure[2] or a motion to suppress a defendant's confession as illegally obtained[3]) and "nonsuppression" motions (e.g., a motion to dismiss the indictment based on a violation of the Double Jeopardy Clause).[4] Many motions filed in criminal cases are uncontested or unopposed (e.g., a motion for a continuance). For our purposes, we are concerned here only with contested motions concerning substantive issues.

Both the prosecution and the defense regularly file pretrial motions in criminal cases, although defense lawyers typically file the bulk of motions. It is helpful to categorize defense motions as "dispositive" or "nondispositive." A dispositive motion is one that, if granted, actually or effectively dismisses the case. A quintessential dispositive motion is a motion to dismiss an indictment based on a constitutional

1. Such motions include, but are not limited to, motions to suppress evidence (including a defendant's confession); motions for change of venue; motions to sever multiple codefendants or multiple charges; motions to disqualify the prosecutor or defense counsel because of a conflict of interest; motions to recuse the trial judge because of bias or appearance of bias; motions to compel discovery; motions to disclose the identity of a confidential informant; motions to dismiss the indictment for failure to charge an offense; motions to dismiss the indictment because the underlying penal statute is unconstitutional; motions to dismiss the indictment based on a violation of the defendant's statutory or constitutional right to a speedy trial; motions to dismiss the indictment because of an ex post facto violation; motions to dismiss the indictment because of a double jeopardy violation; motions to dismiss the indictment because the prosecution or police have destroyed potentially exculpatory evidence; motions to dismiss the indictment because of racial or gender discrimination in the selection of the grand jury; motions in limine to exclude particular types of evidence at trial as inadmissible under the rules of evidence; motions to close the courtroom to the public; motions for appointment of an expert witness for an indigent defendant. *See, e.g.*, 1 Federal Defenders of San Diego, Inc., *Pretrial Motions, in Defending a Federal Criminal Case*, 6-281, *et seq*. (2010).

2. *See, e.g.*, Arizona v. Hicks, 480 U.S. 321 (1987).

3. *See, e.g.*, Miranda v. Arizona, 384 U.S. 436 (1966).

4. Harris v. Oklahoma, 433 U.S. 682 (1977).

challenge to the underlying criminal statute (e.g., a claim that a penal statute violates the First Amendment because it criminalizes constitutionally protected conduct).[5]

Although nondispositive in their nature, certain other motions can effectively be dispositive—such as a motion to suppress a defendant's confession. In many cases, without evidence of a defendant's confession, the prosecution will not have sufficient remaining evidence to proceed to trial, and as a result of the motion being granted, the prosecution will very likely dismiss the case.

Some motions (such as a motion to dismiss the indictment based on a facially unconstitutional statute) do not require an evidentiary hearing because there are no factual disputes or no need for further factual development. Other motions (such as a motion to suppress a defendant's confession) typically require an evidentiary hearing unless all the relevant facts are undisputed, which is rare. A motion must make allegations that are specific enough to create the equivalent of a "genuine dispute as to any material fact"[6] to avoid summary denial by the court without an evidentiary hearing.[7] Put another way, the allegations must be "sufficiently definite, clear, and specific to enable the trial court to conclude that contested issues of fact exist,"[8] thus requiring an evidentiary hearing.

Hypothetical One: Pretrial Motions

United States v. Peterson

The indictment in this case alleges that on September 8, **Walter Peterson**, **Oscar Little**, **Jake Woodhouse**, **Brett Bartels**, and **Roland Jones** conspired to rob First National Bank located in the 5700 block of Westheimer Street in Nita City.[9]

The indictment further alleges that the five men drove Peterson's ten-year-old, four-door Cadillac sedan to a parking lot in a strip mall adjacent to the bank at 8:19 a.m. Inside the car were three loaded pistols and three ski masks. The indictment further alleges that the five men waited for the first bank employee (head teller **Gina DeBlanc**) to open the bank's doors (which usually occurred around 8:30 a.m.).[10]

The police report in this case states that DeBlanc arrived at the bank at 8:28 a.m. and immediately got out of her car and approached the bank's back door with keys in hand. The police report also states that off-duty Nita City Police Department (NCPD) officer **Juan Hernandez** happened to be driving down that

---

5. *See, e.g.*, United States v. Reidel, 402 U.S. 351 (1971).
6. *Cf.* Fed. R. Civ. P. 56(a) (the standard for avoiding summary judgment in civil cases).
7. *See, e.g.*, United States v. Harrelson, 705 F.2d 733, 737 (5th Cir. 1983).
8. United States v. Ramirez-Garcia, 269 F.3d 945, 947 (9th Cir. 2001).
9. The indictment alleged a conspiracy (18 U.S.C. § 371) to violate 18 U.S.C. § 2113(a) and (d).
10. The bank opened its doors to customers at 9:00 a.m.

block of Westheimer at 8:29 a.m. when he noticed Peterson, Little, and Woodhouse placing ski masks on their faces as they were sitting in the Cadillac—which raised Officer Hernandez's suspicions, considering that the weather was warm and humid. (None of the five men in the Cadillac noticed Hernandez, who was in plain clothes and driving his private car.) Bartels and Jones remained in the Cadillac as the other three men got out of the car. Officer Hernandez called NCPD's main number on his cell phone and informed the dispatcher that he believed a bank robbery was about to occur.

On-duty NCPD officer **Mark Hamby** was patrolling in a marked police car in the 5300 block of Westheimer when a dispatcher sent out a call to all officers at 8:30 a.m. Within one minute of hearing this radio call, Officer Hamby arrived at the bank's parking lot, where he got out of his car and pointed his gun at Peterson, Little, and Woodhouse, who were walking in the bank's parking lot and wearing ski masks (approximately twenty-five feet from the bank's back door, which DeBlanc was then unlocking). Peterson, Little, and Woodhouse raised their hands in the air and surrendered without incident. At the time they were arrested, each man had a loaded pistol tucked in his waistband hidden from sight. Officer Hamby and other NCPD officers who had arrived at the scene arrested the three men, separated them, and placed them in the back of three different patrol cars.

As the police officers were arresting Peterson, Little, and Woodhouse, Bartels and Jones drove away in the Cadillac but were apprehended by NCPD officers within ten minutes and taken into custody. Bartels had driven the car, and Jones had been a passenger in the front seat.

Officer Hamby interrogated Peterson after reading him *Miranda* warnings. Peterson stated that he, Little, Woodhouse, and Bartels had conspired to rob the bank. Peterson stated that he, Little, and Woodhouse were going to follow the head teller (i.e., Ms. DeBlanc) into the bank, where they had planned to tie her up and "take all the money we could get our hands on" before the bank's manager and other tellers arrived, which usually occurred around 8:45 a.m. Peterson said that Bartels was to be the getaway driver (the "wheel man"). Peterson admitted that he, Little, Woodhouse, and Bartels had "cased" the bank during the prior week and knew the normal arrival times of the head teller, bank manager, and other bank employees. Peterson stated that Roland Jones was Bartels's cousin and was "simply along for the ride." Peterson stated that Jones had not been part of the planning of the robbery and did or said nothing during the ride to the strip mall parking lot to indicate that he had joined the conspiracy.

After they were read *Miranda* warnings, the remaining defendants invoked their right to silence and refused to give statements to the police officers.

After the indictment was returned, the assistant U.S. attorney (AUSA) announced to the district judge that the government intended to try all five defendants together at a joint trial. All five defendants pleaded not guilty; none will plead guilty. When asked by the district court at a pretrial conference, all five defendants, through their respective defense counsel, unequivocally stated that they will not be testifying at trial.[11]

As part of the government's pretrial discovery process, the AUSA states the government's intention to offer Peterson's post-arrest, out-of-court confession into evidence at the joint trial. Anticipating a *Bruton*[12] objection or a motion to sever the other codefendants from Peterson, the prosecutor provides all defense counsel with the following redacted[13] confession by Peterson (which, the AUSA proposes, will be read into evidence by Officer Hamby, but not offered in written form) and states that the government will agree to a limiting jury instruction that will instruct jurors only to consider Peterson's post-arrest statement against him and not any of the other four defendants:

> Me [Little, Woodhouse, Bartels, and his cousin, Jones] *and some other people* drove to the bank on the morning of September 8. [Little, Woodhouse, Bartels] *Some other people* and me had cased the bank during the previous week and knew the schedules of the lady teller and the other employees including the manager. [Little, Woodhouse, and me] I put on [ski masks] *a ski mask* and walked toward the bank when the lady teller arrived at 8:30 a.m. [We] I carried *a pistol* [pistols]. [We were planning to] *Some other people and I* agreed that [we] *I* would tie up the lady teller and take as much money as [we] *I* could get [our] *my* hands on before the manager and other bank employees arrived at 8:45 a.m. [Bartels was the wheel man.] [Deleting the portion of the statement regarding Roland Jones.] /s/ Walter Peterson

Prosecutor 1: Prosecute all five defendants (including Woodhouse); seek to offer into evidence Peterson's confession at a joint trial with the foregoing redactions and with the agreement that a limiting jury instruction will be submitted; this instruction will restrict the jurors' consideration of the confession solely to Peterson's case and will instruct jurors not to consider Peterson's confession against any of the other four defendants (including Woodhouse).

Defense Counsel 1: Represent Woodhouse; you have filed a pretrial motion in limine to exclude Peterson's confession in its original or redacted form or, in the alternative, a motion to sever Peterson from the joint trial (to prevent the prosecution from offering Peterson's redacted confession into evidence).

---

11. Assume that each of the five defendants has a prior felony conviction that would be admissible to impeach them if they chose to testify but otherwise would be inadmissible if they chose not to testify.
12. Bruton v. United States, 391 U.S. 123 (1968).
13. The italicized portions of the confession were added by the prosecutor. The [bracketed] portions are the portions that will be deleted from the original confession and not introduced to jurors at the proposed joint trial.

To prepare for this hypothetical exercise, read *Gray v. Maryland*, 523 U.S. 185 (1998) (majority opinion only).

Prosecutor 2: Prosecute Jones; you have filed a pretrial motion in limine seeking to prevent Jones's counsel from offering the portion of Peterson's post-arrest, out-of-court statement referring to Jones.

Defense Counsel 2: Represent Jones; argue against the AUSA's motion in limine and seek to offer into evidence the portion of Peterson's confession that refers to Jones as having no role in the conspiracy.[14]

Assume for the sake of this particular role-playing assignment that the portion of Peterson's statement referring to Jones does not fall within any exception to the hearsay rule and is not otherwise admissible under any provision of the Federal Rules of Evidence with respect to Jones's case.[15]

To prepare for this hypothetical exercise, read *Holmes v. South Carolina*, 547 U.S. 319 (2006) (majority opinion only), and *Rice v. McCann*, 339 F.3d 546 (7th Cir. 2003) (majority and dissenting opinions).

Hypothetical Two: Pretrial Motions

United States v. Parker

On May 6, **Sammy Parker** approached a U.S. Postal Service mail carrier, **Milton Harrison**, on his route in Nita City. Parker ordered Harrison to "[g]ive me the keys to your mail truck." Parker brandished a handgun and said, "Don't make this a homicide." Harrison gave him the mail truck's keys. Parker drove the mail truck to a motel, rented a room, and searched through the stolen mail for credit cards and checks. He found numerous credit cards and one package of unused checks. When he finished going through the mail, he threw it away and abandoned the stolen mail truck. Parker then obtained a fake identification card with the same name as the one on the stolen checks (but the first name was misspelled).

---

14. Assume solely for the sake of this particular roleplaying assignment (i.e., Prosecutor 2 and Defense Counsel 2) that the district court, over the objection of Little, Woodhouse, and Bartels, already has ruled that the redacted version of Peterson's confession was admissible.

15. In particular, assume that the trial court has ruled that, under the Federal Rules of Evidence, Peterson's statement about Jones is inadmissible in Jones's case because 1) the exculpatory statement regarding Jones was not a statement against penal interest regarding Peterson (Fed. R. Evid. 804(b)(3)), and 2) the statement about Jones did not fall under the rule of optional completeness (Fed. R. Evid. 106) as the jury would be instructed only to consider the other portion of Peterson's confession against Peterson and not against any other defendant, including Jones. Also assume the trial court ruled that Peterson's confession was not admissible under the "residual exception" to the hearsay rule (Fed. R. Evid. 807). However, the trial court has asked the lawyers to address whether, notwithstanding the inadmissible nature of Peterson's remark about Jones under the rules of evidence, the Due Process Clause requires the admission of Peterson's comment about Jones *as a constitutional matter* in Jones's case.

Later that same day, Parker drove his own car to a Sears store in Nita City, where he used one of the stolen checks to purchase a big-screen television. The clerk who waited on Parker was suspicious based on the discrepancy between the spelling of the account holder's name on the check and the spelling of the name on Parker's fake identification. Although he proceeded with the transaction, the clerk alerted the store's manager to the suspicious purchase after Parker went to the area of the store where the television was delivered from the warehouse. The store manager followed Parker to his car and wrote down his license plate number. The store's security surveillance cameras recorded the transaction. After the check was returned from the bank as fraudulent, the Sears store manager contacted the authorities. Using the license plate number and the tape from the surveillance camera, the police identified Parker, which led to his arrest.

Based on Parker's armed robbery of mail carrier Harrison on May 6, a federal grand jury in Nita City returned an indictment charging Parker with assaulting a mail carrier with the intent to steal mail, in violation of 18 U.S.C. § 2114(a).[16]

Parker, who had a prior criminal record, pleaded guilty. The district court sentenced Parker to seven years in federal prison.

Believing that seven years was insufficient punishment, the U.S. attorney in Nita City later obtained a second indictment against Parker, charging him with "possession of stolen mail [on May 6]" in violation of 18 U.S.C. § 1708.[17] It is undisputed that the charge in the second indictment is based on the stolen checks that Parker possessed as a result of the postal robbery of Harrison. Parker's appointed defense counsel filed a pretrial motion to dismiss the indictment alleging a violation of the Double Jeopardy Clause.

Defense Counsel: Argue in support of your motion to dismiss the indictment as a violation of the Double Jeopardy Clause.

Prosecutor: Argue that Parker's motion should be denied.

---

16. Section 2114(a), entitled "Assault," provides that:

> A person who assaults any person having lawful charge, control, or custody of any mail matter or of any money or other property of the United States, with intent to rob, steal, or purloin such mail matter, money, or other property of the United States, or [who] robs or attempts to rob any such person of mail matter, or of any money, or other property of the United States, shall, for the first offense, be imprisoned not more than ten years [and not more than twenty-five years if the offense is committed with a dangerous weapon or if the victim is injured, or for a subsequent commission of the same offense].

17. Section 1708 provides that:

> Whoever . . . unlawfully has in his possession, any letter, postal card, package, bag, or mail, or any article or thing contained therein, which has been . . . stolen, taken, embezzled, or abstracted . . . [s]hall be . . . imprisoned not more than five years . . .

To prepare for this hypothetical exercise, read *United States v. Dixon*, 509 U.S. 688 (1993) (majority opinion only).

Hypothetical Three: Pretrial Motions

United States v. Rodriguez-Hernandez

On January 12, two miles from the Mexico-U.S. border outside of Eagle Pass, Texas, U.S. Border Patrol agents arrested **Jose Rodriguez-Hernandez** along with fourteen other Mexican citizens who had just crossed the border into the United States from Mexico by illegally crossing the Rio Grande River in South Texas without permission from the U.S. government. Agents suspected that Rodriguez-Hernandez was the "coyote" of the group—a slang term for a smuggler—because he was seen walking at the front of the group of Mexican citizens as they were walking away from the river. After being placed in custody, Rodriguez-Hernandez was interrogated by border patrol agents. Agents read him *Miranda* warnings, which he waived. The agents accused him of being the coyote. Rodriguez-Hernandez denied being the coyote. He stated that he was simply a "pollo"—a term commonly used to refer to a smuggled person. He then asked for a lawyer, and the agents ceased their interrogation.

When border patrol agents interviewed the other fourteen members of the group (the same day that they arrested Rodriguez-Hernandez), only two of the members inculpated Rodriguez-Hernandez as the guide or leader of the group while the remaining members exculpated him, denying that he was the guide or leader. Rather, the latter group stated that their coyote had abandoned them or that they did not have a guide. Border patrol agents retained as witnesses the two persons who had inculpated Rodriguez-Hernandez and three who stated that Rodriguez-Hernandez had no involvement as a coyote or guide. These five were placed in the custody of the Bureau of Immigration and Custom Enforcement. The remaining nine members in the group—who all exculpated Rodriguez-Hernandez—were summarily deported on the same day. The chief border patrol agent working on the case, **Raymundo Cantu**, stated: "We only need to keep three of the twelve who said he was a pollo. That still gives him one more than the two pollos who said he was the coyote."

The following day, Rodriguez-Hernandez was taken to federal court, where he was formally charged by indictment with alien smuggling in violation of 8 U.S.C. § 1324. He was appointed defense counsel. During the pretrial discovery process, his defense counsel discovered that nine members in the group had been deported (all of whom had exculpated Rodriguez-Hernandez), while only three who had exculpated him were not deported (along with two who had inculpated him). Defense counsel had no means of finding the deported persons and bringing them back to the United States to testify for Rodriguez-Hernandez.

Defense counsel filed a pretrial motion to dismiss the indictment based on the fact that the Government had deported the nine of the Mexican citizens and only retained the three who had exculpated Rodriguez-Hernandez. The foregoing facts were undisputed at a pretrial evidentiary hearing.

Defense Counsel: Argue in support of your motion to dismiss the indictment.

Prosecutor: Argue against defense counsel's motion to dismiss the indictment.

To prepare for this hypothetical exercise, read *United States v. Valenzuela-Bernal*, 458 U.S. 858 (1982) (majority opinion only).

Hypothetical Four: Pretrial Motions

State v. Cole

In early 2019, the defendant, **Marvin Cole**, was convicted of bank fraud in federal district court in Nita City and sentenced to thirty-six months' imprisonment. He was sent to the federal prison camp outside of Nita City. He remained there until July 2020, when he was transferred to the nearby federal penitentiary in Nita City. The conditions at the penitentiary were more restrictive than at the prison camp; prisoners could not go outside for recreation, visitation was more limited and regulated, and fewer educational and vocational programs were available. Prison officials informed Cole he was being sent to the penitentiary because a "detainer" had been lodged by Nita County authorities. (A detainer is a formal request by one law enforcement entity, such as a county sheriff's department, to another such entity to hold a prisoner once he discharges his sentence long enough for the first entity to pick up the prisoner and transfer him—in custody—to the first entity.) Prisoners with detainers are not permitted to remain in federal prison camps. The detainer had been lodged by the Nita County sheriff's department based on a pending felony indictment charging Cole with theft (of a car), which had been filed against Cole in early May 2020.

While he was serving the remainder of his federal prison sentence from mid-2020 to late 2021, Cole—who did not have the assistance of an attorney—wrote several letters both to the Nita County district attorney and to the clerk of the Nita County criminal trial court demanding to be "extradited" from federal custody to state custody to "get a speedy trial." His letters explained in detail that the detainer that had been filed "has made my prison conditions much worse." He never received a response to the letters. Instead, on December 31, 2021, when Cole had finally discharged his federal prison sentence, Nita County officials picked him up and transferred him to the Nita County jail to face the theft charges.

Thereafter, Cole, now represented by appointed defense counsel, filed a motion to dismiss the indictment based on the alleged denial of his constitutional right to a speedy trial. The district court held a hearing on the motion. At the hearing, the district court received testimony and evidence establishing the above series of events.

In addition, the parties stipulated that the reason that Cole was not transferred earlier from the federal prison to state custody was negligence on the part of the county prosecutor. It was undisputed that had the county prosecutor filed a simple application requesting a transfer (called a "writ of habeas corpus ad prosequendum"), the transfer from federal custody to state custody would have occurred in less than one week. When asked to explain why he did not respond to Cole's letters, the chief county prosecutor candidly admitted that "as a policy matter, our office never responds to inmate mail." Finally, at the hearing, Cole testified—without contradiction—that "I became very stressed because of the pending state charges. I wanted to deal with them promptly—both because I feared more prison time after my federal sentence was over and because my prison conditions were significantly worsened because the detainer." Cole offered documentary proof that he had repeatedly visited with the staff psychologist at the federal prison and requested—but never received—medication for his growing anxiety and depression. On cross-examination, Cole readily admitted that he could not show that his potential defense at trial was in any way prejudiced by the delay in the case. Indeed, the prosecution offered an audiotape of Cole's confession to the alleged car theft.

Defense Counsel: Argue in support of the motion to dismiss the indictment.

Prosecutor: Argue against the motion to dismiss the indictment.

To prepare for this hypothetical exercise, read *Ruffin v. State*, 663 S.E.2d 189 (Ga. 2008), and *State v. Steeves*, 383 A.2d 1379 (Me. 1978).

Class Five

Pretrial Suppression Motions

5.1 Suppression Motions Generally

The most common type of contested pretrial motion in a criminal case is a motion to "suppress" physical evidence and/or a defendant's confession. There are two main categories of motions to suppress: 1) motions seeking to suppress evidence or a defendant's confession under the Fourth Amendment based on an unconstitutional search, seizure, or arrest; and 2) motions seeking to suppress a defendant's confession as "involuntary," under the Due Process Clause, as having been obtained in violation of the Fifth Amendment requirements of *Miranda v. Arizona*[1] or as having been obtained in violation of a defendant's Sixth Amendment right to counsel.[2]

There are myriad substantive issues concerning the Fourth, Fifth, and Sixth Amendments that are regularly litigated in pretrial suppression motions.[3] We will address only representative "suppression issues" in our hypothetical exercises.

A trial judge generally must conduct an evidentiary hearing on a motion to suppress outside the presence of the jury.[4] In some jurisdictions, the defendant, if unsuccessful at the suppression hearing, may then choose to relitigate a constitutional suppression issue de novo in front of the jury without jurors knowing that the trial judge previously denied the motion.[5] In most jurisdictions (including the federal system), however, a defendant may not relitigate any suppression issue in front of a jury other than whether a defendant's confession was involuntary.[6]

If physical evidence has been seized by law enforcement without a search warrant, the prosecution has the burden (by a preponderance of the evidence) at the suppression hearing to show that the evidence was seized in a constitutional manner.[7] If

1. Miranda v. Arizona, 384 U.S. 436 (1966).
2. *See, e.g.*, Michigan v. Jackson, 475 U.S. 625 (1986).
3. *See generally* Yale Kamisar et al., Modern Criminal Procedure 108–813 (12th ed. 2008).
4. *See, e.g.*, Jackson v. Denno, 378 U.S. 368 (1964).
5. *See, e.g.*, Tex. Code Crim. Proc. arts. 38.22, §§ 6–7 and 38.23.
6. *See, e.g.*, 18 U.S.C. § 3501(a); *see also* Crane v. Kentucky, 476 U.S. 683 (1986) (holding that a criminal defendant is constitutionally entitled to challenge the voluntariness of their confession in front of the jury, including by offering expert testimony about their mental condition at the time of the confession).
7. *See* United States v. Scheffer, 463 F.2d 567, 574 (5th Cir. 1972).

physical evidence was seized with a search warrant, a defendant has the burden (by a preponderance of the evidence) in seeking to suppress such physical evidence under the Fourth Amendment.[8] If a defendant challenges the admissibility of their confession under the Fifth or Sixth Amendments, the prosecution generally bears the burden (by a preponderance of the evidence) to prove that no constitutional violation occurred, at least when the defendant has first made out a prima facie case of a constitutional violation.[9]

5.2 Motions to Suppress Evidence under the Fourth Amendment

In theory at least, under the Fourth Amendment, a law enforcement officer cannot engage in a search for, or seizure of, evidence or arrest a suspect without "probable cause" to do so. Furthermore, under most circumstances, a law enforcement officer theoretically may not seize physical evidence or arrest a suspect without first obtaining a warrant, particularly if the evidence or the suspect is located inside the suspect's residence. If evidence is obtained in violation of either of these Fourth Amendment requirements, then a court theoretically must suppress the evidence—including an officer's testimony about the evidence—unless the search or seizure falls within an exception to the Fourth Amendment's probable cause and warrant requirements.[10]

Theory and reality under the Supreme Court's modern Fourth Amendment jurisprudence, however, are two very different things. Since the days of the Warren Court, when the Fourth Amendment was enforced with the most vigor, a steady stream of exceptions to the probable-cause and warrant requirements appear on the verge of overtaking the rule.[11]

For instance, a police officer generally may engage in a warrantless arrest of a defendant if the officer has probable cause to believe that the defendant has committed a felony offense and the defendant is in public at the time of the arrest (including if the defendant has opened his front door in response to the officer's knocking).[12] Even without probable cause, an officer may engage in a temporary warrantless detention of the defendant to conduct a "pat down" and a limited interrogation (referred to as a "*Terry* stop") based on a lesser quantum of proof referred to as "reasonable suspicion."[13] A full-fledged warrantless arrest is permitted if the

---

8. *See, e.g.*, Franks v. Delaware, 438 U.S. 154, 155–56 (1978).
9. *See* Lego v. Twomey, 404 U.S. 477, 489 (1972).
10. *See, e.g.*, Payton v. New York, 445 U.S. 573, 586 (1980).
11. Florida v. White, 526 U.S. 559, 569 (1999) (Stevens, J., dissenting, joined by Ginsburg, J.) ("the exceptions have all but swallowed the general rule").
12. United States v. Santana, 427 U.S. 38 (1976).
13. Terry v. Ohio, 392 U.S. 1 (1968). "Reasonable suspicion" is defined as something less than "probable cause"; "the police officer must be able to point to specific and articulable facts, taken

officer obtains probable cause during a *Terry* stop.[14] Under the "automobile exception" to the Fourth Amendment's warrant requirement, an officer may engage in a warrantless search and seizure of an automobile if the officer has probable cause to believe that contraband or incriminating evidence is inside the car and the car is in a public place.[15] Under the "exigent circumstances" exception, police officers may engage in a warrantless search or seizure if they have probable cause to believe that evidence will be destroyed or removed before a warrant can be obtained.[16]

Once a defendant has been lawfully arrested (with or without an arrest warrant), a search of the defendant's person and the defendant's immediate surroundings (including inside their car or home, if the defendant was arrested inside or very near their car or residence) is generally permitted without a search warrant to promote officer safety or to "inventory" the arrested defendant's property.[17] Evidence discovered during such a warrantless "protective sweep" or "inventory search" is admissible under the Fourth Amendment.[18] As a general matter, an officer may always seize an item of contraband or incriminating evidence without a search warrant if that evidence is in "plain view" from any vantage point where the officer legally stands.[19]

Even where law enforcement officers violated the Fourth Amendment by engaging in a warrantless search or seizure, the prosecution is permitted to show that evidence that was unconstitutionally obtained is nonetheless admissible if it would have been obtained legally as the result of an "inevitable discovery" or through an "independent source." If the prosecution can establish that the challenged evidence would have been lawfully seized under such circumstances, the evidence will not be excluded because of unconstitutional conduct by a law enforcement officer.[20]

Another common argument prosecutors make when trying to uphold the validity of a challenged arrest, search, or seizure is that a police officer acted in objective "good faith" notwithstanding a Fourth Amendment violation, as seen in *United States v. Leon.*[21] In *Leon*, the Supreme Court held that when a police officer "in good faith" relies on a facially valid warrant that later is determined to be invalid, the evidentiary fruits of a search, seizure, or arrest pursuant to the invalid warrant are nonetheless admissible. After *Leon*, the lower courts grappled with applying

---

together with rational inferences from those facts, [that] reasonably warrant" a temporary seizure in order to investigate suspicious circumstances. *Id.* at 21. "Reasonable suspicion" is, however, more than a mere subjective "hunch." *Id.* at 27.

14. *See, e.g.*, United States v. Dotson, 49 F.3d 227 (6th Cir. 1995).

15. White, 526 U.S. 559.

16. *See* Schmerber v. California, 384 U.S. 757 (1966).

17. *See* South Dakota v. Opperman, 428 U.S. 364 (1976) (inventory searches); Maryland v. Buie, 494 U.S. 325 (1990) (protective sweeps).

18. *See, e.g.*, United States v. Wilson, 306 F.3d 231 (5th Cir. 2002).

19. Texas v. Brown, 460 U.S. 730 (1983).

20. Murray v. United States, 487 U.S. 533 (1988) (independent source exception); Nix v. Williams, 467 U.S. 431 (1984) (inevitable discovery exception).

21. United States v. Leon, 468 U.S. 897 (1984).

this "good-faith exception" to *warrantless* arrests, searches, and seizures.[22] In two recent cases—*Herring v. United States*[23] and *Davis v. United States*[24]—the Supreme Court extended *Leon* to warrantless searches where officers mistakenly but reasonably believed that such warrantless searches were permitted under particular circumstances.[25] Whether the holdings in *Herring* and *Davis* apply beyond their factual situations is an open question currently being litigated in the lower courts.[26]

Hypothetical One: Pretrial Motions

State v. Gonzalez

On Monday, September 8, around 9:30 a.m., **Berry Scoggins**, a white patrol officer with the Nita City Police Department (NCPD), was driving his patrol car down a residential street in Nita City's economically affluent River Oaks neighborhood. This particular area of River Oaks has many homes that are valued at over $1 million. The vast majority of residents of this neighborhood are white. Many of the white families regularly employ Latinx to clean their houses and maintain their lawns. NCPD records show very little criminal activity reported in this area. An occasional burglary or car theft is reported. Compared to the remainder of Nita City, however, River Oaks has relatively little crime. Officer Scoggins, who regularly patrols the River Oaks area, has been aware of the foregoing demographic facts concerning River Oaks since he became a patrol officer fifteen years ago.

That morning, Officer Scoggins noticed **Heriberto Gonzalez**, a twenty-six-year-old Mexican citizen who possesses a valid U.S. green card, walking along a sidewalk in front of a multimillion-dollar home. Gonzalez, who has long hair down past his shoulders, was wearing cut-off jean shorts and a T-shirt with a soccer ball emblem

22. *Compare* United States v. Whiting, 781 F.2d 692, 698 (9th Cir. 1986), *with* United States v. De Leon-Reyna, 930 F.2d 396 (5th Cir. 1991).

23. Herring v. United States, 555 U.S. 135 (2009).

24. Davis v. United States, 564 U.S. 229 (2011).

25. In *Herring*, a police officer reasonably but mistakenly relied on information provided by another police department that the defendant had an outstanding warrant when in fact that warrant had been vacated. *Herring*, 555 U.S. at 137–38. In *Davis*, a police officer reasonably conducted a warrantless search in conformance with existing federal circuit court precedent that later was overruled by the Supreme Court. *Davis*, 564 U.S. at 241.

26. After the Supreme Court's decisions in Herring and Davis, the lower courts have taken inconsistent positions about the breadth of the holdings in those two cases. *See, e.g.*, United States v. Cote, 72 M.J. 41, 46 n.11 (U.S. Armed Forces App. 2013) (declining to apply good-faith exception to an individual officer's negligent but good-faith mistaken belief that he had a right to conduct search beyond the terms of a warrant; distinguishing Herring); United States v. Davis, 690 F.3d 226, 255–57 (4th Cir. 2012) (applying the good-faith exception to an "isolated" and "negligent" warrantless search by a police officer when the governing case law did not clearly address whether such a search was constitutionally permissible; citing Davis); *id.* at 278–80 (Davis, J., dissenting) (disagreeing with the majority concerning whether the good-faith exception applied to the facts of that case).

and Spanish writing on it. He was not carrying any bags or other visible items. Officer Scoggins suspected that Gonzalez "was up to no good." Scoggins, who was wearing standard police dress, drove his patrol car up to the sidewalk where Gonzalez was walking. Scoggins, who speaks "some Spanish," clearly called out: "Do you speak English? ¿Habla Ingles?" In response, Gonzalez looked very nervous and immediately ran away from Scoggins's car. Scoggins jumped out of his car and ran after Gonzalez. Scoggins yelled out in English and Spanish: "Stop! Para! Stop! Para!" Gonzalez did not stop and kept running down the street. Eventually, Officer Scoggins caught up with Gonzalez and tackled him.

When Officer Scoggins tackled Gonzalez, a clear plastic baggie with a number of "rocks" of crack cocaine fell out of Gonzalez's shirt pocket. (A subsequent NCPD lab report showed that the crack cocaine weighed six grams.) Scoggins arrested Gonzalez for possessing crack cocaine, a felony under state law. Scoggins proceeded to drive Gonzalez to the police station, where he was booked and eventually formally charged by an indictment with possession of crack cocaine.

After defense counsel was appointed, counsel filed a motion to suppress the crack cocaine based on an allegedly unconstitutional detention (which resulted in the crack cocaine being exposed to view). The prosecutor filed a response to the motion. The trial court conducted an evidentiary hearing where the foregoing facts were established.

Assume that at the time that the motion to suppress is litigated in this case, the only directly relevant case law concerning the substantive Fourth Amendment issue in this case is *Illinois v. Wardlow*, 528 U.S. 119 (2000).

Defense Counsel: Argue in support of your motion to suppress and contend that the facts of this case did not give Officer Scoggins reasonable suspicion under Wardlow to temporarily detain Gonzalez.

Prosecutor: Defend against defense counsel's motion to suppress. In particular, argue that the facts of this case gave Officer Scoggins reasonable suspicion under Wardlow to temporarily detain Gonzalez.

After making your initial arguments, further assume that the trial court has ruled that Officer Scoggins did *not* possess probable cause or reasonable suspicion to search and seize Gonzalez. The court next has asked counsel to address whether 1) the "good-faith exception" applies to a warrantless search and seizure (as opposed to a search based on what turns out to be an illegal warrant) and 2) assuming it does, whether Officer Scoggins acted in good faith.

Defense Counsel: Argue against application of the good-faith exception as a matter of law; alternatively, argue that even assuming the good-faith exception applies to a warrantless search and seizure, Officer Scoggins did not act in good faith.

Prosecutor: Contend that the good-faith exception applies to warrantless searches and seizures and also that Officer Scoggins acted in good faith in this case.

In addition to *Wardlow*, supra, read *Commonwealth v. Censullo*, 661 N.E.2d 936 (Mass. App. Ct. 1996), and *Herring v. United States*, 555 U.S. 135 (2009).

Hypothetical Two: Pretrial Motions

United States v. Peterson

At 10:45 a.m. on September 12, Nita City Police Department (NCPD) police officer **Myron Fair**, who was on patrol, was instructed by a NCPD dispatcher to investigate an anonymous citizen complaint that had just been called in regarding a group of "white guys" at the corner of Montrose and Hyde Park Streets in Nita City, who allegedly were conducting illegal drug sales. At that time, Officer Fair had ten years of experience with the police department, two of which were with the narcotics division. Officer Fair knew from past experience as a narcotics officer that the location described by the anonymous caller was—in Officer Fair's words—a "hot spot;" a frequent source of complaints about drug deals. Because of delays occasioned by a serious automobile accident and the arrest of one of the drivers for DUI, Officer Fair did not go out to investigate the anonymous complaint until 3:15 p.m. on September 12.

Officer Fair, along with his partner, arrived at the corner of Hyde Park and Montrose in an unmarked police vehicle. As they approached, they saw "at least eight white males standing from the curb to the sidewalk to the top of the driveway" in front of 1564 Hyde Park, which is "about a house length" from the intersection of Montrose and Hyde Park. **Milton Peterson** was one of the individuals in this group. The group did not alter their behavior until the officers got out of their car dressed in police uniforms. At that point, the group walked away while tucking their hands in their pockets. The officers observed one of the individuals—but not Peterson—making a throwing motion towards nearby bushes (although the officers could not see what, if any, object was actually thrown). Seeing this, the officers pulled their firearms and demanded that all of the individuals stop, take their hands out of their pockets, and place them on a nearby vehicle. The officers' command was for the admitted purpose of searching for weapons and drugs and to ensure the officers' safety. Other officers arrived in other police cars shortly thereafter.

Officer Fair conducted a pat-down search of Peterson and found a .40 caliber pistol in his right-side waistband. Peterson was subsequently handcuffed and arrested for the state misdemeanor offense of unlawfully carrying a concealed handgun without a license. A criminal background check later revealed that he was a convicted felon. A federal grand jury in Nita City later returned an indictment charging Peterson with the felony offense of possession of a firearm by a convicted felon in violation of 18 U.S.C. § 922(g)(1). Peterson was appointed defense counsel, who proceeded to file a motion to suppress evidence of the firearm found on Peterson. The district court conducted an evidentiary hearing on the motion. The foregoing facts were established at the hearing.

Defense Counsel: Argue in support of your motion that Officer Fair lacked reasonable suspicion to detain and search Peterson.

Prosecutor: Respond to defense counsel's motion and contend that Officer Fair possessed reasonable suspicion to detain and search Peterson.

To prepare for this hypothetical exercise, read *Florida v. J. L.*, 529 U.S. 266 (2000), and *Illinois v. Wardlow*, 528 U.S. 119 (2000). (For purposes of this exercise, assume that the good-faith exception does not apply because there was no warrant or other circumstances that would require applying the good-faith exception.)

Hypothetical Three: Pretrial Motions

State v. Johnson

At 11:45 p.m. on June 17, the Nita City Police Department dispatched Officer **John Cook** to the corner of Liberty and Highland Streets next to what an anonymous caller described as a "a dive . . . a bar" to investigate a complaint. The anonymous caller—whose speech was slurred, suggesting that he was intoxicated—reported (and the dispatcher advised the responding officers) that "three Black guys" were acting disorderly and "at least one of them had a pistol and was brandishing it at other bar patrons in a threatening way." Assume that under Nita law, brandishing a firearm in a threatening manner is a felony.

The anonymous caller also stated that the three "were getting into a car, and I think they are leaving." The caller described the vehicle as a "white car." The caller then hung up. Sending backup, the police interpreted the report as describing "a high-risk situation with a gun possibly involved." The officers, including Officer Cook, knew from their previous experience that the neighborhood in question was an economically depressed area of town in which drug deals, thefts, and crimes of violence (including crimes involving handguns) were commonplace. Blacks are the vast majority of residents in that area of town.

Seven minutes after receiving the dispatch, Officer Cook and other officers arrived at Big Daddy's Bar—the only such establishment in the area around Liberty and Highland Streets—and observed a white Honda Accord leaving the bar's parking lot. They saw two other white vehicles parked in the immediate vicinity—an older model white Oldsmobile and a white pick-up truck, both of which were parked in front of the bar. No persons were seen in or near the other two white vehicles. The white Honda "pulled out right in front" of Officer Cook, permitting the headlights of his police cruiser to shine directly into the vehicle. Officer Cook clearly saw three Black males in the white Honda. On the basis of the anonymous tip, the officers followed the vehicle and stopped it several blocks away.

Officer Cook approached the car and explained the reason for the stop. Sergeant James Hogan went to the passenger side of the vehicle and shone a light into the car. Terrance Johnson sat in the front passenger seat with his arms folded across his stomach. Officer Hogan noted an unusual bulge underneath Johnson's shirt, which the officer suspected to be a firearm. The bulge, Officer Hogan concluded, "obviously was not part of his body" and was "too big" to be anything smaller than a handgun.

Officer Hogan asked Johnson if he had a gun on him. Johnson said no. Officer Hogan then instructed Johnson to "pull your shirt up so I can be comfortable with us talking, because I believe you have a firearm." In response, Johnson pulled up his shirt "a couple inches and put it back" and then "crossed his arms back across his stomach."

Fearing for his safety, Officer Hogan unholstered his sidearm and ordered Johnson out of the car. After Johnson got out of the vehicle, Officer James Bartley immediately conducted a weapons search and removed a Glock .40 caliber semiautomatic handgun from Johnson in the exact area of the previously noticed bulge. The officers then handcuffed Johnson and placed him under arrest. In a search incident to his arrest, the officers also found less than one gram of crack cocaine in Johnson's pants pocket. Johnson did not possess a license for the handgun.

A state grand jury in Nita City returned an indictment charging Johnson with felony possession of crack cocaine and possession of a handgun without a license. After retaining private counsel, Johnson moved to suppress the evidence of the firearm and drugs, claiming that the police officers 1) lacked a sufficient basis to stop the white Honda and to question its occupants, and 2) had equally insubstantial grounds for searching him for weapons or drugs. At a pretrial evidentiary hearing, the foregoing facts were established.

Defense Counsel: Argue in support of your motion to suppress.

Prosecutor: Respond to defense counsel's motion to suppress.

To prepare for this exercise, read *Florida v. J. L.*, 529 U.S. 266 (2000). (For purposes of this exercise, assume that the good-faith exception does not apply because there was no warrant or other circumstances that would require application of the good-faith exception.)

Hypothetical Four: Pretrial Motions

United States v. DeBeer

On six different days in May 2018 (May 1, 4, 9, 18, 21, and 28), an unidentified masked male wearing gloves robbed six different banks in Nita City. FBI agents investigating the robberies received an anonymous tip that Shaun DeBeer had been the masked robber. DeBeer is 6'2" and weighs 190 pounds. The surveillance videos from the six banks all depict a man who appears around 6'2" and 190 pounds. Agents learned DeBeer's cell phone number from DeBeer's parole officer. (DeBeer was on parole after having served prison time for a 2014 bank robbery.) On June 9, 2018, the FBI agents contacted DeBeer's cell phone provider, American Cellular Service, Inc. (ACSI), and obtained cell site location information (CSLI) about DeBeer's cellular phone—that is, data about which cell towers that DeBeer's cell phone connected to on the dates of the various bank robberies. The agents did not obtain a search warrant from a judge in obtaining the CSLI from ACSI. Instead, the agents merely faxed a letter on FBI letterhead to ACSI's records department, which requested the CSLI about DeBeer's cell phone.

On June 10, 2018, ACSI's records department responded with the requested CSLI about DeBeer's cell phone. The CSLI showed that DeBeer's cell phone had connected to cell towers located near the six banks at the very times the six banks were robbed. None of the six banks were located near each other in Nita City. Each were at least five miles away from any other of the five banks. The cell towers to which DeBeer's phone connected were located 100 to 200 yards from the banks in question. In addition, the CSLI records showed that DeBeer's cell phone approached the cell towers shortly before each robbery and immediately left the areas of the banks after each robbery. Agents also obtained the call records for DeBeer's phone, which showed that his cell phone was used to call his parole officer five minutes after one of the robberies (at 1:10 p.m. on May 18, 2018). The parole officer informed the agents that DeBeer had called the officer on that date "shortly after I finished my lunch hour" in response to a message that the officer had left on DeBeer's phone ten minutes beforehand. The parole officer's phone records confirmed the parole officer's memory. DeBeer had called the officer at 1:10 p.m.

Based on the information collected by the agents, including the CSLI, the agents obtained an arrest warrant from a federal magistrate judge on June 11, 2018, and arrested DeBeer that afternoon. The following week, a federal grand jury indicted DeBeer for six counts of bank robbery. Subsequently, on June 22, 2018, the United States Supreme Court issued its decision in *Carpenter v. United States*, 138 S. Ct. 2206 (2018), which required law enforcement officers to obtain a search warrant in order to obtain at least seven days of CSLI. Assume that, before *Carpenter*, neither the state courts in Nita nor the federal courts in the Twelfth Circuit had ever addressed the issue of whether law enforcement officers needed a search warrant to obtain CSLI about a suspect. Before the Supreme Court's decision in *Carpenter*, several other state and federal lower courts had permitted officers to obtain CSLI without a search warrant.

Defense Counsel: Argue in support of your motion to suppress based on *Carpenter*. Argue that the good-faith exception to the Fourth Amendment's exclusionary rule does not apply.

Prosecutor: Argue against defense counsel's motion to suppress. Argue that the good-faith exception applies based on the pre-*Carpenter* decisions of the other state and federal lower courts.

To prepare for this exercise, in addition to *Carpenter*, read *United States v. Diggs*, 385 F. Supp.3d 648 (N.D. Ill. 2019), and *United States v. Lopez*, 951 F. Supp.2d 657 (D. Del. 2013).

Hypothetical Five: Pretrial Motions

State v. Shaeffer

At 10:45 a.m. on Sunday morning, January 20, Nita City police officer **Beverley Taylor** was driving her patrol car. Officer Taylor received a radio dispatch advising that an anonymous caller claiming to be a "neighbor" of **Linda Beam**—who was described as an "elderly widow" residing at the Heritage Apartments—had called 911 and reported that Mrs. Beam "has not been seen or heard from in days." The anonymous caller also stated that "Mrs. Beam did not leave her apartment to go to church this morning. The church's pick-up van came to her door and the driver knocked, but when she didn't answer after repeated knockings, the van left. Mrs. Beam always takes the van to the 9:00 a.m. church service. Something must be wrong with her." The radio dispatcher informed Officer Taylor that the unidentified caller had called from a cellphone whose number could not be traced.

Officer Taylor drove to the large apartment complex, which has 140 apartments, and first went to the manager's office. The manager, **Ricky Chavez**, informed her that Linda Beam lived in apartment 106 and confirmed that she was an elderly widow who had lived there for a decade. Mr. Chavez said that he had not seen or heard from Mrs. Beam during the past few days. He also did not believe that Mrs. Beam had left town on a trip. In fact, Mr. Chavez told Officer Taylor that "the last few times that Mrs. Beam has left town for any significant period of time, she informed our office so we could collect her mail for her since the mailboxes in the apartment frequently are broken into." Mr. Chavez informed Officer Taylor that Mrs. Beam does not possess a telephone. "She frequently comes into our office to use our phone."

Officer Taylor and Mr. Chavez proceeded to apartment 106, where Officer Taylor banged on the apartment's door and loudly said, "Mrs. Beam, this is the police. Please come to the door. Are you OK?" After approximately sixty seconds with no response, Officer Taylor again knocked and loudly said, "Mrs. Beam, are you in there?" After no response, Officer Taylor then asked Mr. Chavez to open the door with a key that he possessed as manager. The key only unlocked the regular doorknob but did not permit Chavez to unlock an internal deadbolt lock with no external key access. After Mr. Chavez was unable to open the internal lock, Officer Taylor kicked in the door and went inside the apartment. When she looked in the back bedroom, she saw the defendant, **Harold Shaeffer**, lying on the bed in a deep sleep. On the bedside stand in plain view were a crack pipe and a small baggie of crack cocaine, which Officer Taylor immediately recognized as illegal contraband. Officer Taylor awoke Shaeffer, who was sleeping off his high, arrested him, and seized the drugs and crack pipe.

It turned out that Harold Shaeffer was Mrs. Beam's grandson, who was staying in her apartment (with her permission) during her week-long visit with her sister in another town. Mrs. Beam simply had forgotten to inform her church and the apartment's manager that she was going to be traveling out of town for the week.

A state grand jury indicted Shaeffer for possession of crack cocaine. Because he has two prior felony convictions for drug possession, he faces a lengthy prison sentence if convicted. Court-appointed defense counsel filed a motion to suppress both the crack cocaine and Officer Taylor's testimony about her discovery of Shaeffer's drug possession as fruits of a warrantless search and seizure in violation of the Fourth Amendment. The prosecutor opposed the motion, and the trial court conducted an evidentiary hearing at which the above-mentioned facts were proven.

Defense Counsel: Argue in support of your motion to suppress.

Prosecutor: Argue against defense counsel's motion to suppress.

To prepare for this exercise, read *Brigham City v. Stuart*, 547 U.S. 398 (2006), and *United States v. Huffman*, 461 F.3d 777 (6th Cir. 2006) (portions of majority and dissenting opinions concerning the Fourth Amendment issue in case).[27]

27. Assume that Shaeffer has standing to file the motion because he was an "overnight guest" at his grandmother's apartment. *See* Minnesota v. Olson, 495 U.S. 91 (1990).

Class Six

Pretrial Suppression Motions Continued

6.1 Motions to Suppress Confessions under the Fourth, Fifth, and Sixth Amendments

There are three primary types of motions to suppress a defendant's confession: 1) a motion to suppress the confession based on a *Miranda* violation or a related violation of a defendant's Sixth Amendment right to counsel; 2) a motion to suppress the confession as "involuntary" under the Due Process Clause, and 3) a motion to suppress the confession as "tainted fruit" of an illegal search or seizure in violation of the Fourth Amendment.

It is important to distinguish between violations of the "*Miranda* right to counsel" (which is rooted in the Fifth Amendment) and violations of the Sixth Amendment right to counsel.[1] The *Miranda* right to counsel, just like the *Miranda* right to silence,[2] is triggered once a law enforcement officer subjects a suspect to "custodial interrogation," whether or not the person has been charged with a crime or even formally arrested.[3] Conversely, the right to counsel under the Sixth Amendment "attaches" only with the "initiation of adversary judicial criminal proceedings," "whether by way of formal charge, preliminary hearing, indictment, information, or arraignment"; a mere arrest or interrogation, however, is insufficient by itself to trigger the Sixth Amendment right to counsel.[4] Until the "initiation of adversary judicial criminal proceedings," a defendant has no Sixth Amendment right to the assistance of counsel, although *Miranda* affords some protection of the Fifth Amendment right to counsel if the defendant has been subjected to "custodial interrogation."

Once the Sixth Amendment right to counsel attaches, law enforcement officers cannot interrogate a defendant—whether or not he is in "custody" for *Miranda*

---

1. *See* McNeil v. Wisconsin, 501 U.S. 171 (1991). The Fifth Amendment contains no explicit "right to counsel"; the Supreme Court in *Miranda* created a limited right to the assistance of counsel in the Fifth Amendment context as a corollary to the Fifth Amendment right to remain silent. *See* Miranda v. Arizona, 384 U.S. 436, 444–45, 465–73 (1966).
2. *See* Michigan v. Mosley, 423 U.S. 96 (1975) (discussing the right to silence aspect of *Miranda*).
3. *See* Stansbury v. California, 511 U.S. 318 (1994) (per curiam).
4. Texas v. Cobb, 532 U.S. 162, 167–68 (2001) (citation and internal quotation marks omitted); *see also* Rothgery v. Gillespie County, 554 U.S. 191 (2008).

purposes—unless the defendant first validly waives his Sixth Amendment right to counsel. If law enforcement officers deliberately elicit an incriminating statement from a defendant after his Sixth Amendment right to counsel attaches, then the confession must be suppressed unless a defendant had validly waived his right to counsel.[5] Officers "deliberately elicit" a confession when they directly question the defendant about a charged offense or otherwise make statements designed to prompt the defendant to incriminate himself.[6] Similarly, if a defendant unambiguously invokes his *Miranda* right to counsel—rather than waiving it—an officer must cease questioning him until counsel is present, and any confession obtained thereafter outside of counsel's presence (other than one initiated by the defendant rather than the police) is inadmissible.[7]

Confessions given in violation of *Miranda* also should be distinguished from involuntary confessions. *Miranda* is a "prophylactic" rule that requires a law enforcement officer who subjects a defendant to a custodial interrogation to first secure a valid waiver of a *Miranda* rights—including the right to silence and right to counsel—before a confession will be admissible at a trial.[8] An involuntary confession is one where the defendant's confession was the product of law enforcement "techniques and methods offensive to due process" that interfered with the defendant's free will in giving an incriminating statement, while a confession given without waiving *Miranda* rights is not necessarily (and usually is not) involuntary.[9] Nevertheless, if a confession was obtained in violation of *Miranda*'s prophylactic requirements, the confession is inadmissible even if it was in fact voluntary.[10]

Finally, if a defendant was unconstitutionally arrested or confronted with unconstitutionally seized evidence, a defendant's subsequent confession may be tainted fruit of the antecedent Fourth Amendment violation depending on the circumstances.[11] Even if the confession was voluntary and the defendant waived his *Miranda* rights prior to confessing, a confession that is tainted fruit of a Fourth Amendment violation is inadmissible.[12]

---

5. Brewer v. Williams, 430 U.S. 387 (1977).
6. *See id.* at 399–400. There is a difference between "deliberately eliciting" a confession (for Sixth Amendment purposes) and "interrogating" a suspect (for *Miranda* purposes). *See* Rhode Island v. Innis, 446 U.S. 291, 300 n.4 (1980). It generally is easier for a defendant to prove that officers "deliberately elicited" a confession in violation of the Sixth Amendment than it is for a defendant to prove "interrogation" under *Miranda*.
7. Edwards v. Arizona, 451 U.S. 477 (1981).
8. *See* Miranda v. Arizona, 384 U.S. 436 (1966).
9. Oregon v. Elstad, 470 U.S. 298, 304 (1985) (citation and internal quotations omitted).
10. *Id.* at 307.
11. Brown v. Illinois, 422 U.S. 590 (1975); Fahy v. Connecticut, 375 U.S. 85, 90–91 (1963); *see generally* Wayne R. LaFave, Search & Seizure: A Treatise on the Fourth Amendment, § 11.4(b) and (c) (3d ed. 1996 and 2003 pocket part).
12. *Brown*, 422 U.S. at 602–03.

Hypothetical One: Pretrial Motions

United States v. Liebman

In January 1982, U.S. Naval Ensign **Michael Liebman** (then twenty years old) and U.S. Naval Ensign **Andrew Munoz** were shipmates aboard the U.S.S. *Sam Houston*. Both men were assigned to work in the ship's disbursement office, an area where cash was kept in a safe for purposes of paying the ship's personnel. Sometime in the late evening hours of January 16, 1982, while the ship was moored in Subic Bay, Philippines, Ensign Munoz disappeared. Shortly after Munoz's disappearance, approximately $8,600 was found to be missing from the disbursement office. Naval investigators conducted an investigation and concluded that Munoz had stolen the money from the disbursement office and deserted the Navy.

Having never believed the official conclusion of the Navy, Munoz's sister, **Olivia Rodgers**, convinced Special Agent **Mark Houghton** of the Naval Criminal Investigative Service (NCIS), "Cold Case" Homicide Unit, to reopen the investigation over three decades later, in 2020. On November 19, 2020, NCIS agents interviewed Liebman, by then in his fifties, concerning Munoz's disappearance. The interview occurred at Liebman's home around 7:00 p.m. In early 2020, Liebman had been diagnosed with leukemia and had only recently recovered from six months of chemotherapy; his cancer was in remission at the time that he was questioned by NCIS agents in late 2020. The agents were made aware of Liebman's medical condition.

During the interview, which lasted over two hours, the agents did not directly accuse Liebman of having killed Munoz, but they did ask numerous questions indicating that Liebman was a possible suspect. Liebman was never read *Miranda* warnings and was told at the outset of the questioning that "you are not under arrest and may terminate this interview at any time." Liebman told the agents that he was "glad to answer [their] questions." During the interview, Liebman provided vague answers—none of which incriminated him—and agreed to submit to a polygraph examination (although no examination was ever given).

At the end of the interview, Liebman surprised the agents by stating that he could have "repressed memories" regarding Munoz's disappearance and asked Agent Houghton if he knew of a therapist who could help him reveal the memories. Agent Houghton responded that he did not know of any such therapist, but suggested to Liebman that "counseling would be a good idea." Liebman indicated that he wanted to attempt to recover his repressed memories and asked the agents to allow him that opportunity. The agents agreed to terminate the interview at Liebman's request. On December 16, 2020, Agent Houghton telephoned Liebman to inquire about his progress. Liebman responded that he had not recovered any repressed memories since the last interview and that "this whole thing has me feeling a lot of stress, which is not what I need right now because of the leukemia and chemotherapy." The agents had no further contact with Liebman until the fall of

2021. After the interview in late 2020, Liebman never saw a counselor or otherwise sought professional help to recover any "repressed memories." Liebman also never consulted with an attorney during that time.

At the time of the 2020 interview, Liebman had completed college (in 1989) and one year of law school (before he dropped out in 1991 for financial reasons) and was employed as a project manager for a real-estate sales company making approximately $70,000 per year. He was living with his wife and raising his four-year-old and two-year-old granddaughters. (Liebman's unmarried adult daughter, who suffered from serious emotional problems and a drug addiction, was unable to raise her two children, and Liebman and his wife had assumed custody of them.)

In September 2021, Agent Houghton and two other NCIS agents, **Larry Eaten** and **Tony Gibbs**, decided to talk to Liebman again. The agents believed that Liebman was the primary suspect in Munoz's disappearance, but did not have sufficient evidence to bring criminal charges. The agents engaged in a great deal of planning in advance about how the second interview with Liebman would be conducted (*e.g.*, how they would transport Liebman to the interview and what specific questions they would ask). They also arranged to have enlarged photos of Liebman's family and house, the U.S.S. *Sam Houston* and Liebman's former shipmates, and other scenes from Liebman's life on the walls in the interview room.

On September 21, 2021, Special Agent Eaten (whom Liebman had not met the year before) and Officer **Andy Harrison** of the Nita Highway Patrol drove to Liebman's office, without prior notice, weaning plain clothes. Officer Harrison identified himself to Liebman, vaguely told him they were conducting "an investigation," and asked Liebman to accompany them to the Highway Patrol station. Liebman asked what the investigation was about. Officer Harrison told him that at that point they could not tell him what it was about, but that it had nothing to do with his "family." Liebman, assuming that it had to do with certain alleged criminal actions of his employer (who, coincidentally, recently had been investigated for embezzlement), agreed to accompany the officers. Liebman had his cell phone with him the entire time. Liebman's cancer was still in remission at that time, and he otherwise appeared healthy.

Officer Harrison told Liebman that they would give him a ride to the Highway Patrol station. Liebman offered to drive himself, but the officers told him they would "prefer" that he ride with them. Liebman rode to the Highway Patrol station in the front passenger seat of an unmarked highway patrol car. After arriving at the station, which was located approximately thirty miles away from Liebman's job and home, Liebman was told that he was "not under arrest," and that he was free to terminate the interview and leave the building at any time. "We'll drive you back to your job or home, or you can call a cab," he was told. Despite these assurances that he was not under arrest, Officer Harrison nonetheless read Liebman *Miranda* warnings. Officer Harrison told him that "any time we conduct an interview we read the interviewee his or her rights. It's our standard practice." Liebman signed a standard *Miranda* waiver-of-rights form saying that he understood his rights and agreed to talk to the law enforcement agents. At that point, Liebman still was unaware that he was about to be interviewed concerning Munoz's disappearance.

Agent Eaten, who had not yet identified himself as an NCIS investigator, advised Liebman that he was subject to audio and video recording anywhere in the building. Agent Eaten then led Liebman to a 15' × 15' windowless interview room and closed the door. The walls of the room were covered with the enlarged photos from Liebman's life. Once everyone was seated, Agent Eaten identified himself as an NCIS investigator. Liebman responded in a surprised manner: "Oh. That's what this is about." Agent Gibbs entered a short time later and began the interview. Agents Eaten and Gibbs sat in chairs with armrests and rollers a few feet in front of Liebman, who was seated in a chair without armrests or rollers. No furniture was positioned between the agents and Liebman. The agents were not visibly armed with firearms while in the interrogation room. Liebman was not handcuffed during the interview.

Agents Eaten and Gibbs, by their own admission at the subsequent suppression hearing, began the interview by lying to Liebman about the existence of incriminating evidence. During questioning, Agent Eaten told Liebman: "There is no doubt in my mind that you were responsible for Ensign Munoz's death. Absolutely no doubt about it. Your claim to have suppressed memories is total hogwash. Who do you think you are fooling?" The agents also falsely stated that they had an unnamed eyewitness who had just been located: "It's another sailor who saw you dispose of the body. He never thought anything of it—he didn't realize it was a dead body— until we talked to him last week and explained what we now know." The agents also falsely claimed that Munoz's skeletal remains had been found and identified through DNA analysis, but did not give any specifics. In fact, the agents had neither an eyewitness nor evidence of Munoz's remains.

Agent Eaten stated that "the only issue" he and Agent Gibbs were interested in was whether Ensign Munoz's death was "premeditated or, instead, spontaneous and unplanned." Agent Eaten also told Liebman, "[w]e have evidence against you that is going to result in grand jury proceedings." The agents told Liebman that they were ready to proceed with a premeditated first-degree murder charge against him and that he would be "extradited to Hawaii," where the trial allegedly would occur since it was the closest U.S. state to the Philippines.[13] The agents also said that Liebman's "reputation" would be destroyed, his family's reputation would be destroyed, and "you and your wife will be financially ruined" if he fought the charges.

13. In fact, the trial was authorized to occur in federal court in any state in the United States and did not have to occur in Hawaii (although federal charges could be brought there as well as in Nita City).

The agents next falsely informed Liebman that Munoz's family was planning to file a civil wrongful death suit against him "now that Mr. Munoz's remains have finally been recovered." (In fact, Munoz's remains had not been recovered.) The agents advised Liebman that Munoz's family was then present at the Highway Patrol station and were "prepared to forgive" him and would agree not to sue him if Liebman admitted to a "spontaneous" rather than a "premeditated" killing—and if, in the words of Agent Eaten, "they believe that is really what happened." In the same breath, the agents also told Liebman that if the crime was "manslaughter" rather than "murder," there could be no criminal prosecution under the statute of limitations.[14] However, the agents knew that, if Liebman admitted to killing Munoz during the course of a theft, a felony-murder charge could be brought because there is no statute of limitations for murder (as opposed to manslaughter).[15] The agents never told Liebman that a felony-murder charge could be brought even if Liebman truthfully admitted to killing Munoz as a "spontaneous" act rather than as a "premeditated" act, although the agents never directly claimed the opposite either.

Ensign Munoz's sister and a law enforcement agent masquerading as Munoz's brother were in another room at the station. After being told that there could be no prosecution under the statute of limitations if the prosecutor and judge determined that the only crime that Liebman committed was manslaughter, Liebman

---

14. The following is a verbatim account of this portion of the interview:

Gibbs:	And if you will be man enough and stand up to the plate and say, "You know what, guys, it was spontaneous." [Twenty-second pause.] Although I have not talked to the prosecutor yet, I also think we might just have a problem with the statute of limitations here. It's possible, beyond possible, that you won't be prosecuted at all, if the prosecutor and judge determine that you committed only manslaughter rather than murder.
Liebman:	What?
Gibbs:	Special Agent Eaten?
Eaten:	That's what I think, too, although I'm not a lawyer. You [i.e., Liebman] went to law school. You know as much or more than we do.
Liebman:	What's the statute of limitations on murder?
Gibbs:	There is none for murder. But there is five-year statute of limitations for manslaughter, but none for murder. [Fifteen-second pause.] Now, it was spontaneous; is that right? It was, the choice was, either "I was going to the brig or Ensign Munoz had to die" and that was a selfish act.
Liebman:	So, am I hearing that I won't be prosecuted?
Gibbs:	Let me say it loud and clear: If the prosecutor and judge determine that what you did was only manslaughter rather than murder, you could not be prosecuted because of the statute of limitations.
Eaten:	If it was only manslaughter, you will not—cannot—be prosecuted.
Gibbs:	That's absolutely right.

# # #

15. First-degree murder is premeditated murder, while second-degree murder is felony-murder, i.e., a nonpremeditated killing committed during the course of a felony (including theft). The crime of manslaughter includes a nonpremeditated killing that did not occur during the course of a felony. Assume that Liebman's killing of Munoz, even if "spontaneous," constituted felony-murder rather than manslaughter.

was asked if he wanted to "apologize and make peace" with Munoz's family. Without giving Liebman an opportunity to answer, Munoz's sister immediately entered the interview room, along with Special Agent Bruester of NCIS, who falsely represented to Liebman that he was Munoz's brother. Agents Eaten and Gibbs knew that Liebman had recently battled cancer and told him that the agent posing as Munoz's brother had "terminal lung cancer" and had only a short time to live. Agent Bruester, pretending to be Munoz's dying brother, told Liebman that he wanted to find out everything about his "brother's" death "so I can die in peace."

Within a minute following these remarks, Liebman became emotional, broke down in tears, and for the first time incriminated himself. Looking at Munoz's sister, he said, "I'm so sorry for what I did. I was a scared, dumb kid 2,000 miles away from home. I just flipped when [Munoz] caught me stealing the money. I didn't want to get in trouble. I never intended to kill him. It was spontaneous, not planned. I swear to God." After composing himself, Liebman then asked if he could maintain contact with the family as he "uncovered more memories about the death," but he was advised that he should communicate with the family only through NCIS agents.

After Munoz's sister and "brother" left the interview room, Liebman confessed in greater detail to the murder of Ensign Munoz. He stated that Munoz had walked into the disbursement office while he was stealing money from the ship's safe. According to Liebman, he "panicked" and killed Munoz by strangulation. Liebman then described how he disposed of the victim's body—by placing the body in a large duffel bag loaded down with weights from the ship's gym and throwing it overboard—and even reenacted the murder with Agent Eaten in the role of the victim.

In total, the interview lasted approximately ninety minutes from the time that Liebman was taken into the interview room to the time that he offered his detailed confession. Liebman was arrested and eventually indicted for felony-murder (i.e., second-degree murder) in federal court in Nita City.[16]

After Liebman was appointed defense counsel, he moved to suppress the incriminating statements that he made during the 2021 interview on the ground that they were involuntary. In response, the prosecution argued that all of Liebman's statements were voluntary.

The foregoing facts were proven at a pretrial suppression hearing on Liebman's motion. The entire interview had been recorded by a video camera (including an audio recording) that was concealed in the room. A copy of the video recording

16. 18 U.S.C. § 111. The prosecution proceeded in civilian court rather than in military proceedings. Under federal law, an American citizen who commits a crime against another American citizen in a foreign country may be prosecuted in a federal court in the United States.

was played during the hearing. Although agents occasionally used strong emotion in their voices during the interview, they never shouted or used profanity.

Defense Counsel: Argue that Liebman's incriminating statements were involuntary and thus that the court should suppress them.

Prosecutor: Argue in response that Liebman's incriminating statements were voluntary and thus admissible at trial.

To prepare for this exercise, read *United States v. Syslo*, 303 F.3d 860 (8th Cir. 2002) (majority and dissenting opinions), and *Holland v. McGinnis*, 963 F.2d 1044, 1046–48, 1050–52 (7th Cir. 1992) (portion of opinion addressing the confession issue).

Hypothetical Two: Pretrial Motions

State v. Davis

On September 5, **Adam Davis**, a sixteen-year-old male who had dropped out of high school in the ninth grade and who had a juvenile record for car theft and robbery, broke into the trailer home of **Dorris Brewer**, his elderly neighbor. Once inside the home, Davis brutally raped and murdered Mrs. Brewer. Davis then left her house and stole some of her property. Davis eventually was arrested a week later after he attempted to pawn Mrs. Brewer's television, which had been reported stolen. The pawn shop owner ran the serial number of the television on a computer database and contacted the police, who located Davis sleeping in his mother's mobile home. Davis was arrested pursuant to a valid arrest warrant for possession of stolen property, but the police suspected that he had been involved in Mrs. Brewer's murder.

Nita City Police Department Homicide Detectives **John Marsicano** and **James Iverson** approached Davis, who was being processed in the Nita City Jail on the stolen property charges. Based on a fake ID that Davis had in his possession—that claimed he was eighteen years old—the police honestly believed that Davis was eighteen years old and, thus, a legal adult. Davis possessed the fake ID to buy cigarettes (the purchase of which requires the purchaser to be at least eighteen years old under state law). Therefore, Davis was not treated as a juvenile by the officers.

The two detectives took Davis to the interrogation room at the Homicide Division around 9:30 p.m. The officers spoke with Davis for approximately one hour. At the outset of the interrogation, Officer Iverson read Davis proper *Miranda* warnings, and Davis responded: "I've been arrested twice before. I know the drill. I'll talk to you. I ain't got nothing to hide."

Thereafter, Davis initially denied knowing anything about Mrs. Brewer's death and claimed that "some homeless guy" down the street from his mother's trailer had sold him the television for $10 and that he did not know that it had been stolen from Mrs. Brewer's trailer. At that point, Detective Marsicano stated:

> Look, Adam. You need to know something. We think you committed the capital murder of Mrs. Brewer. If you are convicted, you could get the death penalty based on the fact that the murder was committed during a rape, robbery, and burglary. The DA's office in Nita City is damn good at getting the death penalty. You need to come clean with us. If you confess, then we will tell the DA's office that you were cooperative. We can't promise that the DA won't go after the death penalty, but we'll make sure he knows you cooperated. But if you lie to us, and we then prove that you are the murderer—which we will be able to do once the DNA test comes back—then we will tell the DA's office that you were not cooperative and that you lied to us. It's your choice. Come clean, man.

In fact, as the case later progressed, the county medical examiner was unable to obtain any DNA samples from Mrs. Brewer's body (other than her own DNA). At the time of the interrogation, the detectives, however, did not know that DNA samples—or any other physical evidence linking Davis to the murder—would not be recovered from the crime scene or the victim's body.

In response to the detective's statements, Davis began to cry and stated: "I killed her. I was high on speed. I didn't really know what I was doing. I was so high. Please ask the DA not to go after the death penalty. I'm so sorry, man." Davis then broke down and cried heavily; he also asked to call his mother. He was permitted to do so.

The following week, Davis was indicted for capital murder and was certified to be tried as an adult. However, under state law, because he was only sixteen years old at the time of the murder, he is ineligible for the death penalty and, instead, faces a maximum sentence of life imprisonment if convicted. Under state law (as well as the U.S. Constitution), defendants convicted of capital murder must be at least eighteen years old at the time of the offense to be eligible for the death penalty.

Davis's appointed counsel filed a pretrial motion to suppress his confession. The prosecutor filed a response. A pretrial evidentiary hearing established the foregoing facts concerning the interrogation.

Defense Counsel: Contend that Davis's confession was involuntary.

Prosecutor: Argue in response that Davis's confession was voluntary.

To prepare for this portion of the exercise, read *United States v. Harrison*, 34 F.3d 886 (9th Cir. 1994), and *United States v. Braxton*, 112 F.3d 777 (4th Cir. 1997) (en banc).

Hypothetical Three: Pretrial Motions

State v. Tindall

On February 6, a masked man with a pistol robbed a jewelry store in Nita City. There had been a number of robberies in this area of town by a robber wearing a mask, and the police had initiated an intensive manhunt in an effort to apprehend the robber. **Jesse Jacobs**, who was at that time incarcerated on unrelated charges, told a police officer that "he had heard that **Omar Tindall** was involved in the robbery." Jacobs had never before given similar information to any police officer, did not tell the officer where he had heard this information, and did not provide any details of the crime. This tip was insufficient to give the police probable cause to obtain a warrant or to arrest Omar Tindall (whose criminal record consisted of a single misdemeanor conviction for shoplifting a few years earlier).

Nonetheless, on the basis of this information, two Nita City Police detectives, **Gerry Jones** and **Marty Mills**, arrested Tindall without a warrant on February 9, at 10:45 a.m. They told him that he was being arrested in connection with the jewelry store robbery, searched him, and took him to the police station for questioning. At the station, the officers read Tindall *Miranda* warnings, which he acknowledged that he understood. Tindall never asked for an attorney or stated that he wished to remain silent.

Tindall then was fingerprinted, re-advised of his *Miranda* rights, and placed in a lineup. The victims of the robbery were unable to identify him in the lineup. Officer Jones then told Tindall that a fingerprint examiner would be comparing Tindall's fingerprints with latent prints recovered from some of the items stolen during the jewelry store robbery (which had been recovered from a pawn shop). Officer Jones urged Tindall to cooperate with the police before the results of the fingerprint test came back,[17] but carefully refrained from making him any promises—only stating that at most he could inform the DA and judge of Tindall's cooperation. "If you confess after your prints are linked to the stolen property, I won't tell the DA and judge that you cooperated," Officer Jones stated. Tindall continued to deny involvement in the robbery.

At that point, Tindall's girlfriend, **Wendy Chen**, arrived at the police station and asked to see Tindall. After a short visit with Chen—outside of the police officers' hearing—Tindall was again read his *Miranda* warnings, which he waived. He then offered a detailed confession admitting to the robbery at 11:00 p.m. A grand jury subsequently charged Tindall with armed robbery. Tindall's appointed defense counsel filed a motion to suppress Tindall's confession under the Fourth

17. As it turned out, the fingerprint examination performed the following day did not reveal that Tindall's prints were on any of the stolen items.

Amendment as tainted fruit of the illegal arrest. The prosecutor filed a response. The trial court conducted a hearing, at which the foregoing facts were established.

Defense Counsel: Argue in support of your motion to suppress.

Prosecutor: Argue against defense counsel's motion to suppress.

To prepare for this hypothetical exercise, read *Brown v. Illinois*, 422 U.S. 590 (1975).

Hypothetical Four: Pretrial Motions

United States v. Porto

On the morning of September 11, 2020, the First National Bank of Nita was robbed by a lone masked man. The robber took $10,460 at gunpoint, then fled the scene. Later that day, based on an uncorroborated tip by an anonymous informant that **Willie Porto** had committed the robbery, FBI agents went to Porto's rural property. Without a search warrant, the agents approached Porto (without arresting him), told him that "we know you robbed the bank this morning," and asked for his consent to search his property. After they told Porto that "we will get a search warrant so you might as well let us search now," Porto consented. The agents found the money that had been taken from the bank hidden in Porto's barn. The agents were able to identify the money as being that stolen from the bank by its serial numbers.

Porto was arrested and that same day was taken to FBI headquarters in Nita City. There, FBI Agent **Sheila Smalley** read Porto his *Miranda* warnings, which he waived by signing a written waiver form. Agent Smalley then told Porto: "Look, your goose is cooked. We recovered the bank's money from your property. We've traced the serial numbers on those bills to the bank robbery that happened earlier that day." Porto made no statements in response and asked to use the restroom.

While in the bathroom at the FBI's offices, Porto escaped by crawling through a vent. He eventually was apprehended in New Orleans, Louisiana, on April 24, 2021, after being legally arrested for DWI. FBI agents in New Orleans, including Agent **Mark Richards**, learned of Porto's arrest on state DWI charges and went to the local jail to interview Porto. At the outset of the interview with Porto, Agent Richards advised him of his *Miranda* rights before questioning him, and Porto signed a waiver-of-rights form. The agents said nothing to Porto specifically about the bank's money that had been recovered from Porto's property. Rather, Agent Richards only said, "We want to talk to you about the bank robbery in Nita City last September." Before discussing the bank robbery, Porto asked to make a phone call to his mother in Nita City. The agents permitted him to make an unmonitored call to his mother. After Porto returned from the jail cell in which he had made the phone call (which had lasted six minutes), Porto immediately offered Agent Richards a detailed oral confession to the First National Bank robbery in Nita City.

After defense counsel was appointed, counsel filed a motion to suppress both the money (including evidence of Porto's fingerprint) and also Porto's April 24 confession under the Fourth Amendment (i.e., based on the agents' warrantless search and seizure of the bank's money). The prosecutor filed a response. The district court conducted a pretrial evidentiary hearing on the motion at which the foregoing facts were established. The district court held that the warrantless search of Porto's barn was unconstitutional because Porto's consent to search had been involuntary (based on the agents' threat to obtain a search warrant when in fact they knew that they did not have probable cause to do so at that juncture). The remaining issue was whether Porto's April 24, 2021, confession should be suppressed as tainted fruit of the September 11, 2020, unconstitutional search and seizure.

Defense Counsel: Argue that Porto's confession should be suppressed under the Fourth Amendment. (Assume that Porto's arrest in New Orleans, Louisiana, on April 24, 2021, was constitutional.)

Prosecutor: Argue against defense counsel's motion to suppress Porto's confession.

To prepare for this hypothetical exercise, read *Kaupp v. Texas*, 538 U.S. 626 (2003) (per curiam), and *State v. Abdouch*, 434 N.W.2d 317 (Neb. 1989).

Hypothetical Five: Pretrial Motions

State v. Ross

Alan Ross and **Robert Clark** were acquaintances whose relationship primarily revolved around using methamphetamine. On the morning of July 9, a mutual acquaintance, **Paula Kuykendall**, discovered that her car had been stolen. Ross and Kuykendall suspected that Clark was involved and later that morning confronted him at Kuykendall's house. Kuykendall began yelling at Clark, but Ross remained calm. When Clark denied that he stole the car, he appeared edgy and nervous. As Kuykendall left the room to call the police, Clark left the house. Ross left shortly thereafter, stating that he was going to "find Clark and get the car back."

Clark's body was discovered by the side of a road later that afternoon. He had been shot in the head four times. Investigators found a methamphetamine pipe lying between Clark's arm and body. A cigarette lighter was resting on Clark's stomach under his right hand. Pieces of a partially-eaten hamburger and a fresh cigarette butt were also near the body.

The police asked Ross to come in for an interview two days later, July 11. Ross agreed to do so and voluntarily drove himself to the police station. During the interview, Ross stated that on the day of the murder he saw Clark at Kuykendall's apartment in the morning, but that he had been unable to find him once he left Kuykendall's apartment that day. Ross denied having had anything to do with

Clark's death. At that point, the police told Ross that he was free to leave. He drove himself home.

The following day, however, the police took Ross into custody for an unrelated parole violation.[18] One of the officers read Ross *Miranda* warnings off a standard card; Ross responded that he was willing to "waive [his] rights and talk." At the outset, Ross again denied having anything to do with Clark's death. Instead, Ross claimed to be "very upset about it." The following colloquy then occurred between the lead officer, Arthur Winkler, and Ross:

Officer Winkler:	You act like you're cryin' like a baby, and you can't cry for someone that was a no good . . . and I bet you killed him for a good reason.
Ross:	No way! No way. You know what, I don't even wanna talk about this no more. We can talk about it later or whatever. I don't want to talk about this no more. That's wrong. That's wrong.
Officer Winkler:	Right now, you're showing me your remorse. Come on. Tell me what really happened.

Immediately after this exchange, the officer continued to interrogate Ross about his drug use on the day of the murder, including whether Ross had used a "meth pipe" on the day of Clark's murder. Ross said, "I might have. I use a meth pipe pretty much every day. You know that." Officer Winkler then said: "Come on. We know you killed Clark. A meth pipe was found near his body." In response to this questioning, Ross stated that he was "through with this." He then said: "Just take me into custody. I plead the Fifth." The following exchange between Officer Winkler and Ross then occurred:

Officer Winkler: "Plead the Fifth." What's that?

[Ross looked at Officer Winkler but said nothing in response to this question.]

Officer Winkler:	Why did you kill him? For drugs? Come clean, man.
Ross:	[After first letting out a heavy sigh and pausing for twenty seconds.] I killed him because he stole my dope as well as Paula's car. When I confronted him about it, we got into a fight. I pulled my gun and shot him. I was high.

After confessing to killing Clark, Ross was charged with murder. After the court appointed counsel, counsel filed a motion to suppress Ross's confession as being a violation of *Miranda v. Arizona*, 384 U.S. 436 (1966). Assume that it is undisputed

18. Ross was on parole after having served prison time for a methamphetamine conviction.

that at the time of the interrogation, Officer Winkler truly did not know the meaning of "plead the Fifth."

Defense Counsel: Argue in support of your motion to suppress.

Prosecutor: Argue against the defendant's motion to suppress.

To prepare for this exercise, read *Davis v. United States*, 512 U.S. 452 (1994), and *Michigan v. Mosley*, 423 U.S. 96 (1975).

Class Seven

Voir Dire

One of the most important stages of a criminal prosecution is jury selection or "voir dire" (which literally means "to speak the truth" in old French[1]). Because in most criminal trials the jury rather than a judge renders the verdict, the composition of the jury is critically important to both the prosecution and defense.

7.1 Educating Prospective Jurors during Voir Dire

Voir dire practices in criminal cases vary widely in this country. Some trial judges, particularly in state courts, permit the lawyers themselves to address and question prospective jurors (referred to collectively as "the venire"). Other trial judges, particularly in federal court, only permit limited questioning by the lawyers, and a small percentage of judges entirely handle the questioning themselves. In the vast majority of noncapital cases, questioning of prospective jurors occurs in the presence of the entire venire. Individual voir dire (questioning of individual members of the venire outside of the presence of other members of the venire) usually occurs in noncapital cases only concerning a sensitive topic (e.g., a member of the venire has been a victim of a serious crime and as a result may have a bias against criminal defendants generally). Conversely, in capital cases, where emotionally charged questions about the death penalty are the focus, individual voir dire is the rule, not the exception.

In all types of criminal cases, both the prosecution and the defense should ensure that prospective jurors are educated about—and then questioned in a follow-up manner about—the basic "ground rules" in a criminal case. Those ground rules are as follows: 1) the prosecution's never-shifting burden[2] to prove each and every element of the charged offense "beyond a reasonable doubt,"[3] 2) a criminal defendant's presumption of innocence,[4] and 3) the important corollary of a criminal defendant's right to remain silent and the concomitant requirement that this silence

---

1. Black's Law Dictionary 1746 (8th ed. 2004).
2. Sandstrom v. Montana, 442 U.S. 510 (1979) (discussing the prosecution's burden of proof in a criminal case, which cannot be "shifted" to the defendant at any point during the trial).
3. Victor v. Nebraska, 511 U.S. 1 (1994) (discussing the "reasonable doubt" quantum of proof).
4. Taylor v. Kentucky, 436 U.S. 478 (1978) (discussing the defendant's presumption of innocence in a criminal case).

not be considered against them.[5] Both sides have an interest in seeing that members of the jury are able to follow these rules fairly.

Effective voir dire on these ground rules requires counsel to speak to the members of the venire in layperson's terms. Avoid legalese and sophisticated vocabulary. At the same time, effectively convey the legal concepts to prospective jurors and avoid simplistic or trite explanations of those important matters. Many citizens have little or no prior knowledge of—and, indeed, many citizens have misconceptions about—the legal rules that apply to criminal cases. For instance, many laypersons erroneously believe that criminal and civil cases are governed by the same burdens of proof. And even those laypersons who do understand the legal rules in criminal cases may nonetheless be unable or unwilling to follow those rules because of an ideological bias. Most such biased jurors are prejudiced against criminal defendants. However, a growing minority of biased jurors are prejudiced against law enforcement or the government generally.

Although the purpose of voir dire is not the same as the purpose of an opening statement or closing argument—and, therefore, counsel should not refer to the specific facts involved in the case or make factual or legal arguments—treat voir dire as an opportunity to *educate* prospective jurors about the legal rules that apply to the case. For instance, if as defense counsel you know in advance that your client will not be testifying, make sure that the venire members are informed of the defendant's Fifth Amendment right to silence and also do your best to expose and remove any venire members who would hold the defendant's silence against them at the trial. Explain the right to silence in a manner that underscores its historical pedigree and its admirable purposes[6]—thus seeking to prevent jurors' perceiving it as a "technicality" that favors "criminals." Similarly, as a prosecutor, seek to expose and remove all prospective jurors who believe that the prosecution has a burden to prove a defendant's guilt "beyond a shadow of a doubt" or "beyond all doubt"—a higher standard than proof beyond a reasonable doubt.

In sum, an effective voir dire will 1) adequately explain the legal ground rules to the venire members and 2) seek to expose and remove those members who are unable to—or are unwilling to—fairly apply those rules during the trial.

---

5. Carter v. Kentucky, 450 U.S. 288 (1981) (discussing the defendant's right to remain silent and the need to instruct jurors that they cannot consider the defendant's silence against him or her at trial). Defense counsel should make sure that this issue is addressed during voir dire, even if the defendant intends to testify on her own behalf during the trial, because the defendant may change her mind and not testify during trial.

6. As the Supreme Court has said of the right to silence: "[O]ne of the Fifth Amendment's basic functions . . . is to protect innocent men . . . who might otherwise be ensnared by ambiguous circumstances. [T]ruthful responses of an innocent witness, as well as those of a wrongdoer, may provide the government with incriminating evidence from the speaker's own mouth." Ohio v. Reiner, 532 U.S. 17, 21 (2001) (per curiam) (citations and internal quotation marks omitted).

7.2 Removing Objectionable or Undesirable Members of the Venire

Jury selection is a misnomer. The parties do not in fact *select* jurors. Rather, they *remove* objectionable or undesirable members of the venire through the use of peremptory challenges or "strikes" (which can be made on any basis except for race, ethnicity, or gender)[7] and challenges "for cause" (which can be made based on a prospective juror's bias against one of the parties or the prospective juror's refusal to follow the applicable legal rules).[8] Depending on the jurisdiction, each side is given a set number of peremptory challenges to use during voir dire.[9] There is no limit to the number of for-cause challenges that can be made. Appellate courts tend to be extremely deferential to a trial judge's legal rulings on challenges for cause.[10]

One of the most common legal issues that arises during the parties' exercise of their peremptory challenges is a "*Batson* claim"[11]—an argument by one side that the opposing side used one or more of its strikes in a discriminatory manner. The U.S. Supreme Court has held that peremptory strikes cannot be used on the basis of a prospective juror's race, ethnicity, or gender.[12] The Court also has held that defense counsel as well as prosecutors cannot use peremptory strikes in a discriminatory manner; likewise, the Court has extended *Batson* to lawyers in civil cases.[13] Finally, any party—regardless of race or gender—has standing to challenge the opposing side's improper use of a peremptory challenge in violation of the Equal Protection Clause.[14]

7.3 Voir Dire Exercises

There will be two types of voir dire exercises during this class. The first will involve two hypotheticals involving *Batson* issues, which are set forth in the following pages.

---

7. *See* J.E.B. v. Alabama, 511 U.S. 127 (1994).
8. For a discussion of juror misconduct, see Class 13, *infra*. Sometimes a prospective juror reveals their bias during voir dire; other times the bias of a juror is not detected until after a defendant has been convicted following a jury trial. In the former situation, the trial court is required to rule on the question of whether a prospective juror is biased during voir dire; in the latter situation, the trial court is required to determine whether a juror (who actually sat in judgment of the defendant) was biased in ruling on a motion for a new trial or other post-conviction challenge to a defendant's conviction.
9. *See, e.g.*, Fed. R. Crim. P. 24(b)(1)–(3) (specifying the number of peremptory challenges given to the prosecution and defense in capital cases, noncapital felony cases, and misdemeanor cases).
10. *See, e.g.*, Wainwright v. Witt, 469 U.S. 412 (1985).
11. Batson v. Kentucky, 476 U.S. 79 (1986); *see also* Snyder v. Louisiana, 552 U.S. 472 (2008) (discussing *Batson*).
12. *See J.E.B.*, 511 U.S. 127 (gender); *Batson*, 476 U.S. 79 (race and ethnicity).
13. *See* Georgia v. McCollum, 505 U.S. 42 (1992); Edmonson v. Leesville Concrete Co., 500 U.S. 614 (1991).
14. *See* Campbell v. Louisiana, 523 U.S. 392 (1998).

The second set of exercises for this class will require the remaining students to roleplay either a prosecutor or defense counsel during voir dire. The point of this exercise is to educate the panel of prospective jurors (played by the other members of the class) on the ground rules of a criminal case. Although the prosecution, as well as the defense, is governed by these ground rules during a trial, obviously the defense will try to benefit from the ground rules, which place hurdles for the prosecution to surmount during a trial. Therefore, in a typical voir dire, the defense will tend to overstate the importance of each ground rule, while the prosecution will attempt to portray the ground rules as routine components of a criminal prosecution that are not insurmountable. Neither side, however, should describe a particular ground rule in a way that misstates the law.

In explaining these legal ground rules during voir dire, neither the prosecutor nor defense counsel may comment on the specific facts of the case. Rather, the prosecutor and defense counsel should simply explain the rules to the panel to 1) educate prospective jurors on the rules (from the differing perspectives of the prosecution and defense) and 2) root out those members of the venire who (from the defense's perspective) are unwilling or unable to follow the ground rules or who (from the prosecution's perspective) will apply the ground rules too strictly. Avoid using legalese and try to use commonsense, real-life examples when explaining your point. Feel free to ask the panel of prospective jurors about the rules after you have explained them (e.g., "Does everyone understand the definition of 'reasonable doubt'? Is there anyone who feels as if they could not follow it?"). Although voir dire is not the same thing as closing arguments, lawyers will often use voir dire to *explain* the ground rules in a manner that plants the seeds for what they intend to *advocate* during closing arguments.

Students will be divided into three groups for the jury explanation exercises. The first group will explain to prospective jurors the concept of the prosecution's burden of proof in a criminal case as well as the related concept of a defendant's presumption of innocence. The second group will explain to prospective jurors the "reasonable doubt" quantum of proof. The third group will explain to prospective jurors the constitutional rule that a criminal defendant's silence cannot be considered against them when arriving at a verdict.

Hypothetical One: *Batson*

State v. Gerger

A grand jury in Nita City returned an indictment charging the defendant, **Abraham Gerger**, with grand theft. Gerger is an Orthodox Jew. He both dresses and wears his hair and beard according to Orthodox Jewish custom. During voir dire, defense counsel used peremptory challenges to remove both members of the forty-person venire who had written "Islam" in response to the question, "What is your religion (if any)?" on the written jury questionnaire that was given to members of the venire at the beginning of the voir dire process. During the oral question-and-answer portion of the voir dire, neither the trial judge nor the lawyers asked the two Muslim venire members about their religious beliefs. When the trial judge asked the entire panel of prospective jurors whether "for any reason there are any of you who could not be fair and impartial jurors if selected to serve in this case," neither Muslim member of the venire raised his hand.

After the defense exercised its peremptory challenges, the prosecutor objected to the strikes against the two Muslim members of the venire on the ground that the defense attorney had violated the Equal Protection Clause of the Fourteenth Amendment. The trial judge asked defense counsel to respond to the objection. Defense counsel stated: "I struck those two people because they identified themselves as Muslims, and I feared that they would have a bias against my client, who is obviously an Orthodox Jew. It is common knowledge that there is tremendous tension between Muslims and Jews. That is the sole reason for my strikes against the two Muslim members of the venire. I had no other reasons for striking them."

The trial court then asked the lawyers to address the issue of whether the Equal Protection Clause was violated by defense counsel's exercise of peremptory challenges in this manner.[15]

Prosecutor: Argue that there was an Equal Protection violation.

Defense Counsel: Argue that there was not an Equal Protection violation.

To prepare for this exercise, read *State v. Purcell*, 18 P.3d 113, 118–22 (Ariz. Ct. App. 2001), and *State v. Davis*, 504 N.W.2d 767 (Minn. 1993) (majority and dissenting opinions).

Hypothetical Two: *Batson*

State v. Edwards

A grand jury returned an indictment charging the defendant, **Reginald Edwards**, with possession of marijuana. The thirty-member panel of prospective jurors was made up of twenty-four whites, three Latinos, and three Blacks. During voir dire, the prosecutor used three of his six peremptory challenges to remove all three Black members of the venire; the remaining three prosecution peremptory strikes were used on white members of the venire.

Defense counsel objected to the prosecutor's strikes of the three Blacks as a violation of the Equal Protection Clause. The trial judge asked the prosecutor to respond to the objection. The prosecutor stated as follows: "I struck each of the three Black

15. Assume that, if the trial court were to conclude that the Equal Protection Clause was violated, then the remedy would be to seat the two Muslim venire members as jurors in this case.

prospective jurors for a variety of reasons. Race was not my sole motivating factor for any of them. But to be candid, the fact that they were Black did have some role in my decision-making process for each of them. I believe that a Black juror might be more likely to vote to acquit a Black defendant simply because Blacks have been treated unfairly in our criminal justice system in the past."

The trial judge then asked the prosecutor to list the specific reasons for striking each of the three venire members in question. The prosecutor gave a variety of race-neutral reasons (e.g., all three were members of labor unions) as well as the foregoing racially motivated reason regarding each of the three Black venire members. The trial judge then found that the prosecutor's racial motive was "a factor, but not the sole factor—and not even the primary motivating factor—regarding any of the three members of the venire." The trial judge then asked the lawyers to address whether, based on this finding, there was an Equal Protection violation.[16]

Prosecutor: Argue that there was not an Equal Protection violation.

Defense Counsel: Argue that there was an Equal Protection violation.

To prepare for this exercise, read *Payton v. Kearse*, 495 S.E.2d 205 (S.C. 1998) (majority and dissenting opinions), and *Guzman v. State*, 85 S.W. 3d 242 (Tex. Crim. App. 2002) (majority and dissenting opinions).

Jury Explanation Exercises

To prepare for the second set of exercises, students should read Kevin F. O'Malley et al., 1A FEDERAL JURY PRACTICE AND INSTRUCTIONS, §§ 12.10, 15.14, pp. 167–68, 451–52 (5th ed. 2000), quoted in relevant part below.[17] In addition, depending on your particular assignment, you also should read the cases assigned below.

---

16. Assume that if the trial court were to conclude that the Equal Protection Clause was violated, then the remedy would be to seat the three Black venire members as jurors in this case.

17. **§ 12.10 Presumption of Innocence, Burden of Proof, and Reasonable Doubt**

I instruct you that you must presume the defendant to be innocent of the crime charged. Thus the defendant, although accused of a crime in the indictment, begins the trial with a "clean slate"—with no evidence against him. The indictment is not evidence of any kind. The law permits nothing but legal evidence presented before the jury in court to be considered in support of any charge against the defendant. The presumption of innocence alone, therefore, is sufficient to acquit the defendant.

The burden is always upon the prosecution to prove guilt beyond a reasonable doubt. The burden never shifts to a defendant, for the law never imposes upon a defendant in a criminal case the burden or duty of calling any witnesses or producing any evidence. The defendant is not even obligated to produce any evidence by cross-examining the witnesses for the government.

It is not required that the government prove guilt beyond all possible doubt. The test is one of reasonable doubt. A reasonable doubt is a doubt based upon reason and common sense—the kind of doubt that would make a reasonable person hesitate to act. Proof beyond a reasonable doubt must, therefore, be proof of such a convincing

Prosecution's Burden of Proof/Defendant's Presumption of Innocence

Also read *Sandstrom v. Montana*, 442 U.S. 510 (1979) (majority opinion only); *Taylor v. Kentucky*, 436 U.S. 478 (1978) (majority opinion only).

Reasonable Doubt Definition

Also read *Victor v. Nebraska*, 511 U.S. 1 (1994) (majority opinion only).

Defendant's Right to Remain Silent

Also read *Carter v. Kentucky*, 450 U.S. 288, 299–303 (1981) (majority opinion only).

---

character that a reasonable person would not hesitate to rely and act upon it in the most important of his or her own affairs.

Unless the government proves, beyond a reasonable doubt, that the defendant has committed each and every element of the offense charged in the indictment, you must find the defendant not guilty of the offense . . .

§ **15.14 Effect of the Defendant's [Decision not to] Testify**

The defendant in a criminal case has an absolute right under our Constitution not to testify. The fact that the defendant did not testify must not be discussed or considered in any way when deliberating and in arriving at your verdict. No inference of any kind may be drawn from the fact that a defendant decided to exercise his privilege under the Constitution and did not testify. As stated before, the law never imposes upon a defendant in a criminal case the burden or duty of calling any witnesses or of producing any evidence.

Class Eight

Legal Objections During Trial

After the trial court has ruled on all pretrial motions and the jury has been selected, the trial on the merits begins in a criminal case where a defendant has persisted in their plea of not guilty.[1] Beginning with the opening statements of the lawyers, continuing through the presentation of testimony and evidence, and finally during closing arguments, there are many disputed legal issues that can arise during a criminal trial. These issues are typically raised in the form of an oral objection by defense counsel or the prosecutor—usually the former.

For our purposes, we divide these objections into two types: constitutional and nonconstitutional objections. The most common constitutional objections during trial implicate the Self-Incrimination Clause of the Fifth Amendment (such as a prosecution witness's comment on the defendant's silence after arrest or during trial)[2] and the Confrontation Clause of the Sixth Amendment (such as that "testimonial" hearsay is generally inadmissible).[3] The most common types of nonconstitutional objections implicate the rules of evidence (e.g., whether evidence is relevant under Rule 401 or unduly prejudicial under Rule 403). Sometimes an objection will have both constitutional and nonconstitutional dimensions (such as an objection to hearsay under both the Rules of Evidence and the Confrontation Clause).

Objections occur most frequently during closing arguments, usually in the form of an oral objection from defense counsel to a remark made by the prosecutor. Claims of impermissible comments on a defendant's right to silence,[4] mischaracterizations of the reasonable doubt standard,[5] and the improper shifting of the burden

---

1. It should be noted that in the modern era, well over 90 percent of criminal convictions on felony charges occurred as a result of guilty pleas. See, e.g., Bureau of Justice Statistics, U.S. Dep't. of Justice, FAQ Detail, http://www.bjs.gov/index.cfm?ty=qa&iid=405 (last visited on December 14, 2022).
2. *See, e.g.*, Doyle v. Ohio, 426 U.S. 610 (1976).
3. *See, e.g.*, Crawford v. Washington, 541 U.S. 36 (2004).
4. *Doyle*, 426 U.S. 610 (prosecutor's comment on defendant's post-*Miranda*, post-arrest silence violated defendant's Fifth Amendment right to remain silent); Griffin v. California, 380 U.S. 609 (1965) (prosecutor's comment on defendant's invocation of right to silence during the trial violated Fifth Amendment).
5. *See, e.g.*, Randolph v. State, 36 P.3d 424, 431 (Nev. 2001).

of proof to the defense[6] are the most common objections in this context.[7] Prosecutors, too, occasionally object to defense counsel's closing arguments, although less frequently. The most common objection by a prosecutor is a complaint that the defense lawyer has misrepresented the evidence offered during trial.

The immediate purpose of a legal objection is to rectify the prejudice caused by the error—which usually means having the trial court sustain the objection and instruct jurors to disregard the objectionable matter or "strike" something from the record. Occasionally, however, counsel may believe that an instruction to disregard is insufficient to cure the taint from the error (or that an instruction to disregard actually will exacerbate the error by calling further attention to it) and thus a mistrial is required. Under these circumstances, counsel will couple an objection with a motion for a mistrial.

The secondary purpose of an objection is to preserve a legal issue for review on appeal where the trial court does not afford the corrective action requested at trial.

Legal objections, whether constitutional or nonconstitutional in nature, must be made in a specific and timely manner. Failure to make a timely objection that clearly and specifically states the legal point at issue generally will "procedurally default" or "waive" a claim of error on a subsequent appeal.[8] Merely stating "objection" is insufficient. The specific ground for the objection must be articulated.[9] Furthermore, counsel must assure that a trial court rules on an objection, even if counsel fully expects the trial court to deny it. Failure to obtain an adverse ruling on an otherwise meritorious objection likewise may prevent reversal on appeal.[10]

Occasionally, competent counsel will make the strategic judgment that an objection in the presence of jurors would be unwise because the jurors may perceive an objection as an attempt to distort the truth by limiting jurors' information or the jurors may view counsel as being obstreperous. This is rarely a valid reason for not objecting. Instead, raise the objection in a manner that limits the perceived prejudice that could result from an objection in the presence of jurors. The best way to do this would be to ask to "approach the bench," and make the objection outside of the hearing of jurors. Never forego a good-faith, nonfrivolous objection merely because of fear of irritating the trial judge.

---

6. *See, e.g.*, People v. Hill, 952 P.2d 673, 689 (Cal. 1998).
7. *See generally* Andrew M. Hetherington, *Thirty-First Annual Review of Criminal Procedure: III. Trial: Prosecutorial Misconduct*, 90 Geo. L.J. 1679, 1680–88 & n. 1740–64 (2002); Paul J. Spiegelman, *Prosecutorial Misconduct in Closing Argument: The Role of Intent in Appellate Review*, 1 J. App. Prac. & Process 115, 132–39 (1999).
8. *See, e.g.*, United States v. Olano, 507 U.S. 725 (1993); Saldano v. State, 70 S.W.3d 873, 887–89 (Tex. Crim. App. 2002).
9. Osborne v. Ohio, 495 U.S. 103 (1990).
10. *See, e.g.*, McKinney v. Estelle, 657 F.2d 740 (5th Cir. 1981).

Hypothetical One: Legal Objections During Trial

State v. Reno

The defendant, **Jake Reno**, was charged with theft. He pleaded not guilty and proceeded to a jury trial.

The prosecution's main witness, Nita City police officer **Dani Stephens**, testified that on December 4, they first encountered Reno outside of a department store in downtown Nita City. Store employees had called the police department after they witnessed Reno appear to shoplift clothing items from the men's department. Officer Stephens confronted Reno in the parking lot and asked if he would voluntarily go inside the store and answer some questions. Stephens agreed, and the two went back inside the store. Prior to asking Reno questions, Officer Stephens first read Reno *Miranda* warnings. Reno stated that he understood his rights and agreed to talk.

Officer Stephens further testified that after reading Reno his *Miranda* warnings, Officer Stephens explained that store employees had accused Reno of shoplifting. Reno responded, "I didn't steal these" and proceeded to pull two silk ties out of his jacket. Reno then stated, "I bought these last week as a Christmas present for my father and decided to take them back to the store to return them. I think my dad won't like them." Officer Stephens asked Reno, "Do you have a receipt for the ties showing that you purchased them last week?" to which Reno responded, "I think I dropped it in the store" after he looked through his wallet and pockets. Officer Stephens then examined the two ties, including their price tags. Officer Stephens walked over to the store's manager, engaged in a brief conversation about the ties, and returned to Reno.

Officer Stephens testified that they then went back to Reno and said to him: "The manager says these ties were placed on the display for sale last night. You couldn't have purchased them last week. Come clean with me." According to Stephens, Reno appeared nervous and distressed at that point. Stephens testified that Reno responded, "I've said everything that needs to be said. I don't want to say anything more."

Part A

Defense counsel objected to Officer Stephens's trial testimony that Reno allegedly had said: "I've said everything that needs to be said. I don't want to say anything more."

Part B

Assume for purposes of Part B of this exercise that the trial court overruled the foregoing objection by defense counsel and the trial continued. Later, during the defense's case, Reno took the stand and denied having told Officer Stephens that he'd purchased the ties during the previous week. Reno testified that, instead, he told Officer Stephens that he had purchased the ties earlier that same day and had lost the receipt. Reno was never asked by either the prosecutor or defense counsel—and never stated during his testimony—whether Officer Stephens had "lied" in his testimony about what Reno supposedly told him.

After both sides rested their respective cases at trial, the trial court instructed the jury on the applicable rules of law. Among the court's instructions was the following:

> The prosecution has the burden of proof in this case and must prove the defendant's guilt beyond a reasonable doubt in order for you to convict the defendant. That burden never shifts to the defendant. If you conclude that the prosecution failed to meet that burden, you must return a verdict of not guilty.

During closing arguments that followed the trial court's jury instructions, the prosecutor made the following statement to jurors:

> If you believe Officer Stephens's testimony about what the defendant told him, then you must find the defendant guilty as charged. But if you believe that the defendant is telling the truth and that Officer Stephens is lying, then you must acquit the defendant. It's that simple—if Officer Stephens is a liar, then the defendant is not guilty.

At that point, defense counsel stood up and objected to the prosecutor's closing argument.

Defense Counsel

Part A. Argue that Officer Stephens's testimony violated Reno's right to silence and requires a mistrial.

Part B. Argue that the prosecutor's closing argument impermissibly shifted the burden of proof to the defense and requires a mistrial.

Prosecutor

Part A. Respond to defense counsel's objection to Officer Stephens's testimony during trial.

Part B. Respond to defense counsel's objection to your closing argument.

To prepare for Part A of this hypothetical exercise, read *United States v. Velarde-Gomez*, 269 F.3d 1023 (9th Cir. 2001) (en banc) (majority and dissenting opinions). To prepare for Part B, read *United States v. Spencer*, 25 F.3d 1105, 1110 (D.C. Cir. 1994), and *Atkins v. State*, 878 So. 2d 460 (Fla. Dist. Ct. App. 2004).

Hypothetical Two: Legal Objections During Trial

State v. Herman

On December 31, **Margy Thompson** and **Alan Herman** were seen together at a New Year's Eve party. According to informed observers, Thompson and Herman met for the first time at the party. The two were seen leaving the party in Herman's car shortly after midnight. At 3:00 a.m. on New Year's Day, Thompson appeared at a local hospital's emergency room wearing torn clothes. She said Alan Herman raped her. Hospital employees called the police, who came to the emergency room. A "rape kit" was administered, which showed semen inside Thompson. There was no noticeable bruising or tears in her vaginal area or on any other part of her body. A DNA test was performed on the semen, which was shown to have come from Herman. (A sample of Herman's blood was obtained through a search warrant the following day.) Herman was arrested and charged with rape.

During the prosecution's case-in-chief, Thompson testified that Herman forcibly raped her after she refused to go beyond kissing. Herman's defense at trial was that he and Thompson had consensual sex at a time when both were very intoxicated. During the defense's case, he testified that he and Thompson had unprotected sexual intercourse shortly after 1:45 a.m. in the backseat of his car. He further testified that prior to having unprotected sex, he asked Thompson whether she was on the pill, to which she responded, "Yes." According to Herman's testimony, after the sex was over, Thompson stated: "I really want a baby. I hope it happens this time. I'm not really on the pill. I'm sorry I lied to you. I just really want a baby. You seem like the perfect man to be the father." At that point, Herman testified, he became very angry and told Thompson: "You're crazy. You can't play games with people's lives like that. You better not get pregnant. Get out of my car." Herman testified that the next morning the police came knocking on his door with a search warrant for a blood sample.

During the prosecution's rebuttal case, she testified that Herman's version of events was entirely untrue. She broke down in tears and screamed out, "He's lying. Oh, my God, he's lying."

When Thompson testified during the prosecution's case-in-chief, the courtroom gallery was occupied by approximately two dozen spectators, including one woman wearing a button adorned with pink ribbons, which was attached to her shirt. The button, which was three inches in diameter, read: "Sexual Assault Survivors (SAS) Task Force." Defense counsel did not object to the woman's presence in the courtroom. During the prosecution's rebuttal case, shortly before Thompson was recalled to testify, eight female spectators entered the courtroom. All eight were wearing (SAS) Task Force buttons. Defense counsel, who was reading documents and not paying attention to the courtroom gallery, did not notice the eight women at that point. Only after Thompson finished her tear-filled testimony and left the courtroom did defense counsel notice the eight women wearing the buttons. When Thompson left the courtroom, all eight women got up and followed her outside the courtroom.

Defense counsel asked that the jury be excused, and the trial judge ordered a recess. Defense counsel then moved for a mistrial based on the eight women's presence in the courtroom. The prosecutor opposed the mistrial motion. It is undisputed that no member of the prosecution team had advance notice that the eight women wearing the buttons would come into the courtroom during Thompson's testimony. The SAS Task Force is a local organization of women who, according to their website, "support victims of sexual assault during the emotionally devastating days, weeks, months, and years following the horrible experience of sexual assault."

Defense Counsel: Argue in support of your motion for a mistrial.

Prosecutor: Argue against defense counsel's motion for a mistrial.

To prepare for this hypothetical exercise, read *State v. McNaught*, 713 P.2d 457, 466–68 (Kan. 1986), and *State v. Franklin*, 327 S.E.2d 449, 474–75 (W. Va. 1985).

Hypothetical Three: Legal Objections During Trial

State v. Angel

In the early morning hours of January 14, the tenants of an apartment building located in Nita City heard scuffling noises coming from an apartment rented to **Neil Davis**. **Theresa Warner**, who lived above Davis, was one of the tenants who heard the commotion.

Approximately thirty minutes later, Ms. Warner went to her window and saw two unidentified men carrying "something large" from the apartment building and putting it in the trunk of Neil Davis's car. Before the men drove away, Ms. Warner heard the sound of kicking or pounding coming from the trunk of Davis's car.

Thereafter, around 7:00 a.m. on January 14, the owner of the apartment building, **Philip Rowe**, was awakened by a phone call from one of his tenants, who had spotted blood in the driveway leading to the building. Mr. Rowe went to the building and saw a pool of blood in the parking space for Neil Davis's car and a trail of blood from the porch of the building to Davis's apartment. He entered Davis's apartment and saw three pools of blood. He then called the police.

While the police searched Davis's apartment, two bystanders—the defendant, **Jamie Angel**, and Theresa Warner's adult son, **Victor Warner**—appeared to be unusually curious about the investigation. At one point, Angel volunteered to the police officers who had come to the apartment that in his opinion, Neil Davis had committed suicide. Angel also told the police that he and Warner had visited Davis on the previous evening to help Davis clean up his apartment after a burglary, which had occurred the day before. Angel stated that Davis was highly intoxicated and had received three prank phone calls.

Davis's car was found the following day with traces of blood in the trunk and in the front passenger seat. On January 16, following some highly suspicious statements made by Angel to the press regarding undisclosed police material (such as how much blood was found in Davis's car), the police interviewed him again. Angel volunteered that in his opinion, Davis was dead and that he had been transported in the trunk of his car and either dumped in a river or buried.

On January 18, Angel requested another interview with the police because he was disturbed that they had interviewed his girlfriend. During Angel's interview, he was told that the police suspected that Warner had killed Davis and that Angel "somehow had been involved in the killing." After waiving his *Miranda* rights, Angel told the police that he wanted to give them a statement. Angel stated that on the date of the murder, he and Victor Warner had been drinking and taking Valium and had gone to Neil Davis's apartment. Davis and Warner began to fight after Davis grabbed Warner by the testicles. Angel stated that Warner then pulled out a pistol and beat Davis repeatedly on his head until Davis became unconscious. Angel said that he and Warner assumed that Davis was dead at that point.

Angel told the police that he and Warner decided to get rid of Davis's body. They put Davis in the trunk of Davis's car and drove away. After they started to drive, however, Angel said that they started to hear Davis's repeated pounding and yelling coming from the trunk. Angel claimed that at that point he "begged" Warner to stop and let Davis out of the trunk. Angel further claimed that in response, Warner pulled out his pistol and told Angel that if he did not help Warner "get rid of" Davis, Warner would kill Angel. Angel told police that he and Warner proceeded to drive to a nearby bridge where they threw Davis, who had again become unconscious, into the river under the bridge. Angel's oral account was memorialized by a police officer into a written statement. Angel then reviewed and signed it.

Later that same day, Davis's body was recovered from the river. A subsequent autopsy performed by the county's medical examiner revealed that Davis had suffered eleven lacerations to his head and face, which were "consistent" with being struck with the barrel and handle of a gun. The medical examiner opined that drowning associated with injury to the head was the cause of death.

Following Angel's statement and the discovery of Davis's corpse, both Angel and Warner were arrested on first-degree murder charges. After he was arrested, Warner was shown Angel's typed statement. Warner told police that Angel had falsely switched the roles of the two men with respect to Davis's murder. Warner claimed that it was Angel, not Warner, who initially had beaten Davis with the pistol and further that it was Angel, not Warner, who (brandishing the pistol) demanded that the other help dispose of Davis's body. Warner claimed that he never intended to kill Davis and that he had helped Angel dump Davis's body into the river "because I was scared for my life."

The trial court originally scheduled back-to-back, separate jury trials for Warner and Angel. Each man's announced defense was to blame the other in a manner consistent with their respective pretrial confessions. Prior to their respective trials, however, both Angel and Warner agreed to take polygraph tests administered by a police officer. According to the officer who administered the exams, Warner passed his test whereas Angel failed his.

Although the results of such tests are inadmissible at a trial under Nita's rules of evidence, they are influential in plea bargaining. As a result of passing his lie-detector test, Warner was offered the opportunity to plead guilty to a reduced charge of being an accessory-after-the-fact in connection with Davis's murder and receive a five-year prison sentence, the maximum term for that offense. Warner accepted the prosecution's plea offer; the murder charge against him was dismissed, and he pleaded to the lesser charge, receiving a five-year prison sentence. As part of his plea bargain, Warner also agreed to testify against Angel in exchange for the murder charge being dismissed. The written plea agreement specifically provided that:

> In the event that you [i.e., Warner] do not testify truthfully as a prosecution witness against defendant Angel at his murder trial, then the murder charge against you will be reinstated and the State will prosecute you for that charge.

At Angel's trial, Warner testified in a manner consistent with his pretrial statement to the police. Warner admitted on direct examination that his plea bargain with the prosecution had resulted in the dismissal of the murder charge against him. At the outset of defense counsel's cross-examination, defense counsel stated, "Mr. Warner, I want to discuss with you now your sentencing exposure—that is, the maximum penalty for murder that you avoided by entering into this plea bargain with the prosecutor." At that point, the prosecutor objected and asked to approach the bench. The trial court asked the jury to go to the jury room.

In a conference outside of the presence of the jury, defense counsel expressed an intention to cross-examine Warner about the fact that by entering into the plea bargain, he avoided being exposed to a sentence of life without parole, the maximum penalty for murder under the applicable law. The prosecutor objected to this question on the ground that such a question was "improper" because, among other things, it effectively informed the jurors that Angel faced such a maximum penalty if convicted of murder. Under the applicable law, jurors in a murder case (where the death penalty is not being sought) are not permitted to be informed of the penalty range in the event of a conviction.

Prosecutor: Argue that the trial court should sustain your objection and that doing so would not violate the Confrontation Clause.

Defense Counsel: Argue that the trial court should overrule the prosecutor's objection and that prohibiting the proposed question from being asked would violate the Confrontation Clause.

To prepare for this hypothetical exercise, read *United States v. Chandler*, 326 F.3d 210, 216–27 (3d Cir. 2003) (portion of majority and dissenting opinions concerning the Confrontation Clause issue).

Hypothetical Four: Legal Objections During Trial

State v. Flatley

Susan Perkins was sexually assaulted by a male stranger, who fled following the rape. Afterwards, Perkins was transported to a local hospital, where she was examined by medical personnel. In the process of collecting biological evidence, medical personnel used a "rape kit" to collect, among other things, a blood sample, a genital swab, two vaginal swabs, and an anal swab from Perkins. Additionally, Perkins was interviewed by officers from the Nita County sheriff's office and she helped them create a composite sketch of the attacker from her memory.

The physical evidence collected, including the rape kit, was sent to the Federal Bureau of Investigation (FBI) laboratory for serological testing. A serological examiner identified semen on parts of the swabs and detailed the findings in serological examination notes. Despite the testing and investigation, the case remained unsolved for three years.

Three years after the rape, the sheriff's office submitted the rape kit to the FBI laboratory for additional forensic analysis. The laboratory generated a DNA profile of the suspect, consisting of thirteen genetic markers (thirteen "loci"), from the DNA in the biological material found on the vaginal swabs. This profile was entered into the FBI's national database and matched **Alan Flatley**'s existing profile (from a prior, unrelated rape case). The sheriff's office obtained a search warrant to seize additional DNA from Flatley. A buccal swab from inside Flatley's cheek was sent to the FBI laboratory to create a new "reference DNA sample" as well as verify that Flatley's profile in the FBI database was accurate. The second test also identified Flatley as Perkins's assailant. Thereafter, a grand jury returned an indictment charging Flatley with various sex-related crimes against Perkins.

At Flatley's jury trial, the prosecution called a number of witnesses, including Perkins, the nurse who performed much of Perkins's examination at the hospital (including collecting the rape kit evidence), and three law enforcement officers who participated in investigating the rape and collecting and handling the forensic samples taken from the Perkins and Flatley. Additionally, through its witnesses, the prosecution offered, and the court received into evidence, a composite sketch of her attacker that Perkins gave shortly after the rape. The sketch vaguely resembled Flatley.

Additionally, the State called **Jennifer Luttman**, a forensic DNA examiner for the FBI. Both parties accepted Luttman as an expert in forensic serology and forensic DNA analysis. In her testimony, Luttman provided background information about DNA, how it is analyzed and how DNA profiles are created, and how those profiles are used by the FBI to find the source of a DNA sample. Additionally, Luttman testified that DNA testing is performed by teams consisting of examiners, serologists, and DNA biologists.

After providing background information, Luttman testified about the present case. Luttman testified that her role was to compare known and unknown DNA samples, do the statistical calculations, and write a report; that her team participated in the actual analysis of some, but not all, of the DNA in the case; and that she reached her conclusions after reviewing the bench work[11] of both the DNA analysis conducted by her team and that performed by analysts she did not supervise.

At that point, defense counsel asked the trial judge to remove the jury from the courtroom so counsel could voice an objection—on Confrontation Clause grounds—to further testimony by Luttman. The trial judge removed the jury from the courtroom and asked the prosecutor to proffer further testimony by Luttman so that the judge could rule on defense counsel's objection. In the proffered testimony that followed, Luttman identified and explained the DNA profiles from the DNA tests of the biological material taken from Perkins and Flatley. In addition, Luttman introduced the results of the DNA testing on the pieces of biological evidence in the rape kit. Luttman additionally testified about how the FBI determines the rarity of a DNA profile using the "product rule." Luttman explained that this approach entails "basically . . . multiplying the frequencies across all [thirteen loci of particular DNA] to get the probability of selecting someone at random from the general population that would have the same DNA that's found on the evidence."

Finally, in her proffered testimony, Luttman presented her conclusions. First, she stated that the DNA taken from the vaginal swabs from Perkins matched the DNA taken from Flatley "at all thirteen DNA locations." Luttman testified that "[t]he probability of selecting an unrelated individual from the general population that would have the same DNA profile that was found on the [vaginal swabs]" was more than one in a quadrillion. Next, Luttman concluded, based on the serology report and serology notes from the original serological test, that the biological material on the vaginal swab was semen. Additionally, the original examination notes from the original serological examination of Flatley's rape kit evidence was proffered by the

11. With regard to the meaning Luttman attached to the term "bench work," she stated: "The biologists are the people who go into the laboratory and actually do what we call the wet chemistry. They're the ones who look at the items of evidence and then examine those items for blood and semen and then do the DNA testing. They then give me all of their results, and I'm the one who does all of the interpretation."

prosecutor. Thereafter, Luttman gave her final conclusion, "to a reasonable degree of scientific certainty," "that the DNA specimen from Flatley's sample is the source of the DNA found on the biological material collected in Perkins's vaginal swab."

It is undisputed that Luttman did not conduct or supervise the original serological testing or the original DNA testing of the rape kit. Further, Luttman did not perform the actual DNA testing that occurred thereafter, and while she supervised or reviewed her team's analysis, she did not observe the bench work at the time it was performed by her team. The results of these tests, however, were presented as the basis for Luttman's proffered testimony that Flatley was the source of the DNA found on the victim.

The prosecution has contended that all of the prior serology and DNA testing results are admissible under the business records exception to the hearsay rule[12] and that Luttman, a qualified expert witness, is permitted to testify about the testing and the results pursuant to Nita Rule of Evidence 703[13] as the basis for Luttman's expert opinion. At trial, the prosecution has stated that it does not intend to call either the serological examiner or the FBI DNA analysts who performed the DNA tests. Assume that the prosecution's arguments about the nonconstitutional rules of evidence are meritorious and the only issue for the trial court is whether her expert testimony, if admitted, would violate the Confrontation Clause.

Prosecutor: Argue that Luttman's expert testimony, if admitted, would not violate the Confrontation Clause.

---

12. Nita Rule of Evidence 803(b)(6) encompasses the "business records exception," which delineates those statements that are considered "[r]ecords of regularly conducted business activity" and are, therefore, admissible as an exception to the hearsay rule:

> A memorandum, report, record, or data compilation of acts, events, conditions, opinions, or diagnoses if (A) it was made at or near the time of the act, event, or condition, or the rendition of the diagnosis, (B) it was made by a person with knowledge or from information transmitted by a person with knowledge, (C) it was made and kept in the course of a regularly conducted business activity, and (D) the regular practice of that business was to make and keep the memorandum, report, record, or data compilation.

13. That rule provides that:

> The facts or data in the particular case upon which an expert bases an opinion or inference may be those perceived by or made known to the expert at or before the hearing. If of a type reasonably relied upon by experts in the particular field in forming opinions or inferences upon the subject, the facts or data need not be admissible in evidence.

However, the rule also provides that:

> If determined to be trustworthy, necessary to illuminate testimony, and unprivileged, facts or data reasonably relied upon by an expert pursuant to section (a) may, in the discretion of the court, be disclosed to the jury even if those facts and data are not admissible in evidence. Upon request, the court shall instruct the jury to use those facts and data only for the purpose of evaluating the validity and probative value of the expert's opinion or inference.

Defense Counsel: Argue that Luttman's expert testimony, if admitted, would violate the Confrontation Clause.

To prepare for this exercise, read *Williams v. Illinois*, 567 U.S. 50 (2012) (plurality, concurring, and dissenting opinions), and *Stuart v. Alabama*, 139 S. Ct. 36 (2018) (Gorsuch, J., dissenting from denial of certiorari, joined by Sotomayor, J.).

Hypothetical Five: Legal Objections During Trial

State v. Brooks

According to the indictment, **Gary Brooks**, acting in complicity with **Diane Wood,** Brooks's then-girlfriend, robbed a cab driver in Nita City. The indictment alleges that Brooks used a knife to cut the throat of the cab driver, and during the struggle that followed, he also slashed and stabbed the cab driver in the face and on his hands and arms. A confidential informant contacted the Nita City Police Department and told them that he had been present when Brooks planned the crime and that Brooks showed him a sum of money and told him that he and the others committed the robbery. This informant then helped the police by wearing a wire and obtained incriminating statements from Wood. The cab driver/victim positively identified Brooks during a pretrial lineup.

During its case-in-chief at trial, the prosecution did not call the informant to testify. Instead, the prosecution relied primarily on the testimony of the cab driver, who identified Brooks as the primary assailant. At the trial, Brooks testified in his own defense and denied planning or committing the robbery. He testified that the other individuals, including the informant,[14] had committed the robbery. He also denied telling the informant that he committed the robbery or driving him to the scene of the occurrence. Brooks also testified that the cab driver had mistaken him for the real robber.

During the prosecution's rebuttal case, the prosecution sought to introduce a court reporter's transcription of, and the court reporter's audio recording of, Wood's prior testimony at the preliminary hearing (at which she testified that she and Brooks had robbed the cab driver).[15] The prosecution informed the trial court that Wood, who was incarcerated at the time of trial and who was on the prosecution's witness list, had "broken down mentally" on the morning of the second day of trial and, thus, was unavailable to testify as a live witness during the prosecution's rebuttal case.

In a hearing outside of the presence of the jury, the prosecution called **Dr. Sam Wainwright** as a witness. Dr. Wainwright, a psychologist employed by the Nita City jail, testified that Wood appeared emotionally distraught and "is suffering

14. Although the informant did not testify at trial, Brooks's defense voluntarily elicited the fact during the prosecution's case-in-chief that an informant had implicated Brooks in the robbery.

15. At the preliminary hearing, Brooks had been represented by counsel, who vigorously cross-examined Wood.

from a major depressive disorder." Dr. Wainwright opined that, "It would not be in her interests, from a medical standpoint, to be forced to testify against a man whom she fears will retaliate against her if she testifies against him at the trial. It would only make her fragile mental condition all the worse." He also stated, "I cannot imagine that she will ever overcome her extreme fear of the defendant, at least where he potentially will be released from jail. My strong medical advice is that she should not be forced into court as a witness against the defendant. The preliminary hearing traumatized her enough." By Wood's own admission, Brooks has never threatened her; however, she honestly believes he will cause her death in retaliation for her testimony if he is released from custody. When asked whether Woods qualified as "mentally incompetent," Dr. Wainwright responded, "No, not incompetent, but very, very scared of the defendant."

Before making a ruling on whether Wood's prior testimony was admissible, the trial court asked the defense if they wanted to move for a mistrial and a new trial date after a few months had passed to give Wood's mental condition time to improve (to see if she could serve as a live witness at some later point in time). Defense counsel responded that after consulting with Brooks, the defense did not wish for a mistrial and, in fact, would oppose a mistrial and contend that a retrial following a mistrial would violate the Double Jeopardy Clause.[16] Defense counsel stated that Brooks should not be forced to stand trial twice and that the court should refuse to admit Wood's prior testimony. The prosecutor stated that the State also would not move for a mistrial (fearing a prosecution motion would result in a double jeopardy bar to a retrial) but would not oppose a motion for a mistrial filed by the defense.[17] The prosecutor urged the trial court to admit Wood's prior testimony under the circumstances. The trial court stated that, based on the position of the parties, no mistrial would be granted and that the court would make a ruling on the admissibility of Wood's prior testimony after hearing legal argument from both sides.

Prosecutor: Argue in support of the admission of Wood's prior testimony.

Defense Counsel: Object, on Confrontation Clause grounds, to the admission of Wood's prior testimony.

To prepare for this exercise, read *State v. Kuone*, 757 P.2d 289 (Kan. 1988) (majority and dissenting opinions).

---

16. Defense counsel should assume that Brooks insisted that counsel oppose a mistrial and "roll the dice" in terms of the trial court's ruling on the admissibility of Wood's prior testimony under those circumstances. Assume for the sake of this hypothetical that defense counsel decided to respect Brooks's request.

17. If the defense—as opposed to the prosecution—moved for a mistrial, then Brooks would have no basis to argue that a second trial would be barred by the Double Jeopardy Clause. *See* Oregon v. Kennedy, 456 U.S. 667 (1982).

Class Nine

Motions for Judgment of Acquittal

After the prosecution has rested its case, defense counsel will typically move for a judgment of acquittal. Closely analogous to a motion for a directed verdict in a civil case, a motion for a judgment of acquittal in a criminal case is a procedural device whereby defense counsel requests—usually in an oral motion—that the trial court "take the case away from the jury" and render a not-guilty verdict based on legally "insufficient" evidence.[1]

9.1 The *Jackson v. Virginia* Standard

The standard governing the trial court in ruling on a motion for judgment of acquittal is the same standard governing an appellate court asked to reverse a conviction based on insufficient evidence—namely, whether, viewing the evidence in a *light most favorable to the prosecution*, a rational jury could conclude that the prosecution proved each element of the charged offense beyond a reasonable doubt.[2]

After viewing the evidence in such a light, a trial court, if it concludes that no rational jury could find each and every element of the charged offense(s) beyond a reasonable doubt, will take the case away from the jury and enter a judgment of acquittal.[3]

This *Jackson v. Virginia* standard erects a high hurdle for defendants. Motions for judgment of acquittal are thus infrequently granted. Nevertheless, defense counsel should make such a motion in every case, even if only in a perfunctory manner. The prosecution occasionally makes a critical mistake—overlooked by the parties and the trial judge—by failing to offer some piece of evidence that later turns out to be a basis for reversal on appeal.[4]

---

1. *See, e.g.*, Fed. R. Crim. P. 29(a).
2. *See* Jackson v. Virginia, 443 U.S. 307 (1979); *see also* Glasser v. United States, 315 U.S. 60, 80 (1942).
3. Sometimes, trial courts grant motions for judgment of acquittal on some counts of the indictment, but not on others. In such cases of "partial acquittals," the remaining counts of the indictment are submitted to the jury for deliberation.
4. *See, e.g.*, United States v. Schultz, 17 F.3d 723 (5th Cir. 1994) (federal bank fraud conviction reversed based on insufficient evidence as a result of the prosecution's failure to offer readily available proof that bank was FDIC-insured on date of fraud).

If a trial court grants a motion for judgment of acquittal, it usually does so before the jury has deliberated and returned a verdict. Occasionally, however, a trial judge inclined to grant a motion will allow a jury the opportunity to return a not-guilty verdict first and, if the jury fails to do so, then the judge will enter a judgment of acquittal after the jury's guilty verdict[5] or after a mistrial following a hung jury. The critical difference between a trial court's judgment of acquittal granted before a jury returns a verdict and one granted after a guilty verdict from the jury is the possibility of double jeopardy issues. A pre-verdict judgment of acquittal by the trial court prevents a retrial under the Double Jeopardy Clause and also prevents an appeal of the court's ruling by the prosecution; a post-verdict judgment of acquittal does not prevent an appeal by the prosecution, which, if successful, will reinstate the jury's guilty verdict.[6]

In some jurisdictions, a trial court also has the option of granting a new trial after concluding that a jury's guilty verdict is unjust because it is "against the great weight and preponderance of the evidence," even if there was legally sufficient evidence to support the verdict under the *Jackson v. Virginia* standard.[7] Such a post-verdict ruling does not apply the *Jackson* "legal sufficiency" standard, but instead applies a less deferential "factual sufficiency" standard that permits the judge to reweigh the evidence. That is, a court does not review the evidence in a light most favorable to the prosecution, as it does under *Jackson*. Instead, the court acts to some degree as a "thirteenth juror."[8] A finding of factual insufficiency does not bar a retrial under the Double Jeopardy Clause.[9]

In many jurisdictions, to preserve a sufficiency issue for appeal, the defense not only must make a motion for judgment of acquittal immediately after the prosecution has rested its case-in-chief, but it also must renew the motion after both sides have rested following the close of all the evidence in the case (assuming that the defense does not rest its case without putting on any evidence).[10] If defense counsel fails to renew its motion at the close of all the evidence, then an appellate court either will refuse to address a claim of insufficient evidence or will engage in some type of appellate review more limited than de novo review.[11]

---

5. Such a post-verdict judgment of acquittal is analogous to a "judgment notwithstanding the verdict" in a civil case.
6. *See* United States v. Scott, 437 U.S. 82, 91 n.7 (1978).
7. *See, e.g.*, United States v. Ashworth, 836 F.2d 260, 266 (6th Cir. 1988) (*discussing* FED. R. CRIM. P. 33).
8. United States v. Washington, 57 M.J. 394, 403 (Armed Forces App. 2002).
9. Tibbs v. Florida, 457 U.S. 31 (1982).
10. *See, e.g.*, United States v. Burton, 324 F.3d 768, 770 (5th Cir. 2003).
11. *See, e.g.*, United States v. Carpenter, 95 F.3d 773, 775 (9th Cir. 1996).

9.2 Direct and Circumstantial Evidence

In theory at least, most courts, when ruling on motions for judgment of acquittal, treat "direct evidence" cases and "circumstantial evidence" cases[12] in the same manner.[13] Traditionally, however, some courts have applied what has been referred to as the "reasonable hypothesis of innocence analytical construct," whereby circumstantial evidence that permits *any* reasonable hypothesis of innocence as well as a hypothesis of guilt is necessarily deemed insufficient as a matter of law, even if the greater weight of circumstantial evidence supports the hypothesis of guilt.[14] The vast majority of courts have abandoned this standard in circumstantial evidence cases.[15]

Nonetheless, some courts still conclude that where the prosecution's circumstantial evidence shows "equal or nearly equal circumstantial support to a theory of guilt and a theory of innocence," the evidence is necessarily insufficient under the *Jackson v. Virginia* standard.[16] Similarly, in criminal cases involving charges that a defendant illegally possessed contraband (e.g., a controlled substance or an illegal firearm), courts faced with circumstantial evidence that the defendant was present in a place jointly occupied by other persons and that the contraband was not in plain view will find insufficient evidence as a matter of law if there is no proof specifically linking the defendant to the hidden contraband.[17] Likewise, circumstantial evidence of a defendant's mere association with, or proximity to, other persons engaging in criminal activity does not, by itself, prove beyond a reasonable doubt that the defendant also was engaging in that criminal conduct.[18]

Conversely, in cases in which direct evidence was introduced concerning each element of the charged offense—such as testimony from an eyewitness or accomplice—it is highly unlikely that a trial court will take the case away from the

12. "'Direct evidence' is the testimony of one who asserts actual knowledge of a fact, such as an eyewitness. 'Circumstantial evidence' is proof of a chain of events and circumstances indicating that something is or is not a fact." Fifth Circuit Pattern Jury Instructions, § 1.07 (2001).
13. *See, e.g.*, Geesa v. State, 820 S.W.2d 154 (Tex. Crim. App. 1991), *overruled on other grounds by* Paulson v. State, 28 S.W.3d 570 (Tex. Crim. App. 2000).
14. *Geesa*, 820 S.W.2d at 157; *see also* State v. Derouchie, 440 A.2d 146, 148–49 (Vt. 1981); State v. Bell, 560 P.2d 925 (N.M. 1977).
15. *See Geesa*, 820 S.W.2d at 160–61; *see also* State v. Grim, 854 S.W.2d 403 (Mo. 1993); United States v. Jackson, 863 F.2d 1168, 1173 (4th Cir. 1989); United States v. Bell, 678 F.2d 547 (5th Cir. 1982).
16. *See, e.g.*, United States v. Coplan, 703 F.3d 46, 69 (2d Cir. 2012); United States v. Morillo, 158 F.3d 18, 22–23 (1st Cir. 1998); McRee v. State, 732 So. 2d 246, 250 (Miss. 1999).
17. *See, e.g.*, United States v. Mergerson, 4 F.3d 337, 349 (5th Cir. 1993) ("[W]here . . . a residence is jointly occupied, the mere fact that contraband is discovered at the residence will not, without more, provide evidence sufficient to support a conviction based upon constructive possession against any of the occupants. [S]omething else (e.g., some circumstantial indicium of possession) is required besides mere joint occupancy before constructive possession is established.") (internal citations and quotation marks omitted); Guiton v. State, 742 S.W.2d 5 (Tex. Crim. App. 1987).
18. *See, e.g.*, United States v. Starks, 309 F.3d 1017, 1025–26 (7th Cir. 2002); United States v. Perry, 624 F.2d 29, 31 (5th Cir. 1980).

jury and enter a judgment of acquittal under the *Jackson v. Virginia* standard. This is because "[a]ssessing the credibility of witnesses and weighing the evidence is the exclusive province of the jury."[19] Even substantial inconsistencies between the testimony of two witnesses or internal inconsistencies in a witness's testimony will not ordinarily render the evidence insufficient concerning one or more elements of the charged offense. Only if the testimony of a witness is incredible on its face (e.g., it defies the laws of nature) will a reviewing court discredit the testimony as a matter of law.[20] Therefore, unless direct evidence offered by the prosecution simply fails to address one or more essential elements of a charged offense, a trial court ordinarily must assume that jurors could believe direct evidence in reaching a guilty verdict and allow the case to go to the jury.

Hypothetical One: Motions for Judgment of Acquittal [Class Nine] and Closing Arguments [Class Eleven]

United States v. Doggett

A federal grand jury in Nita City returned an indictment that alleged that **Martin Doggett**, **Charles Gray**, **Barbara Gaston**, and **Martin Solis** conspired to import heroin into the United States in violation of 21 U.S.C. § 963.[21] The following facts were established by the evidence presented at trial.

On August 25, **Maria Vasquez**, a porter at an airport outside of Mexico City, Mexico, met Martin Solis and three other persons, who were later identified as Martin Doggett, Barbara Gaston, and Charles Gray, as they arrived together at the front door of the airport. Although Vasquez had known Solis for a long time from his position with the Mexican Customs Department, a position that he still held at that time, Vasquez had never before seen the other three people with him that day. The group had four pieces of luggage, three black and one red, and a handbag. Solis handed Vasquez the three pieces of black luggage, and she placed them at the counter where the luggage would first clear Mexican Customs and then go through U.S. Customs onto an international flight to Nita City, Nita. By the time Vasquez had done this and returned, Gaston and Gray had left Solis and Doggett, and they were checking in with the airline.

---

19. United States v. Greenwood, 974 F.2d 1449, 1457–58 (5th Cir. 1992); *see also* United States v. Necoechea, 986 F.2d 1273, 1282 (9th Cir. 1993).

20. Greenwood, 974 F.2d at 1457–58; *see also* State v. Hornsby, 858 S.W.2d 892 (Tenn. 1993).

21. Section 963 states: "Any person who . . . conspires [with another person or persons] to commit any offense defined in this title [including section 952] shall be subject to the same penalties as those prescribed for the offense, the commission of which was the object of the attempt or conspiracy." Section 952 states that: "It shall be unlawful to import . . . into the United States from any place outside thereof, any controlled substance." Heroin is a controlled substance.

Solis, with Doggett still standing beside him, asked Vasquez to take the red suitcase around customs and place it on the trolley that held luggage for the flight to Nita City. Although it was clearly violating customs procedures, Vasquez did as Solis requested. Vasquez later testified that she had never been asked to take luggage around customs before and that Solis gave her a $100 tip for doing so. Between the time when Vasquez took the red suitcase around customs and Doggett, Gaston, and Gray were next seen, Doggett checked in at the ticket counter. Solis was not heard of or seen again (and remains a fugitive in both Mexico and the United States).

The next witness to have any contact with this group was **Ben Kenney**, a U.S. Bureau of Immigration and Customs (BICE) official whose responsibilities include preclearance of people and their luggage flying from Mexico into the United States. Kenney and **Robert Boeman**, a BICE inspector whose responsibilities were identical to Kenney's, were clearing two separate lines of people flying to Nita City, the lines being positioned about ten feet apart. Gaston and Gray were standing in Kenney's preclearance line. Doggett was standing in Boeman's preclearance line. As Gaston and Gray moved up in their line to Kenney's station, Doggett left his place in Boeman's line, walked over to Gaston and Gray "to get a key, or something, from them," and then returned to his position in his own line.

Thirty minutes later, Doggett was undergoing preclearance at Boeman's station. Doggett identified himself to Boeman as **Feton Sutton**—an alias—and presented for Boeman's inspection one of the black suitcases and the handbag brought to the terminal by Solis, Doggett, Gaston, and Gray. After accepting Doggett's written customs declaration, which was in the name of Feton Sutton, Boeman asked Doggett for proof of his United States citizenship. While Doggett was searching through his pockets for some type of identification, Boeman saw a U.S. passport in the handbag, which was lying partially open on the preclearance table. Boeman took the passport and told Doggett, "This is all you need." At that moment, Doggett produced another passport in response to Boeman's initial request for identification. The latter passport was that of "Feton Sutton." The passport that had been in the bag was in the name of Martin Doggett.

In response to Boeman's questions about whose passport and luggage he was carrying, Doggett (falsely claiming to be Feton Sutton) told Boeman that the passport, the luggage, and its contents belonged to a friend of his. Doggett said that he and a friend ("Doggett") had shared a hotel room in Mexico City the night before. According to Doggett (still claiming to be Sutton), earlier that morning his friend had departed the hotel for an undisclosed destination and had asked him to carry his personal effects with him to Nita, as his friend was returning to Nita City that same day.

Boeman thereupon commenced a search of the black suitcase. A close examination of the inner breast pocket of a white suit revealed a small residue of a grass-like substance, which was field tested and proved to be marijuana. Because of the positive results of the field test, Doggett was required to undergo a strip search. This was conducted by a Mexican police officer with Boeman present and observing. The search produced nothing. Doggett was again questioned about the whereabouts of the owner of the suitcase. In response to Doggett's answers that the owner might have gone to Nita City, the passenger lists of ticket stubs were checked to see if anyone by the last name of "Doggett" had flown from the airport that morning. No such name was found.

Before leaving, Doggett asked Boeman if he could give him a signed statement to present to customs in Nita City that Doggett had been cleared by customs in Mexico to avoid being checked again (and subject to a strip search) in Nita City. Boeman told him that it was not possible to do that. Doggett was then released to go to the restroom. He did not board the flight to Nita City. How he returned to the United States is unknown. (Doggett was subsequently arrested in Nita City after being stopped for a traffic violation.)

As Boeman was returning to his preclearance station, an airline porter came off the ramp with a red suitcase and presented it to Boeman for customs inspection. The porter knew the red suitcase had not cleared customs inspection because it did not have a preclearance stamp, which all properly customs-inspected luggage receives. Boeman opened the red suitcase, which was the same one that Solis had asked Vasquez to carry around customs. It contained what proved to be eight kilos of heroin. Boeman put everything back into the red suitcase, relocked it, placed it onto the baggage cart for the flight to Nita City. Boeman's customs supervisor then telephoned the BICE office in Nita City, notifying the BICE supervisor, **Carlos Arango**, what Boeman had discovered and requesting surveillance on the red suitcase when it was picked up in Nita City.

At the airport in Nita City, Arango set up a surveillance unit to cover the incoming flight from Mexico. He told his agents to look for the red suitcase. Arango's agents saw the red suitcase as it was unloaded from the flight from Mexico, placed on the baggage cart, and wheeled to the baggage claim area. Arango saw Gray pick up the red suitcase, carry it approximately twelve or fifteen feet, and set it alongside several black suitcases. Gaston then came into the baggage claim area and looked around as she was approaching the red suitcase. She picked up the red suitcase and was subsequently arrested by Arango near the front entrance of the airport.

A voter registration card bearing the name Feton Sutton, Doggett's alias, was found on Gaston, as were several personal papers belonging to Doggett and an address book with the initials "M.D." Gray was also arrested as he was leaving the airport; Solis's business card was discovered in his possession. No one saw the real Martin Doggett disembark in Nita City from the flight. (As noted, the prosecution offered no proof concerning how Doggett returned to the United States.)

At Doggett's trial,[22] in addition to offering proof of the foregoing facts, the prosecution also offered a DEA agent, who testified that fifteen months before the heroin smuggling in this case, Doggett had been in Gray's house in Nita City when heroin was being sold. The agent testified that although Gray was involved in an earlier heroin deal on that occasion, the agent had no knowledge whether Doggett knew that a heroin deal was in progress when he was in Gray's house. The agent admitted that he could only say that Doggett was present in Gray's house on that occasion.

The defense offered no evidence at trial. Doggett did not testify on his own behalf.

Defense Counsel: Move for a judgment of acquittal. Contend that the evidence is legally insufficient to prove beyond a reasonable doubt that Doggett is guilty of conspiracy.

Prosecutor: Argue against defense counsel's motion for judgment of acquittal.

To prepare for this hypothetical exercise, read *United States v. Morillo*, 158 F.3d 18 (1st Cir. 1998).

Hypothetical Two: Motions for Judgment of Acquittal [Class Nine] and Closing Arguments [Class Eleven]

United States v. Willie

A federal grand jury returned an indictment charging **Brian Willie**, **Bert Willie**, and **Luis Gil** with participating in a drug (cocaine) conspiracy in violation of 21 U.S.C. § 846.[23] Brian Willie and Luis Gil pleaded guilty before trial, but did not testify at Bert Willie's trial. Bert Willie pleaded not guilty and proceeded to trial. He did not testify at trial.

According to prosecution's evidence offered at trial, in late 2017 Brian Willie approached Luis Gil and offered his services in the drug-related business. Brian Willie informed Gil, a large-quantity cocaine dealer, that he had contacts with "legit" shipping companies that could help Gil ship large quantities of cocaine (dozens and sometimes hundreds of kilograms) to his buyers in various parts of the

22. After their arrests, Gaston and Gray pleaded guilty, but did not cooperate with the prosecution or testify at Doggett's trial. (Solis, as noted, is a fugitive who has never been arrested.)

23. Section 846 states: "Any person who . . . conspires to commit any offense defined in this title [including section 841] shall be subject to the same penalties as those prescribed for the offense, the commission of which was the object of the attempt or conspiracy." Section 841 states that it is illegal to "distribute . . . or possess with the intent to . . . distribute . . . a controlled substance." Cocaine is a controlled substance.

country. Sometime later, Brian Willie began using legitimate freight companies[24] to ship boxes that contained Gil's cocaine; from the outside, those boxes looked like ordinary freight. Each of the delivered boxes rested on a pallet, was wrapped in industrial cellophane, and was marked "fragile." Brian Willie told the shipping companies that the boxes contained ceramic goods.

Brian Willie usually used a forwarding company (SGT) to arrange the details with shipping companies to transport the freight. When dealing with SGT, Brian Willie said that he worked for Ceramics Enterprises—a fictional entity. Typically, a person working for SGT would meet either Brian Willie or his brother, Bert Willie, at the shipping company with the paperwork. Bert Willie sometimes delivered the drug-filled boxes to the shipping company on his own. SGT employees testified that Bert Willie appeared on behalf of his brother on approximately six occasions from 2017 to 2020.

The illicit drug trafficking was uncovered by DEA agents in April 2021 when a forklift operator at one of the shipping companies accidentally punctured one of Brian Willie's boxes. Rather than broken ceramics, cocaine poured out of the box, and the worker called the local police, who in turn contacted the DEA. DEA agents replaced the punctured box with an identical, undamaged one and arranged to have the box shipped under controlled supervision to its planned destination. Because the shipment was delayed, Brian Willie called the company that had arranged the shipment (SGT) and asked about the freight's whereabouts. An SGT employee told DEA agents of the inquiry. This, in turn, led the DEA to discover Brian Willie's identity. Before arresting Brian Willie, however, DEA agents observed him orchestrating two other drug deliveries. The boxes in these two deliveries each contained a total of over fifty kilos of cocaine (per shipment) with a street value of over $1,000,000 (per shipment). Bert Willie arranged the second delivery for his brother, Brian.

The second delivery—monitored by the DEA—occurred on June 18, 2021. DEA agents observed Bert Willie dropping off the freight at the shipping company. When Bert Willie arrived at the shipping dock, no one was around to accept the freight. After waiting for a short time (approximately ten to twenty minutes), Bert Willie left his (correct) name and cell phone number in a note attached to the boxes; the notes asked SGT employees to call him about the boxes, which he left on the dock. The police followed Bert Willie to a McDonald's restaurant, where he met three unidentified men. The three men left in the truck that Bert Willie had taken to drop off the boxes, and Bert Willie left in his own automobile. Agents, accompanied by local police officers, arrested Bert Willie as he drove away from

24. The freight companies that Brian Willie used included Herman Miles Trucking, ABF Freight, and C. F. Motor Freight Co. Brian Willie also used a shipping broker (called a freight forwarding company) to handle the details of the shipping arrangements. This company is named SGT.

McDonald's. He did not attempt to flee the agents or police officers. He made no statement to the agents after he was arrested.

After further investigation, the authorities discovered that Brian Willie had a Mexican bank account containing $2,000,000. (Brian Willie reported an income of less than $20,000 for each of the years 2017 through 2020.) It was undisputed that Brian Willie paid his brother Bert Willie $100 for each time that Bert Willie took boxes to be shipped on behalf of his brother. A DEA agent who testified for the prosecution at trial admitted on cross-examination by defense counsel that such a relatively small sum was not disproportionate to the ostensible task at hand (i.e., delivering ceramics) by which Bert Willie might have become suspicious of the true nature of his assignment.

At trial, there was uncontroverted evidence all of the cocaine shipments bore no outward indication that they contained illegal drugs, i.e., they had no odor and the packaging suggested nothing untoward; in fact, the shipments were packaged in industrial cellophane to discourage any investigation into their contents.

At trial, a DEA agent characterized as "suspicious" the manner in which Bert Willie had delivered the shipment on the day that he was arrested. Bert Willie met three unidentified men at a restaurant, took their loaded vehicle to the forwarding company, and then returned the empty vehicle to them at the restaurant after he had dropped off the boxes at the forwarding company.

Defense Counsel: Move for a judgment of acquittal. In particular, argue that there is legally insufficient proof that Bert Willie knowingly assisted his brother in the drug shipments and, thus, that there is insufficient evidence that he is guilty of conspiracy.

Prosecutor: Argue against defense counsel's motion for judgment of acquittal.

To prepare for this hypothetical exercise, read *United States v. Morillo*, 158 F.3d 18 (1st Cir. 1998).

Hypothetical Three: Motions for Judgment of Acquittal [Class Nine] and Closing Arguments [Class Eleven]

United States v. Nixon

A federal grand jury charged **Jonathan Nixon** with 1) possession with intent to distribute crack cocaine in violation of 21 U.S.C. § 841 and 2) possessing a firearm in furtherance of drug trafficking (i.e., the crack cocaine) in violation of 18 U.S.C. § 924(c).[25] Nixon pleaded guilty to the § 841 charge, but proceeded to trial on the

25. Section 924(c) provides in pertinent part that: "[A]ny person who, during and in relation to any . . . drug trafficking crime . . . for which the person may be prosecuted in a court of the United States, uses or carries a firearm, or who, in furtherance of any such crime, possesses a firearm, shall, in

§ 924(c) charge, which carries an extra five years of prison time in the event of conviction. The following evidence was offered at trial.

On June 12, Nixon and his girlfriend, **Jane Whitt**, were involved in an argument, and officers with the Nita City Police Department were called to intervene. The police left after receiving assurances from Whitt that she was fine and that the argument was resolved. However, after the police left, the fight resumed, and Nixon hit Whitt. She ordered him to leave, and he started packing his belongings with the help of two friends. While he was removing his belongings, Whitt called the police again to report the assault. When the police arrived, about an hour after their previous visit, Nixon was in the parking lot of the apartment building with two males near a truck. The truck contained a bed and some furniture, as well as some other personal items belonging to Nixon. One officer went upstairs to talk to Whitt. The officer observed a mark on Whitt's face. At that time, Whitt told the officer that Nixon had drugs in his pocket. Due to the mark on Whitt's face, the officers arrested Nixon.

The police searched Nixon's pockets. In his pockets, the police found 10.5 grams of crack cocaine,[26] a small amount of marijuana, a small amount of powder cocaine, a small scale, and $2,230 cash in his wallet. After arresting Nixon, the officers obtained Nixon's valid consent to search the truck. In the truck, police found two guns. One of the guns, a loaded nine-millimeter semiautomatic handgun, was in a closed shoe box in the back portion of the cab of the truck, but within the driver's reach. The other gun was an unloaded 12-gauge shotgun, which was inside a gun case located in the bed of the truck.

Neither of the guns was reported stolen. Records showed that Nixon, who had no prior criminal record, legally purchased the nine-millimeter pistol the year before from a pawn shop. No drugs or drug paraphernalia were found in Nixon's truck. Nixon made no statement to police after he was arrested and did not testify at trial.

At the trial, a DEA agent admitted on cross-examination that the prosecution had no direct proof that Nixon's guns were being used in furtherance of his drug-trafficking activities (e.g., no proof that Nixon had been seen carrying a gun during a drug deal), but testified that as a general matter, "guns are tools of the trade for drug traffickers." The agent noted that "we often see nine-millimeter pistols carried by drug dealers. They are small, but powerful guns, and they are relatively inexpensive."

Defense Counsel: Move for a judgment of acquittal on the § 924(c) charge.

Prosecutor: Argue against defense counsel's motion for a judgment of acquittal.

---

addition to the punishment provided for such . . . drug trafficking crime . . . [be sentenced to] a term of imprisonment of not less than 5 years." 18 U.S.C. § 924(c)(1)(A)(i).

26. There was no dispute at the trial that Nixon possessed crack cocaine with the intent to distribute it. Indeed, he had pleaded guilty to the drug charge prior to trial.

To prepare for this hypothetical exercise, read *United States v. Ceballos-Torres*, 218 F.3d 409 (5th Cir. 2000).

Hypothetical Four: Motions for Judgment of Acquittal [Class Nine] and Closing Arguments [Class Eleven]

United States v. Watkins

A federal grand jury returned an indictment charging **Horatio Watkins** and **Bobby Lewis** with conspiracy to possess crack cocaine with the intent to distribute, in violation of 21 U.S.C. § 846.[27] The following facts were established at Watkins's trial.[28]

On June 13, narcotics officers with the Nita City Police Department engaged in an undercover sting operation that resulted in the arrest of Watkins and Lewis. Officer **Ralph Chadwick**, acting in an undercover capacity and wearing a hidden microphone (a "wire"),[29] arranged to meet with Lewis during the afternoon at 2816 Gregg Street in Nita City to purchase twelve ounces of crack cocaine. Chadwick was accompanied by a female confidential informant (CI). Lewis was standing next to the open door of a Mazda pickup truck when Chadwick's vehicle arrived.[30] Chadwick's vehicle pulled up behind the truck.

The CI exited Chadwick's vehicle and approached Lewis; the two had a brief conversation. The CI then introduced Lewis to Chadwick, who was sitting in his vehicle. Watkins remained in the passenger's seat of the Mazda truck. Chadwick had no idea who Watkins was and did not anticipate that anyone would be accompanying Lewis. Chadwick did not speak to Watkins at any point. Chadwick asked Lewis about Mr. Watkins and stated that he was nervous about being "ripped off." Lewis responded that, "Everything is cool," which, Chadwick testified, he understood to mean that Mr. Watkins posed no threat. Chadwick testified that he assumed that Watkins was serving as Lewis's lookout during the drug transaction. This conversation between Lewis and Chadwick occurred at Chadwick's vehicle; Chadwick was sitting in his vehicle, and Lewis was standing outside of the vehicle. Watkins neither exited the Mazda truck nor talked or otherwise participated in this conversation on Gregg Street. When cross-examined by defense counsel, Chadwick admitted that Watkins likely could not hear Lewis say, "everything is cool" in response to Chadwick's expressed concern over Watkins's presence in Lewis's truck.

---

27. Section 846 states: "Any person who . . . conspires to commit any offense defined in this title [including section 841] shall be subject to the same penalties as those prescribed for the offense, the commission of which was the object of the attempt or conspiracy." Section 841 states that it is illegal to "distribute . . . or possess with the intent to . . . distribute . . . a controlled substance." Crack cocaine is a controlled substance.
28. Before trial, Lewis pleaded guilty, but did not otherwise cooperate with the prosecution. Lewis did not testify at Watkins's trial.
29. Another NCPD officer, Alan Jones, monitored the hidden microphone through a "monitoring device" similar to a walkie-talkie.
30. At trial, the government presented evidence that the truck was registered in Lewis's name.

During this initial conversation, Lewis told Chadwick to follow Lewis to Sayre Street. Lewis said an unnamed person would deliver the "product" to that location. Chadwick followed Lewis to Sayre Street. When the two vehicles arrived at Sayre Street, Lewis exited his vehicle and told Chadwick to park in a driveway near the location where Lewis had parked the truck. Chadwick refused to park in the driveway, fearing his vehicle would be trapped. Eventually, the two vehicles parked approximately forty to fifty yards from each other on Sayre Street. Lewis exited the truck and approached Chadwick's vehicle. Watkins stayed in the Mazda truck, sitting on the passenger's side. Lewis then entered Chadwick's vehicle and discussed the pending drug deal.

According to Chadwick, while Lewis was in Chadwick's car, Lewis said an unidentified person—referred to as "my man"—would be delivering the drugs to the Sayre Street location. Lewis waited in Chadwick's vehicle for thirty to forty-five minutes. Eventually, the drug courier—whom Lewis identified as "Randy"—arrived in a yellow car. Lewis got out of Chadwick's car and briefly met with Randy. Chadwick lost visual contact with Lewis and Randy. Lewis returned to Chadwick's vehicle and said Randy preferred dealing through Lewis rather than directly dealing with Chadwick. After Chadwick agreed to this procedure, Lewis again exited the vehicle and went back to Randy. Lewis eventually returned to Chadwick's vehicle carrying a brown paper bag containing crack cocaine underneath his clothes.

Chadwick and Lewis got out of the vehicle and went to a nearby tree, where Chadwick inspected the crack cocaine inside the bag. Chadwick told Lewis that Chadwick had to contact another person to bring cash for the drugs. Lewis responded that he would have to "call my man up" to hold "the product" until Chadwick could get the cash. Lewis then waved to Watkins, who was still sitting in the passenger's side of the Mazda truck. Watkins moved into the driver's seat and began to drive toward Lewis and Chadwick. Before Watkins was able to drive the truck over to Lewis, numerous police officers moved in on Lewis to make an arrest. The officers arrested Lewis and seized the crack cocaine, which weighed twelve ounces, from Lewis. Watkins drove the truck away at a fast speed in an apparent attempt to flee the police, who approached him in marked patrol cars with sirens blaring and emergency lights flashing. The police stopped the truck within a few blocks and arrested Watkins.

After the police stopped the Mazda truck and arrested Watkins, they seized 5.9 grams of crack cocaine from an open ashtray in the truck. The crack cocaine was in plain view. Officer Chadwick testified that, in his experience as a narcotics officer, 5.9 grams of crack—by itself—was "right on the border between an amount that a crack user would possess for personal use and the amount that a crack dealer would possess for purposes of selling it."

Watkins did not make any statement to police and did not testify at his trial.

Defense Counsel: Move for a judgment of acquittal.

Prosecutor: Argue against defense counsel's motion for judgment of acquittal.

To prepare for this hypothetical exercise, read *United States v. Morillo*, 158 F.3d 18 (1st Cir. 1998).

Hypothetical Five: Motions for Judgment of Acquittal [Class Nine] and Closing Arguments [Class Eleven]

United States v. Perry

A federal grand jury returned an indictment charging **Charles Perry** with being a felon in possession of a firearm in violation of 18 U.S.C. § 922(g)(1).[31] The following facts were established at the trial.

The government's evidence that Charles Perry, a fifty-nine-year-old man with a forty-year-old felony conviction for burglary, knowingly possessed a firearm was totally circumstantial. On December 6, when officers with the Nita City police department executed a search warrant for unprescribed opioid pain pills at 6102 Highland Drive, apartment #3, in Nita City,[32] they encountered Mr. Perry sitting at a table in the living room, where he was eating a breakfast sandwich purchased from a fast-food restaurant. There were two closed cigar boxes—one stacked on top of the other—located approximately thirty inches from Mr. Perry on the table where Mr. Perry was eating. Inside the top box were cigars and a number of small yellow manila envelopes, each containing two to ten opioid pain pills that had not been prescribed by a doctor. Inside the bottom box was a loaded, nine-millimeter pistol. It is undisputed that the pistol was not in plain view. Mr. Perry was wearing a jacket that contained a small manila envelope—similar in style to the type of manila envelopes inside the top cigar box, but different in color[33]—that contained five opioid pills similar to the types in the cigar box. He also had $200 inside his jacket.

Officers located another cigar box in the kitchen cabinet containing $158, and a box of unused small manila envelopes identical in style and color to the ones found inside the top cigar box (which contained the opioid pills). In the bedroom of the apartment, the officers found a backpack containing clothes and a copy of Mr. Perry's birth certificate.

31. Section 922(g)(1) provides that: "It shall be unlawful for any person who has been convicted . . . of [a felony offense] to [knowingly] possess . . . any firearm" that has traveled in interstate commerce. It is undisputed that the pistol in this case was manufactured outside of the State of Nita and, thus, previously traveled from outside of Nita to within the state. The only disputed issue in this case is whether Charles Perry knowingly possessed the pistol found in the apartment.

32. The search warrant was based on a confidential informant's information that marijuana was being sold from the apartment.

33. The envelopes inside the cigar box were yellow in color. The single envelope in Mr. Perry's jacket was brown in color.

At trial, it was undisputed that at the time of his arrest Mr. Perry was a temporary resident in the apartment, which was leased by his two sons, and that both Mr. Perry and his sons regularly sold unprescribed opioid pills from that apartment. Although the apartment was leased to Michael and Jason Perry, Charles Perry's sons, a third, unnamed person also lived in the apartment with the Perrys, and other people regularly "hung out" at the apartment during that time.

According to the informant, Sherry Williams (who testified at trial), Mr. Perry was a small-scale drug dealer who typically sold opioid pills for $5 per pill. Williams had purchased opioids from Mr. Perry on approximately five occasions before his arrest and had purchased opioid pills from his sons on approximately five prior occasions. On some of the occasions when Williams bought drugs in the apartment from Mr. Perry's sons, Mr. Perry was not present.

At trial, the government offered no evidence that Mr. Perry had admitted to knowing that the firearm was located inside the bottom cigar box. There also was no testimony from any witness (including Sherry Williams) claiming to have seen Mr. Perry with a firearm or claiming to have seen a firearm in plain view in the apartment on any prior occasion. Nor were Mr. Perry's fingerprints found on either on the firearm or on the cigar boxes on the table. The ATF agent who testified for the prosecution at trial stated that the prosecution had never tested the gun or cigar boxes for fingerprints.

The government's evidence offered to prove that Mr. Perry had knowledge of the firearm was the fact that he was sitting in close proximity to the loaded pistol and that he was an admitted drug dealer.[34] An NCPD officer also testified that, as a general matter, "guns are tools of the trade for drug dealers."

Defense Counsel: Move for a judgment of acquittal.

Prosecutor: Argue against defense counsel's motion for a judgment of acquittal.

To prepare for this hypothetical exercise, read *United States v. Mergerson*, 4 F.3d 337, 340–41, 348–49 (5th Cir. 1993) (portion of decision concerning insufficiency of the evidence supporting the 18 U.S.C. § 922(g)(1) charge).

34. Prior to the federal trial on the § 922(g)(1) charge, Mr. Perry had pleaded guilty in state court to the misdemeanor charge of possessing the opioid pills found inside his jacket.

CLASS TEN

JURY INSTRUCTIONS

After both sides have rested following the close of all the evidence, but prior to the jury's deliberations, a trial court will instruct the jurors—usually in a multipage written set of instructions that also is read aloud to jurors—on the legal rules applicable to criminal cases generally and also on the law relating to the specific charges at issue in the case.[1] This is called "jury instructions" or the "jury charge."

Most parts of the jury instructions are taken from boilerplate, standardized "pattern" jury instructions. Some pattern jury instructions have received the official imprimatur of a court, while others have been drafted by a legal scholar and were not prepared under the official auspices of a court.[2] In most cases, the parties are generally satisfied with the pattern jury instructions and only tend to request the submission of specifically tailored instructions in light of the particular evidence presented at the trial. For instance, defense lawyers often submit requested nonpattern "theory of the defense" instructions based on a particular defense presented at trial. In most jurisdictions, such instructions are not required unless the trial court's charge as a whole failed to convey adequately to the jurors the requested theory of defense.[3]

One of the most common disputes about jury instructions concerns what are referred to as "lesser-included offenses." A lesser-included offense is an uncharged lesser crime (such as theft) that is a subset of a more serious, charged offense (such as robbery). The defense and/or the prosecution may request such an instruction where the evidence would permit a rational jury to find the defendant not guilty of the greater offense, but guilty of a lesser offense.[4] Usually, the defense requests such an instruction over the objection of the prosecutor, although occasionally the prosecutor requests a lesser-included offense instruction over the objection of the

---

1. In most jurisdictions, the jury instructions are read aloud to the jury prior to closing arguments by the attorneys. In some jurisdictions, the lawyers must give closing arguments prior to the reading of the jury instructions.
2. *Compare* 2019 Fifth Circuit Criminal Jury Instructions (available at https://www.lb5.uscourts.gov/viewer/?/juryinstructions/Fifth/crim2019.pdf), with STATE BAR OF TEXAS, TEXAS CRIMINAL PATTERN JURY CHARGES (2020).
3. *See* United States v. Storm, 36 F.3d 1289, 1294–95 (5th Cir. 1994).
4. *See, e.g.*, Keeble v. United States, 412 U.S. 205, 208 (1973).

defense (who believe that they stand a good chance of an acquittal on the greater offense, but a conviction on a lesser offense, if so charged).[5]

Another common species of defensive instruction concerns "affirmative defenses." An affirmative defense contends that the defendant is not guilty not because the prosecution has failed to prove one or more essential elements of a charge but, instead, because of some other factor that exculpates the defendant. Common affirmative defenses include entrapment, self-defense, necessity, duress, and justification.[6] In some jurisdictions, a defendant has the initial burden to produce enough evidence to make out a prima facie case of an affirmative defense—which entitles the defendant to a jury instruction on the affirmative defense—at which point the burden shifts to the prosecution to disprove the affirmative defense beyond a reasonable doubt.[7]

Hypothetical One: Jury Instructions

United States v. Burns

Alan Burns is the pastor of Holy Spirit Church in Nita City. In early 2019, the church began construction on an 80,000 square foot building, financed through $7 million of private bonds, which required monthly payments of approximately $65,000. The church also owned and operated five largely unprofitable radio stations in Nita, into which it had invested approximately $1 million over three years. In late 2019, due to financial difficulties arising from these obligations, the church issued bonds and sought short-term, unsecured loans.

Burns met in May 2020 with **John Knowles**, a self-proclaimed financial consultant. During this meeting, Burns decided to pursue a limited private offering in the amount of $10.8 million to retire the church's outstanding debt. The church trustees approved the plan, and the offering began in September 2020, but there were few responses, and no money was raised. Shortly after the offering began, Knowles met **Roy Clark**, a financier, in October 2020, and Knowles gave Clark a copy of the private offering prospectus. In February 2021, Clark told Knowles that he knew of some "South American investors" who might be interested in Holy Spirit Church and its operations.

Concerning those supposed investors, while Burns had been attempting unsuccessfully to secure financing for his church, undercover federal agents had been conducting a money laundering investigation of Clark. Beginning in October

5. *See, e.g.*, Hampton v. State, 109 S.W.3d 437 (Tex. Crim. App. 2003).
6. *See, e.g.*, United States v. Bailey, 444 U.S. 394 (1980) (discussing the affirmative defenses of necessity and duress); Mathews v. United States, 485 U.S. 58 (1988) (discussing the affirmative defense of entrapment).
7. *Compare* Dixon v. United States, 548 U.S. 1 (2006), *with* Bishop v. State, 519 S.E.2d 206 (Ga. 1999).

2020, around the time that Knowles first met with Clark, DEA Special Agent **Michael Gonzalez** met several times with Clark, who was suspected of laundering illegal drug proceeds. Working in an undercover capacity, Agent Gonzalez identified himself as a Columbian narcotics trafficker seeking to launder money from cocaine sales.

In early March 2021, Clark contacted DEA Agent **Julian Cisneros**, who was operating undercover as Agent Gonzalez's accountant, and informed Agent Cisneros that he had a "major big-time guy" from "a church group" who was very interested in talking to Cisneros and wanted to close the deal the following weekend.

On March 17, 2021, Agents Gonzalez and Cisneros met with Clark at a hotel in Nita City. Clark said he knew a minister who was interested in raising large amounts of money to finance his church, that "I bet he'd be willing to launder the cocaine money," and that the minister's financial advisor was in town and eager to meet with them. At this time, the agents did not know the identity of either Burns or Knowles. Agent Gonzalez told Clark that he did not want any innocent people involved in the operation and asked if the minister (Burns) knew Gonzalez was a cocaine trafficker looking to launder cocaine proceeds. Clark said the minister, who was "in big trouble financially," and his financial advisor, who was "very greedy," "wouldn't care" where the money came from.

That same afternoon, Clark brought Knowles to the hotel to meet the agents. Knowles told them he represented the minister and wanted to negotiate a deal. Early in the conversation, the agents told Knowles that Agent Gonzalez was a Colombian drug trafficker; that Agent Cisneros was the accountant for the drug organization; and that the deal involved laundering money from cocaine sales. Knowles responded that he knew this and that he'd told Burns that "the money is drug proceeds," but that neither Burns nor Knowles were concerned about the money's source.

Knowles explained that Burns's nonprofit corporation, New Life Fellowship, Inc., d/b/a Holy Spirit Church, could launder the money without arousing suspicion because a minister was involved. Knowles provided a copy of the private offering prospectus for Holy Spirit Church. Agent Gonzalez told Knowles that the agents (acting in their undercover capacities) needed to meet with Burns to ensure that he understood that they were drug traffickers seeking to launder cocaine proceeds. Knowles said Burns would gladly meet with them and could do so within twelve hours.

Over the next few days, Clark left telephone messages with Agent Cisneros that Knowles and Burns were ready to meet with the undercover agents. On March 23, 2021, Agents Gonzalez and Cisneros met Burns, along with Clark and Knowles, in a hotel room. Gonzalez said he was authorized to "invest" up to $10 million, but that Knowles and Burns would first need to launder some test amounts, in amounts of approximately $100,000.

Burns quickly agreed, assuring that he would do whatever was necessary to accomplish his goal and satisfy Gonzalez's organization. The agents said they needed to "go into the delicate issues," so that "there [were] no misunderstandings" or "confusion as to where the money [was] coming from." During the meeting, Agent Cisneros stated: "[Agent Gonzalez] plainly puts it . . . the money is from the sale of cocaine trafficking. It is narcotics money, and he is asking you to launder money."

Burns responded: "I have monies come to the church. I don't have a questionnaire . . . where these monies come from." Burns told the agent that he knew he had received funds "from questionable sources." Burns then stated: "I prayed to God . . . because I wanted to know if I was supposed to do this." According to Burns, "God said He helped put this together." Finally, Burns told the agents: "I appreciate that you want to be very straightforward and upfront with me . . . but that does not concern me, really."

Burns and Knowles said they would need some time to figure out how long it would take to transfer and repay $10 million. Agent Gonzalez explained that he would give various denominations of cash to Knowles and Burns, and they responded that they had already discussed those matters, although the agents had never before met with Burns. Gonzalez agreed to pay Burns, Knowles, and Clark 6 percent of the transferred amount. Burns assured the agents that he was ready to transfer the test money, but Agent Gonzalez told him to have patience and wait.

A month later, on April 24, 2021, Knowles telephoned Agent Cisneros, informing him that Burns was ready to take the first test money. Knowles said he and Burns had already "contrived a system" to quickly deposit and transfer the first $100,000.

Two days later, Agent Cisneros met with Burns and Clark. At the beginning of the meeting, Agent Cisneros told Burns that the Colombian organization had just "crossed" three tons of cocaine into the United States and explained, "[s]o . . . now there's a lot of profit." Agent Cisneros gave Burns the account number for an undercover account in a London bank. Burns said he would wire the $100,000 from his Nita City bank, but suggested transferring the money instead to a domestic bank because it would clear faster and because Holy Spirit Church had not previously transferred money to a foreign bank. Agent Cisneros told Burns that "the Colombians" probably would not change the destination account, but that all other details of the transaction were left to Burns.

Burns also discussed how the $10 million would be repaid: he planned to make payments of $50,000 per month for the first two years; of $100,000 per month for the next two years; and then pay the balance. During this meeting, two other undercover agents, **Ed Gallman** and **Rob Pineda**, gave Burns $100,000 in cash. Agent Cisneros offered Burns two opportunities to withdraw from the transaction, but Burns declined both times.

Burns enlisted **Mark Rozen**, a staff member at Holy Spirit Church, to (unwittingly) help launder the money, giving him specific instructions to obtain cashier's checks with different remitters from certain banks and to deposit them in specific accounts. Burns also instructed Rozen to use cashier's checks in amounts less than $10,000 each to avoid the banks' reporting the transactions to the IRS.[8]

Burns successfully transferred this first test amount to the London account and told Cisneros that he was ready to transfer the next test amount. Knowles telephoned Agent Cisneros on May 3, 2021, and told him that Burns received $3,000 as his share for the first test transfer.

Two days later, on May 5, Agents Cisneros and Gallman met with Burns to discuss the second test transfer. Burns was told to make a transfer to a domestic account, ostensibly Agent Gallman's. Burns said that there were no difficulties running funds through his church's accounts because they were listed as offerings or donations. Burns also suggested that to avoid suspicion, they not transfer the same amount again.

Burns told Agent Gallman that he would account for the money transfers in installments, carried on his books as a loan, and would assimilate it over time through church offerings. Burns explained that, because Holy Spirit Church was a "section 501(c)(3) corporation," the books were not public records. Burns informed the agents that he would explain the next test transfer as an advance payment on interest for the large loan he would soon be receiving. Burns indicated that his involvement in this operation was "supposed to happen" and, "The fact is that I'm not getting a whole lot of respect. I almost have to go to bankers and show them that I do not need the money for them to loan it to me. Frankly, I'm just tired of being somebody's whipping dog."

After receiving the second $100,000 test amount, Burns commented to the undercover agents, "I have a feeling that neither one of you has ever come across a pastor like me." Burns confirmed that he would again receive $3,000 as his commission. (Burns had excluded Clark from this meeting because of potential disagreement over how to split the 6 percent commission.)

When Burns received the second $100,000, he directed Rozen to research cash reporting requirements to see if there was a way to avoid using numerous cashier's checks in small amounts. Rozen told Burns that his research indicated that Burns was engaging in illegal money laundering, but Burns assured him this was not true. Burns, again with Rozen's assistance, successfully transferred the money from the church's bank to a domestic bank.

---

8. Under IRS regulations, anytime a person engages in a cash transaction exceeding $10,000, the financial institution must report the transaction to the IRS. *See* 31 C.F.R. § 103.22(a).

After the second test transfer, Knowles told Agent Cisneros that Burns had eleven accounts set up through which he could move $4 million in thirty days. Knowles said that Burns was willing to make another test transfer and that "$10 million is just the tip of the iceberg that we can put through Holy Spirit Church. It's turning into a washing machine real fast." In a subsequent telephone conversation between Agent Cisneros and Burns, Burns reiterated Knowles's information about the eleven accounts and said that he had acquired a large safe in which to store the money.

On May 12, 2021, Agent Cisneros met with Burns, Knowles, and Clark and delivered the last test amount, this time for $150,000. Agent Cisneros stated that "the Colombians" would soon start with $5 million of the "big money," which would include a bonus for Burns. Burns responded that he had someone researching "what raises eyebrows overseas" and that he could transfer the test amount using accounts at three separate banks. Agent Cisneros emphasized that the Colombians were dangerous dope dealers.

Burns and Knowles successfully transferred the third test amount. Burns told Rozen that Knowles handled the transfer because Burns, "wanted [Knowles] to be as involved in it as he was."

On May 18, 2021, Knowles telephoned Agent Cisneros and told him that he and Burns were ready to do the "big deal" (even though Agent Cisneros had not arranged for it to happen then). Burns telephoned Agent Cisneros later and apologized for appearing too anxious. Agent Cisneros delayed further action, repeatedly emphasizing that the Colombians were ruthless drug dealers, so that Burns and Knowles would have an opportunity to "cool down" and withdraw. During this cool-down period, Burns repeatedly tried to contact Agent Cisneros by telephone.

On June 16, 2021, Agent Cisneros had a telephone conversation with Burns and Knowles. Knowles said that he and Burns, after working together for forty-eight hours, had the necessary equipment to transfer the money. Burns added that he had several suitcases of different sizes and asked how the money was packaged. Agent Cisneros responded that the Colombians were thinking about waiting awhile, to which Burns replied: "I'm not going anyplace. You know, I'm ready just like you to finish it. I've got my things in place. I'm prepared. In fact, I'm probably overconservative and overkilled as far as protection and as far as making sure of safety and moving things."

On June 21, 2021, Burns and Knowles met with undercover agents in a parking lot in Nita City and accepted three canvas bags filled with paper clippings approximating the weight of $10 million in cash. Burns and Knowles left the parking lot in Burns's car with the bags and were arrested immediately. The arresting agents found a .380 caliber semiautomatic pistol in the backseat of Burns's car, along with a fully loaded magazine. Burns had bought the pistol the day before his arrest because he thought that "the Colombians" expected him to protect the money.

A federal grand jury returned an indictment charging Burns, Knowles, and Clark with conspiracy to commit money laundering and attempted money laundering in violation of 18 U.S.C. §§ 371, 1956, and 1957. Knowles and Clark pleaded guilty prior to trial. At Burns's jury trial, the foregoing facts were not disputed. Burns, who testified at the trial, admitted to having engaged in the conduct discussed above—almost all of which was captured on undercover video and audiotape recordings—but asserted the affirmative defense of entrapment.

At the conclusion of all the evidence, defense counsel requested the trial court to submit a proposed jury instruction on "positional" and "dispositional" entrapment in accordance with the Seventh Circuit's decision in *United States v. Hollingsworth*.[9] The prosecutor opposed a jury instruction on any type of entrapment.[10]

For purposes of this hypothetical, assume that there is no Twelfth Circuit case law on point and that instead, the most relevant authority is the en banc Seventh Circuit's nonbinding decision in *Hollingsworth*.

---

9. 27 F.3d 1196 (7th Cir. 1994) (en banc).

10. Defense counsel's proposed jury instruction is as follows:

> The defendant asserts that he was a victim of entrapment. Where a person has no previous intent or purpose to violate the law, and/or because of a lack of training or experience or lack of any prior criminal associations is not in the position to commit the charged offense, but is induced or persuaded by law enforcement officers or their agents to commit a crime and/or provided the means to do so (when such means did not previously exist independently of the government's provision), that person is a victim of entrapment, and the law as a matter of policy forbids that person's conviction in such a case. On the other hand, where a person already has the readiness and willingness to break the law and is so situated by reason of previous training or experience or as a result of their existing criminal associations that it is likely that if government agents had not induced them to commit the crime some criminal would have done so, then the defendant was not entrapped.
>
> If, then, you should find beyond a reasonable doubt from the evidence in the case that before anything at all occurred respecting the alleged offense involved in this case, the defendant was ready and willing to commit a crime such as charged in the indictment, was in the position to do so as a result of his prior training or experience or as a result of his existing criminal associations, whenever opportunity was afforded, and that government officers did no more than offer the opportunity, then you should find that the defendant is not a victim of entrapment. On the other hand, if the evidence in the case should leave you with a reasonable doubt about whether the defendant had the previous intent or purpose to commit an offense of the character charged, apart from the inducement or persuasion of some officer of the government, and/or if you have a reasonable doubt about whether the defendant was in the position to commit the crime as a result of his prior training or experience or as a result of his existing criminal associations prior to the involvement of government agents, then it is your duty to find the defendant not guilty. The burden is on the government to prove beyond a reasonable doubt that the defendant was not entrapped.

Defense Counsel: Relying on the majority opinion in *Hollingsworth*, argue to the trial court that it should submit your proposed instruction on both "positional" and "dispositional" entrapment.

Prosecutor: Relying on the dissenting opinions in *Hollingsworth*, argue that the evidence at trial does not warrant the submission of the defendant's requested entrapment instruction.

Hypothetical Two: Jury Instructions

United States v. Fernandez-Ochoa

A federal grand jury indicted **Raul Fernandez-Ochoa** on two counts: 1) conspiracy to possess with intent to distribute more than fifty kilograms of marijuana, a violation of 21 U.S.C. § 846, and 2) possession with intent to distribute more than fifty kilograms of marijuana in violation of 21 U.S.C. § 841(a)(1). The following facts were established at his jury trial.

Border Patrol Agent **Mario Ruiz** testified that he and his drug-detection dog, Rudy, were working the Laredo, Texas, Border Patrol checkpoint on December 21, 2021, when Rudy alerted to a tractor-trailer driven by Fernandez-Ochoa. Agents directed the truck to a secondary inspection point. After obtaining the keys from Fernandez-Ochoa, who "was visibly nervous . . . his hands shaking," agents placed Rudy in the trailer, where he alerted to a group of boxes. Agents found marijuana in the boxes, which were mixed in with many more boxes containing new women's jeans that had been manufactured in Mexico. They arrested Fernandez-Ochoa and escorted him to the checkpoint trailer. Fernandez-Ochoa's wife and children remained in the cab of the truck.

Agents advised Fernandez-Ochoa of his *Miranda* rights and placed him in a holding cell at the checkpoint. He waived his rights and agreed to an interview. He told Agent Ruiz that neither he nor his wife had anything to do with—or had any prior knowledge of—the marijuana found in the boxes. He also declared he was willing to talk about the person who hired him to drive the truck. "The person who hired me is probably the one who placed the drugs in the rig; it was not me," he said.

Fernandez-Ochoa told the agents that his employer, **Julian Ramirez**, of Ramirez Trucking Company, had asked him to drive the truck from Laredo to New York City. Ramirez had instructed Fernandez-Ochoa to pick up the trailer at a gas station in Laredo on December 20. Ordinarily, Fernandez-Ochoa picked up trucks that he was to drive at the businesses that loaded the rig with the products that were to be transported. Fernandez-Ochoa had a check from Ramirez Trucking Company in his wallet. The check was for $3,000 and dated December 20. Fernandez-Ochoa admitted that Ramirez paid him $3,000, which Fernandez-Ochoa admitted was "three times what I am normally paid to drive a rig from

South Texas to the Northeast." When asked whether the larger-than-normal pay aroused any suspicion, Fernandez-Ochoa said: "To be honest, I was so excited that I would be getting that much money that I didn't think anything was wrong. It's Christmastime, and I need money to buy my family nice gifts. I thought it must be a Christmas bonus from my boss."

The agents checked out Fernandez-Ochoa's story. They found phone calls to and from Ramirez on Fernandez-Ochoa's cell phone. A bill of lading found in Fernandez-Ochoa's truck reflected that Ramirez had picked up the trailer from a clothing manufacturer in Laredo on December 20. Agents learned that Fernandez-Ochoa had begun working for Ramirez only two months earlier and that Ramirez had a drug-trafficking conviction in 2012.

Records introduced at trial showed that the clothing company had loaded the truck with women's jeans at a warehouse in Laredo on December 20. Ramirez, who was alone and not accompanied by Fernandez-Ochoa, had brought the trailer to the warehouse and left with it sometime between 7:30 and 8:00 p.m. The trailer was locked and sealed when it left the warehouse, as per shipping custom.[11]

Michel Bosco, an employee of the clothing company, testified that he inspected the trailer after it was seized by the Border Patrol, and he believed someone had tampered with the lock and opened the doors, but did so without breaking the seal that had been placed on the doors by the employee before Ramirez had picked up the truck. When asked by defense counsel whether it was "obvious to just anyone" that such tampering had occurred, Bosco responded, "Probably not. I noticed it because I'm the one who locked the door and put the seal on."

At trial, the Government had DEA Special Agent **Kai Warzecha** qualified as an expert witness on narcotics trafficking. They testified that the marijuana seized was worth $77,600 in Laredo and about $135,000 in New York. They described the cultivation, wrapping, and packaging of the drugs. They also described how traffickers usually recruited people who needed the money to transport the drugs and enticed them with a "quick payday." They testified that many truck drivers passed through Laredo, and some were susceptible to the lure of drug trafficking. When the prosecutor asked if drug traffickers ever concealed an expensive load of drugs in a truck without telling the driver it was there, the agent stated: "Rarely do they do that; usually they don't. They at least imply to the driver that the load contains drugs or other contraband and that the drivers need to play stupid if the cops stop them." The agent also testified that it was possible to put the drugs in the trailer without disturbing the seal. They also recalled that they had investigated cases in which children were involved in smuggling and suggested smugglers were

11. It is industry custom for the company that loads its goods into a third-party truck to seal the back door of the truck so as to assure that the goods will not be tampered with before their arrival at their destination.

under the impression that law enforcement personnel were not inclined to suspect individuals with children of smuggling drugs.

Agent Warzecha then testified that Ramirez had a history of narcotics trafficking, including a 2012 conviction involving over 1,000 pounds of marijuana. Warzecha also explained that DEA agents had seized $368,000 in cash from Ramirez in Dallas, Texas, in October 2021 and opined that the money was drug related (although because no drugs were found in Ramirez's truck, he was never charged with any offense). At the time of that seizure of the money, Ramirez had been traveling with Fernandez-Ochoa. DEA Agent Sharon Brown testified that she was one of the agents who searched Ramirez's truck in Dallas and had interrogated both Ramirez and his passenger, Fernandez-Ochoa, about whether they had been hauling drugs on that trip. Brown testified that Fernandez-Ochoa was well aware at that time that the DEA suspected that he and Ramirez had been hauling drugs. "Back in October in Dallas, I point-blank told them both that I thought they were drug transporters and that they were lucky that we didn't find any evidence of drugs in their truck when we searched it," she testified.

After the prosecution rested its case, the defense put on no evidence and rested its case. The prosecutor requested a "deliberate ignorance" instruction, which defense counsel opposed. That proposed instruction read:

> You may find that the defendant acted knowingly if you find beyond a reasonable doubt that the defendant was aware of a high probability that drugs were in the vehicle driven by the defendant and deliberately avoided learning the truth. You may not find such knowledge, however, if you find that the defendant actually believed that no drugs were in the vehicle driven by the defendant or if you find that the defendant was simply careless.

Prosecutor: Argue in support of your proposed jury instruction.

Defense Counsel: Argue against submission of the prosecution's proposed jury instruction.

To prepare for this hypothetical exercise, read *United States v. Heredia*, 483 F.3d 913, 917–21 (9th Cir. 2007) (en banc); *id.* at 924–30 (Kleinfeld, J., concurring in the result); *id.* at 930–32 (Graber, J., dissenting, joined by Pregerson, Thomas, and Paez).

Hypothetical Three: Jury Instructions

United States v. Shields

A federal grand jury in Nita City returned an indictment charging **Michael Shields** with bank fraud, in violation of 18 U.S.C. § 1344. The indictment alleged that Shields knowingly served as a "straw purchaser" in six fraudulent land transactions, in which another person actually supplied the down payments for the land purchases. The indictment also alleged that Shields falsely completed loan applications for the six purchases, in which he falsely claimed that his income was $200,000 per year and also falsely claimed that he was purchasing each property to live at (as opposed to purchasing them for investment purposes). The following facts were established at the jury trial.

Shields, who was a second-string running back for a professional football team before retiring with injuries, currently works as a records custodian at a large intellectual property law firm in Nita City. Shields has a BA in business from the University of Nita, which he had attended on a football scholarship. His grade point average in college was 2.56. Shields's current job, which he has held for a decade, "does not require much education or brains," according to his boss. "Mike's probably got an average I.Q., but is pretty simple in his outlook as well as being naïve," his boss testified. "He is in charge of the storage and retrieval of tens of thousands of pages of paper. It's a laborious job, but not one that requires a rocket scientist." Shields makes $57,000 per year at his job. Because he only played professional football for three years (at a time when professional athletes were not paid exorbitant salaries), he did not amass much money as a professional athlete. His net worth (at the time of the allegations in the indictment) was only approximately $150,000—primarily equity in a townhouse in which he lives with his girlfriend.

At trial, the prosecution presented evidence that on six separate occasions during a one-week period, Shields submitted mortgage loan applications that contained falsehoods about his income level (claiming he made $200,000 per year from the law firm) and also claiming that he would be living in each house that he was purchasing. Because each loan application was submitted to a different lender during a relatively short period of time and Shield's credit reports were not updated until a week or so later, none of the banks were aware that Shields had purchased the other properties. Each bank approved his requested loans, believing that Shields was purchasing each home as his primary residence. The signature lines on the various forms were located within as little as six inches from the false information stated on the forms.

At trial, it was undisputed that Shields's signature appeared on each of the documents containing falsehoods. In addition to offering proof of various documents signed by Shields, the prosecution presented testimony that a man named **Frank May** was the "ringleader" of a major real estate fraud scheme in Nita City, whereby "straw borrowers" (such as Shields) signed mortgage paperwork containing material falsehoods and that May provided them with the down payment money. After each transaction, May used a fraudulent real estate appraiser and "flipped" each property in another transaction, the first straw purchaser selling the property to another straw purchaser for an inflated price (usually twice the original price). Such "land flips" netted May tens of thousands of dollars per property. May's scheme, which involved over 300 properties in and around Nita City, eventually came crashing down—and was discovered by the FBI—when the straw purchasers did not make mortgage payments on the "flipped" land.

At trial, May (who was cooperating with the government as part of a plea bargain) explained to jurors how his fraudulent scheme worked (as outlined above). When asked on cross-examination whether he had ever told Shields that his scheme was fraudulent, May said: "I never told him that. One of my associates, **Jim Verona**, dealt with Mr. Shields. I don't know what Verona told him." Verona, who invoked his right to silence under the Fifth Amendment, did not testify for either the defense or prosecution at Shields's trial. At the trial, it was undisputed that fraudulent documents (including false W-2 forms and bank statements) were submitted to the lenders along with the loan applications signed by Shields, but the defense claimed Shields had nothing to do with making those fraudulent documents. There was no proof that Shields was even aware of the fraudulent documentation that was submitted along with his loan applications.

After the prosecution rested its case, Shields testified on his own behalf. He denied knowingly participating in the fraudulent scheme. He claimed that his "good friend" Verona had told him that

> [T]his was a legitimate real estate investment opportunity. You know, like the ones that you see advertised on cable TV late at night. The main one, which I've seen many times, is Carlton Sheets's "no money down" program where you actually get cash back at closing. It's all based on buying what they call "distressed" properties at well below market value and then refinancing them at their actual value and taking the equity out at the front end of the deal.

Shields explained that he trusted Verona, a licensed real estate agent, and did what Verona told him to do. According to Shields, Verona told him that May and Verona had handled all the details and all Shields had to do was show up at a title company and sign the paperwork at the real estate closing. Shields said he never read any of the paperwork that he signed, including the loan applications (which he signed at Verona's office). He said he had provided Verona with his bank statements and W-2 forms from his job at the law firm and that Verona had filled out the loan applications on a computer. He testified: "All I did was sign. I honestly never read anything put before me. I just signed where they told me to." Shields specifically denied that he knowingly had signed paperwork that 1) falsely claimed that his income was $200,000 and 2) certified that he would reside in the homes (as opposed to buying them for investment purposes). "I really thought I was buying investment properties."

Shields admitted that Verona gave him $7,500 after each closing. Shields stated that he believed that this was "all part of the investment program." Shields explained that Verona told him that May's "real estate management company" would be "taking care of all the details, including getting rent payments from tenants of the properties and making the mortgage payments." Shields testified that Verona had assured him that May was a "master" at locating valuable properties at "well below market value" and then "taking out the built-in equity at closing." "That's what I thought was happening at the time," Shields testified. He testified that only later—when mortgage companies started calling him and sending him overdue notices—did he realize that it was a "Ponzi scheme" and "that I was a chump."

When asked on cross-examination by the prosecutor how he thought he was able to purchase six homes on a salary of $57,000 per year and with a net worth of only $150,000, Shields responded: "The real estate programs on cable TV involved just that—people who don't have a lot of money purchasing many properties with 'no money down' and getting cash back at the closings. I've seen testimonials from postal employees, nurses, you know . . . ordinary middle-class folks like me. I never understood how it worked. But because it's been on TV for many years, I honestly thought it was legit."

The prosecutor also cross-examined Shields about the $7,500 that he had received immediately after each of the six closings. When asked how he could make a profit "without paying a single dime out of your pocket," Shields testified, "I know it seems too good to be true, but I believed it at the time. It was just like Carlton Sheets's 'no money down/cash at closing' real estate investment program." When asked by the prosecutor whether he had actually ordered Sheets's materials that were advertised on late-night cable TV, Shields responded: "No. I didn't see a point in doing so. I thought Verona and May knew what they were doing. I knew my credit rating was at risk because I was the purchaser, but Verona assured me that everything would work out OK and that I'd become a millionaire one day based on May's expertise."

After both sides have rested their respective cases, the prosecutor requests a "deliberate ignorance" jury instruction from the trial court, which defense counsel opposes. That instruction reads as follows:

> The government may prove that the defendant acted "knowingly" by proving, beyond a reasonable doubt, that the defendant deliberately closed his eyes to what would otherwise have been obvious to him. No one can avoid responsibility for a crime by deliberately ignoring what is obvious. A finding beyond a reasonable doubt of intent of the defendant to avoid knowledge or enlightenment would permit the jury to find knowledge. Stated another way, a person's knowledge of a particular fact may be shown from a deliberate or intentional ignorance of or a deliberate or intentional blindness to the existence of that fact. You may not conclude that the defendant had knowledge, however, from proof of a mistake, negligence, carelessness, or a belief in an inaccurate proposition.[12]

Prosecutor: Argue in support of your requested instruction.

---

12. The prosecution's proposed instruction was taken from Kevin F. O'Malley et al., 1a Federal Jury Practice & Instructions, § 17.09, at 653–54 (5th ed. 2000).

Defense Counsel: Argue against the prosecutor's requested jury instruction.

To prepare for this hypothetical exercise, read *United States v. Heredia*, 483 F.3d 913, 917–21 (9th Cir. 2007) (en banc); *id.* at 924–30 (Kleinfeld, J., concurring in the result); *id.* at 930–32 (Graber, J., dissenting, joined by Pregerson, Thomas, and Paez).

Hypothetical Four: Jury Instructions

United States v. Moncrief

A federal grand jury returned an indictment charging **Lamont Moncrief** with 1) possession with intent to distribute cocaine and 2) possession with intent to distribute ecstasy (chemically known as MDMA), both in violation of 21 U.S.C. § 841(a)(1). The following facts were established at a jury trial.

On June 25, Nita City police officers **Edward Hart** and **Jack Roberts** recognized Moncrief as the driver of a Chevrolet Tahoe registered to a person named **Vicky Creek**. Officer Hart testified that he recognized Moncrief because he had received information the week before that Moncrief's license had been suspended and that there were outstanding traffic warrants for Moncrief. The officers stopped the vehicle operated by Moncrief, which also contained two other passengers, and arrested him for driving with a suspended driver's license. A search of Moncrief incident to the arrest revealed $2,512 in cash and 144.7 grams of cocaine (in a plastic baggie) in his pocket.

A subsequent search of the vehicle uncovered a plastic baggie containing three ecstasy pills behind an air conditioning vent and another baggie with five ecstasy pills in the backseat of the vehicle. A further search at the impound lot using a drug dog yielded another baggie containing five ecstasy pills hidden behind the glove box of the vehicle. On cross-examination, Officer Hart admitted that either the front seat or backseat passenger or anyone else in the vehicle prior to the date on which Moncrief was arrested could have placed the baggies in these locations. The officers also seized a loaded pistol from underneath the driver's seat. The pistol was not in plain view; rather, it was inside a "Crown Royal" velvet bag. Officers were unable to locate Vicky Creek, in whose name the car was registered. Officer Hart admitted on cross-examination that no fingerprint tests had been performed on the baggies or the pistol.

Pursuant to a subsequently obtained search warrant, a search of an apartment in which Moncrief resided yielded an inexpensive battery-operated electronic scale, which, Officer Hart testified, was the type drug dealers often use, three boxes of sandwich baggies (but no food items), and $10,567 in cash. On cross-examination, Officer Hart admitted that Moncrief's name was not on the apartment's lease, and the apartment complex manager testified that the lease was in the name of **Roy Jones**.

The manager further testified that, while he had seen Moncrief living in the apartment during the prior few months, "Other people appeared to be living in that apartment as well." Officer Hart testified that he had not investigated Roy Jones and had never heard that name before.

At trial, Officer Hart further testified that 144.7 grams of cocaine was "consistent" with a drug-trafficking quantity. He also testified that the total amount of ecstasy pills recovered from the car was "by itself consistent" with personal use, "but the fact that the pills were located in various plastic baggies and found along with that much cocaine suggests that it was being possessed for sale and not merely possessed for personal use."

On cross-examination, defense counsel asked Officer Hart, "Isn't it also true that 144.7 grams of cocaine could be 'consistent' with a personal use amount for a person heavily addicted to cocaine," to which the officer responded: "It's very, very unlikely, but I guess not totally out of the question if the person is a total dope fiend with lots of money to buy dope. One hundred forty-four grams is very expensive. I've personally never observed or heard of a cocaine addict carrying around that much dope for personal use." Defense counsel also asked the officer, "Isn't it true that Mr. Moncrief is a cocaine and ecstasy addict?" to which the officer responded, "I have no idea." Officer Hart testified that the police did not run a drug test on Moncrief after he was arrested and that such a drug test could have detected cocaine and ecstasy if they had been used by Moncrief before his arrest.

After the prosecution rested its case, the defense did not call any witnesses or present any evidence. Moncrief did not testify on his own behalf.

After the close of all the evidence, defense counsel requested that the court submit a lesser-included offense instruction on the misdemeanor charges of simple possession of cocaine and ecstasy as well as an instruction on the greater offense of possession of cocaine and ecstasy with the intent to distribute them. The prosecutor opposed such a lesser-included offense instruction and asked the court to submit the greater offense instruction standing alone.[13]

Defense Counsel: Argue in support of your requested instruction.

Prosecutor: Argue against defense counsel's requested instruction.

13. A violation of 21 U.S.C. § 841(a), felony possession with intent to distribute requires (1) knowingly or intentionally, (2) possessing, (3) with the intent to distribute, (4) a controlled substance. (Both cocaine and ecstasy are controlled substances.) A violation of 21 U.S.C. § 844(a), simple possession, a misdemeanor, requires (1) knowingly or intentionally, (2) possessing, (3) a controlled substance. A lesser-included offense instruction on simple possession would only include the three elements of § 844(a) and would omit the "intent to distribute" element contained in § 841(a).

To prepare for this hypothetical exercise, read *United States v. White*, 972 F.2d 590, 592–94, 595–97, 601–05 (5th Cir. 1992) (majority and dissenting opinions concerning lesser-included offense instruction issue).

Hypothetical Five: Jury Instructions

United States v. Weston

A federal grand jury in Nita City returned an indictment charging **Eli Weston** with possession with intent to distribute crack cocaine. The following facts were established at Weston's jury trial.

On December 2, shortly after midnight, two officers with the Nita City police department were patrolling a neighborhood of Nita City where drug sales and drug usage were common. During their patrol, the officers drove to a location where they could maintain surveillance of the area behind an establishment called Sullivan's Lounge. The area behind Sullivan's Lounge was a local hot spot for illegal drug activity where the officers had arrested "dozens if not hundreds" of individuals for violating drug laws on prior occasions in the past few years—arrests for both the illegal use and distribution of drugs, in particular crack cocaine and marijuana. Seeing no one, the officers pulled around to Union Street, which fronts the lounge. Looking down an alley that runs between Sullivan's Lounge and another building, the officers saw the defendant, whom the officers knew as a resident of the neighborhood. Weston was standing in the alley, facing the wall. The officers called out Weston's name, and when Weston saw the officers, he ran around to the back of the building. During the ensuing chase, the officers observed Weston place a plastic bag on a brick wall with his hand. Weston eventually fled into a pool hall, where he was arrested.

The plastic bag that Weston placed on the brick wall contained an eighth of a "cookie"[14] of crack cocaine, which weighed 3.25 grams, an amount that had a street value of $300 and from which at least thirty dosage units or "rocks" could be cut. When Weston was arrested, he was in possession of a razor blade, which field-tested positive for cocaine residue. As the police officers testified, in their experience such razor blades are often used in the crack cocaine business to cut cocaine into "rocks" for distribution. Weston was also found in possession of exactly $135 cash—four $20 bills, three $10 bills, and five $5 bills. According to the testimony at trial, crack cocaine is commonly sold in $10 and $20 rocks. Weston was not in possession of either a crack pipe or scales when he was arrested. A police officer testified that crack cocaine must be vaporized to be ingested and that "crack pipes" are the most common method for vaporizing "rocks" of the drug.

14. One of the officers testified that crack cocaine is typically produced in "cookie" form by mixing powder cocaine, baking soda, and water and then "cooking" it in a microwave oven in a Pyrex dish. Each "cookie" weighs approximately one ounce. "Cookies" are often then divided into "quarters" or "eighths"—which are later broken into "rocks"—for sale.

On cross-examination, both officers admitted that neither one had looked around the area where Weston was arrested to see if there was a crack pipe. One officer was asked whether he'd ever heard of a crack addict possessing as much as an eighth or a quarter of a cookie for personal use, and the officer admitted that "It's certainly not common, but I have heard of it on rare occasion." The officer also admitted that the police had not performed a drug test on Weston after his arrest to see if crack cocaine was in his system. The officer did say that "he didn't seem high on drugs to me." The officer admitted, however, that he was not an expert on the effects of drugs, but that in his experience, he had "dealt with hundreds of people who were high on crack, and I can usually tell you if a person is high on crack."

On further cross-examination of the police officer, defense counsel asked the officer whether Weston possessed any scales when he was arrested. The officer answered no. Defense counsel asked, "Isn't it common for crack dealers to use scales to measure specific amounts of the drug for sale," to which the officer responded, "It depends." The officer then stated that when sales involve street level dealing, small rocks of crack cocaine are cut from larger pieces and are sold on the street by size and not weight. Scales primarily are used for sales of cookies, which are expected to be one ounce, the officer added.

After the prosecution rested its case-in-chief, defense counsel offered into evidence copies of two prior misdemeanor judgments of conviction, showing that Weston had been convicted of possessing small amounts of marijuana on two prior occasions during the past five years. The prosecution offered no evidence that Weston had ever previously been convicted of selling or distributing any type of drug. Weston did not testify at trial, nor did he make any statement to the officers after he was arrested.

After the close of all the evidence, defense counsel requested that the trial court submit a lesser-included offense instruction on the misdemeanor charge of simple possession of crack cocaine as well as an instruction on the greater offense of possession of crack cocaine with the intent to distribute it. The prosecutor opposed such a lesser-included offense instruction and asked the court to submit the "greater" offense instruction standing alone.[15]

Defense Counsel: Argue in support of your requested jury instruction.

Prosecutor: Argue against the submission of defense counsel's requested jury instruction.

---

15. A violation of 21 U.S.C. § 841(a), felony possession with intent to distribute, requires 1) knowingly or intentionally, 2) possessing, 3) with the intent to distribute, 4) a controlled substance. (Crack cocaine is a controlled substance.) A violation of 21 U.S.C. § 844(a), simple possession, a misdemeanor, requires 1) knowingly or intentionally, 2) possessing, 3) a controlled substance. A lesser-included offense instruction on simple possession would only include the three elements of § 844(a) and would omit the "intent to distribute" element contained in § 841(a).

To prepare for this hypothetical exercise, read *United States v. White*, 972 F.2d 590, 592–94, 595–97, 601–05 (5th Cir. 1992) (majority and dissenting opinions concerning lesser-included offense instruction issue).

Class Eleven

Closing Arguments

Closing arguments to a jury involve a different type of legal advocacy than arguments to a trial judge in support of, or in opposition to, a defendant's motion for a judgment of acquittal. The latter often involves legally-based arguments relying on appellate case law and statutory language and applies the "rational jury" standard articulated in *Jackson v. Virginia*.[1] Although both prosecutors and defense counsel will be forced to discuss legal concepts during closing arguments to a jury (e.g., the meaning of "reasonable doubt"), the most effective legal advocacy in closing arguments to jurors avoids legalese and focuses on common-sense explanations of legal matters.

Defense counsel usually must choose between one of two approaches to closing arguments. The first contends that the defendant is "innocent" and that the evidence establishes the defendant's innocence. The second does not assert that the defendant is "innocent" and, instead, contends that the prosecution has not proven the defendant's guilt beyond a reasonable doubt. The latter approach is most often seen in cases where the defense has offered no evidence during the trial and rests its case immediately after the prosecution has rested its case.

Some defense lawyers believe that arguments that rely on "reasonable doubt" and that focus on deficiencies in the prosecution's proof regarding some "element" of the charged offense will have the effect of causing jurors to believe that the defendant is guilty and that his or her lawyer is simply relying on "technicalities" in the law to acquit the defendant. Often, however, such "technical" arguments are all that a defense lawyer has to rely on in a closing argument—particularly in cases in which the defense has offered no evidence and the defendant has invoked his or her right to silence by not testifying at trial. An effective advocate will convey such legal concepts to jurors in a manner that is less "technical," relies more on common sense, and is rooted in fairness.

In anticipation of the exercises, reread *Victor v. Nebraska*,[2] (discussing the reasonable quantum of proof) and the pattern jury instructions concerning the prosecution's burden of proof (including the "reasonable doubt" definition), which are contained in the prior chapter addressing voir dire (discussed in Class Seven).

1. Jackson v. Virginia, 443 U.S. 307 (1979).
2. Victor v. Nebraska, 511 U.S. 1 (1994).

Refer back to the factual hypotheticals in Class Nine, which also will be used for the hypothetical exercises in this class. However, be aware that in closing arguments, the prosecution and defense are not governed by the *Jackson v. Virginia* standard that applies to motions for judgment of acquittal (which requires the evidence to be viewed in a light most favorable to the prosecution). In closing arguments, both the prosecutor and defense counsel in each of the hypothetical exercises should refer to the ground rules discussed in the readings on voir dire with particular emphasis on the definition of reasonable doubt. Students are encouraged to use demonstratives during their closing arguments (such as a poster listing all the elements of the charged offense).

Class Twelve

Sentencing Hearings

Because most criminal cases result in guilty pleas rather than trials, sentencing is the "main event" in most criminal cases. Sentencing issues can range from the very simple to the very complex, especially in capital cases.

12.1 Noncapital Sentencing

In noncapital cases, sentencing procedures vary widely depending on the jurisdiction. The federal system and many states have sentencing guidelines. Sentencing guidelines are point systems whereby a defendant's conduct constituting the offense of conviction and—in some jurisdictions—"relevant conduct" (factually related, uncharged criminal conduct) are given a numerical score based on a variety of aggravating and mitigating factors (e.g., the type and quantity of drugs in a drug-trafficking case; whether the defendant was a minor player in the offense if it involved coconspirators). Generally, when a defendant pleads guilty and accepts responsibility for the offense of conviction, their score is reduced and their resulting guideline range is lower; if, instead, a defendant elects to go to trial and is convicted, their points generally are not reduced and may even be increased if the court finds that the defendant falsely testified at trial. In addition, the defendant is given a separate score based on their criminal record. The two types of points are placed on a grid with a corresponding range of punishment depending on the placement of the two scores on the grid.[1] In most cases, a court sentences a defendant within that range (which is usually narrow), but may depart from the range, upward or downward, if there is some extraordinary factor justifying a departure one way or the other.[2]

The guideline ranges are much more precise (e.g., 46–57 months) than the larger statutory ranges of punishment (e.g., a minimum of probation to a maximum of twenty years in prison for bank robbery under 18 U.S.C. § 2113(a)). In addition to such sentencing guidelines, the federal system and many states also employ

1. *See generally* Mistretta v. United States, 488 U.S. 361 (1989) (discussing the United States Sentencing Guidelines or "USSG"); see also, e.g., Minnesota Sentencing Guidelines and Commentary, available at https://mn.gov/sentencing-guidelines/assets/2021Sept15MinnSentencingGuidelines Commentary_tcm30-497682.pdf (last visited June 1, 2022).
2. *See* Koon v. United States, 518 U.S. 81 (1996).

minimum mandatory statutory sentences—most common in drug-trafficking cases—which trump lesser guideline ranges.[3]

The Supreme Court of the United States has held that there is no constitutional right to have a jury—as opposed to a trial judge—impose sentence in a criminal case.[4] However, any fact (other than a defendant's prior conviction) that increases the statutory maximum sentence, creates a mandatory minimum sentence or raises a mandatory sentencing guidelines range is an "element" of the offense that must be found by a jury beyond a reasonable doubt for such increased punishment to be constitutional.[5] If a particular jurisdiction employs *mandatory* sentencing guidelines, a jury must find at sentencing such facts that increase a defendant's guidelines range. Yet if sentencing guidelines are merely *advisory* in nature—and a judge need only consider the guidelines in imposing sentence, but is free to sentence a defendant anywhere within the larger statutory range of punishment—then the Constitution does not require that juries be used for any purpose during sentencing.[6] The federal sentencing guidelines are advisory in nature. The states that have sentencing guidelines vary from purely voluntary to mandatory in nature.[7]

In some state systems, there are no sentencing guidelines (advisory or mandatory), and judges are governed only by broad statutory ranges of punishment. In these systems, contested legal issues concerning noncapital sentencing are much less common than they are in the jurisdictions with guideline sentencing schemes. The most common sentencing issue in nonguidelines jurisdictions is whether a defendant's prior conviction(s) qualify for an "enhancement" in his or her statutory range of punishment as a "habitual" offender.[8]

Other than issues related to facts that increase a defendant's maximum punishment ("*Apprendi* issues"), there are relatively few constitutional issues that arise in the noncapital sentencing context. Occasionally, a First, Fifth, or Sixth Amendment issue may arise, and, even more rarely, an Eighth Amendment issue.[9] By and

3. *See, e.g.*, 18 U.S.C. § 924(c) (minimum mandatory sentences ranging from five to twenty-five years in prison without parole for possession, use, or carrying of different types of firearms during and in relation or in furtherance of drug-trafficking crimes or crimes of violence); 21 U.S.C. § 841(b) (minimum mandatory sentences of five, ten, or twenty years, or life imprisonment without parole, depending on type and quantity of drugs and whether the defendant has any prior felony drug convictions).

4. *See* Spaziano v. Florida, 468 U.S. 447 (1984).

5. Apprendi v. New Jersey, 530 U.S. 466 (2000) (statutory maximum sentences); Alleyne v. United States, 570 U.S. 99 (2013) (mandatory minimum sentences); Blakely v. Washington, 542 U.S. 296 (2004) (mandatory sentencing guideline ranges); *but see* Almendarez-Torres v. United States, 528 U.S. 224 (1998) (exception for prior convictions).

6. United States v. Booker, 543 U.S. 220 (2005).

7. NCSC, State Sentencing Guidelines: Profile & Continuum (2021), available at: https://www.ncsc.org/__data/assets/pdf_file/0022/25474/state_sentencing_guidelines.pdf (last visited June 1, 2022).

8. *See, e.g.*, Campbell v. State, 49 S.W.3d 874 (Tex. Crim. App. 2001).

9. *See, e.g.*, Mitchell v. United States, 526 U.S. 314 (1999) (sentencing court violated Fifth Amendment right against self-incrimination by increasing defendant's sentence based on his

large, though, in noncapital sentencings, there are few constitutional claims raised because there are relatively few constitutional protections afforded to noncapital defendants at the sentencing stage of a criminal case.[10]

Generally, when there are contested factual issues at a noncapital sentencing hearing—whether in state or federal court—the preponderance standard rather than the reasonable doubt standard applies unless the latter is required by the Supreme Court's *Apprendi* jurisprudence.[11] In addition, the sentencing court may find pivotal sentencing facts based solely on hearsay and other evidence that would be inadmissible under the rules of evidence, assuming such evidence is sufficiently reliable.[12]

12.2 Capital Sentencing

After declaring the existing capital punishment laws to be in violation of the Eighth Amendment's ban on cruel and unusual punishments in the 1972 case *Furman v. Georgia*,[13] the Supreme Court in 1976 upheld the facial validity of most states' capital punishment laws that had been rewritten in the wake of *Furman*.[14] In scores of decisions since *Furman*, the Supreme Court has developed an extremely complex body of Eighth Amendment jurisprudence that applies only in death penalty cases—recognizing that "death is qualitatively different" from any other punishment.[15]

During the capital sentencing phase jurors are asked to find "aggravating" and "mitigating" factors or circumstances and then impose either a life sentence or death sentence. Although the Supreme Court has held that under the Constitution,

---

invocation of right to silence at sentencing); Alabama v. Shelton, 535 U.S. 654 (2002) (defendant's Sixth Amendment right to counsel in a misdemeanor case violated by imposition of a suspended jail sentence when defendant had neither been offered assistance of counsel nor waived right to counsel); Shelton v. State, 41 S.W.3d 208 (Tex. App. 2001) (sentencing court violated First Amendment by increasing the defendant's sentence based on his constitutionally protected conduct that had no relation to the offense); Ewing v. California, 538 U.S. 11 (2003) (discussing the very limited "proportionality" review of noncapital punishment under the Eighth Amendment's cruel and unusual punishments clause).

10. *See, e.g.*, Monge v. California, 524 U.S. 721 (1998) (limited operation of Double Jeopardy Clause in noncapital sentencing context).

11. *See, e.g.*, United States v. Watts, 519 U.S. 148, 156 (1997) (per curiam).

12. *See* Williams v. New York, 337 U.S. 241 (1949) (hearsay admissible at sentencing); *see also* Townsend v. Burke, 334 U.S. 736, 739–41 (1948) (due process violated if unreliable or untrue evidence considered in sentencing).

13. Furman v. Georgia, 408 U.S. 238 (1972).

14. *See, e.g.*, Gregg v. Georgia, 428 U.S. 153 (1976).

15. Woodson v. North Carolina, 428 U.S. 280, 305 (1976) (plurality); *see also* Eddings v. Oklahoma, 455 U.S. 104, 117–18 (1982) (O'Connor, J., concurring) ("[T]his Court has gone to extraordinary measures to ensure that the prisoner sentenced to be executed is afforded a process that will guarantee, as much as is humanly possible, that the sentence was not imposed out of whim, passion, prejudice, or mistake.").

a sentencing jury is not required to render the ultimate decision of whether a death sentence or life sentence is imposed in a capital case,[16] the Court's holding that a jury (as opposed to a trial judge) must find any aggravating factor(s) rendering a defendant eligible for capital punishment[17] means that a jury must be involved in the capital sentencing process.

The Supreme Court's Eighth Amendment jurisprudence has "distinguished between . . . the eligibility phase and the selection phase" of capital sentencing.[18] The eligibility process is concerned with meaningfully narrowing the potential class of capital murderers to a relatively small group who, because of the unusually aggravated nature of their cases, are worthy of consideration for the death penalty.[19]

The selection process—which occurs *after* the eligibility process—is concerned with allowing for a "broad inquiry into all relevant mitigating evidence" and permitting the sentencer to arrive at a sentence only after considering all aggravating and mitigating factors.[20]

A capital sentencer, whether a judge or jury, must "be able to consider," must "not refuse to consider," and must be able to "give effect" to a capital defendant's mitigating evidence under the applicable law and the trial court's jury instructions.[21]

The Supreme Court has broadly defined "mitigating evidence" as being any evidence "which tends logically to prove or disprove some fact or circumstance which a fact-finder could reasonably deem to have mitigating value."[22] Such evidence includes anything that relates to a defendant's character, history, or the circumstances of the offense that would support a sentence less than death, including, for example, a defendant's history of child abuse or an underprivileged childhood; a defendant's relatively young age at the time of the crime (e.g., a nineteen-year-old capital defendant); a defendant's mental or emotional problems at the time of the crime; the fact that a defendant was intoxicated on drugs or alcohol at the time of the crime; and a defendant's good conduct in jail while awaiting his trial.[23]

---

16. *See* Spaziano v. Florida, 468 U.S. 447 (1984).
17. Ring v. Arizona, 536 U.S. 584 (2002).
18. Buchanan v. Angelone, 522 U.S. 269, 275 (1998).
19. *Id.*
20. *Id.* at 275–76; *see also* Tuilaepa v. California, 512 U.S. 967, 971–72 (1994).
21. Hitchcock v. Dugger, 481 U.S. 393, 394 (1987); *see also* Lockett v. Ohio, 438 U.S. 586 (1978); Eddings v. Oklahoma, 455 U.S. 104 (1982); Skipper v. South Carolina, 476 U.S. 1 (1986); Penry v. Lynaugh, 492 U.S. 302 (1989); Penry v. Johnson, 532 U.S. 782 (2001); Tennard v. Dretke, 542 U.S. 274 (2004); Abdul-Kabir v. Quarterman, 550 U.S. 233 (2007).
22. *Tennard*, 542 U.S. at 284 (internal citation and quotation marks omitted).
23. *See, e.g.*, *id.* at 288–89 (low I.Q., even if it does not qualify as mental retardation); *Penry*, 532 U.S. at 788–89, 803–04 (child abuse); Johnson v. Texas, 509 U.S. 350, 367 (1993) (defendant's youth, i.e., nineteen years of age, at the time of the crime); Parker v. Dugger, 498 U.S. 308, 314 (1991) (defendant's "difficult childhood" and intoxication at the time of the crime); Hitchcock, 481 U.S. at 397–99 (underprivileged childhood and mental impairment resulting from childhood substance abuse); Skipper, 476 U.S. at 5 (defendant's good behavior in jail while awaiting trial);

In applying this Eighth Amendment doctrine, the Court has reversed death sentences when there was a "reasonable likelihood" that jury instructions precluded even a single juror (among the twelve) from considering or "giving effect" to mitigating evidence that was introduced during the trial or sentencing phase.[24] Likewise, the Court has reversed death sentences when a trial court excluded such relevant mitigating evidence.[25]

Hypothetical One: Sentencing Hearings

United States v. Waller

A federal grand jury indicted **Steven Waller** for possessing twenty-eight grams of crack cocaine with the intent to distribute it in violation of 21 U.S.C. § 841. It was undisputed that Waller, a nineteen-year-old high-school dropout with a serious crack addiction, had served as a middleman for a large-scale crack dealer in a housing project in Nita City. In exchange for enough crack to feed his own drug habit for a week or so, Waller would deliver distribution-quantities of crack (usually in the form of one-ounce quantities called cookies) from the dealer to other street-level dealers. Waller never received any money for his services; he always received crack cocaine as remuneration, which he always used rather than distributed to anyone else. Waller entered a plea of guilty to the charge in the indictment.

When he was arrested, Waller readily confessed to DEA agents. He also agreed to cooperate with the agents and attempted to set up the crack dealer who supplied Waller with his drugs. Waller told the agents: "I'm a crackhead because of him. I hate that guy for getting me hooked." Waller repeatedly attempted, without success, to set up the dealer. Waller wore a hidden microphone and attempted to have the dealer incriminate himself on an audio recording. The dealer, however, became suspicious of Waller and refused to deal any further with him.

After DEA agents arrested him, a federal magistrate judge released Waller on bond. Waller remained released on bond before and after his plea of guilty to the district court. His sentencing hearing occurred six months after his arrest. During that six-month period, Waller was monitored by the United States Pretrial Services Agency, whose responsibility includes administering drug tests to federal defendants

---

Eddings, 455 U.S. at 115 ("difficult family history," emotional disturbance at the time of the offense, and defendant's youth at the time of the offense).

24. *See, e.g.*, *Penry*, 532 U.S. at 788–90, 803–04 (jury instructions precluded jury from giving mitigating effect to defendant's mitigating evidence of mental impairment and history of child abuse); McKoy v. North Carolina, 494 U.S. 433, 442–44 (1990) (jury instructions impermissibly required jurors to be unanimous about existence of each mitigating factor before it could be considered); *Hitchcock*, 481 U.S. at 397–99 (jury instructions precluded jurors from considering defendant's mitigating evidence of a mental impairment and disadvantaged childhood).

25. *See, e.g.*, Skipper, 476 U.S. at 7–9 (trial court improperly excluded mitigating evidence of defendant's good behavior in jail while awaiting trial).

released on bond. The pretrial services officer assigned to Waller's case administered thirteen biweekly drug tests to Waller during the time that he was on bond. Waller failed the first—testing positive for crack cocaine—but passed the next eleven tests. After failing the first test, he was placed in an inpatient drug rehabilitation clinic as a condition of his bond. He stayed there for thirty days and thereafter was released based on what the clinic's director referred to as "an extraordinary willingness to recover from his crack addiction." After being released from the inpatient clinic, Waller continued to receive outpatient drug counseling as a condition of his bond.

Two days before the sentencing hearing was scheduled to occur, Waller was given his thirteenth (and final) drug test prior to sentencing. As was customary, the pretrial services officer asked Waller prior to the test whether he had been using any illegal drugs during the time since his last drug test. Waller responded, "No." After the drug test came back positive for marijuana, Waller initially denied having used it. He told his pretrial officer: "I live in a drug-infested apartment complex where people smoke pot all day long. I must have accidentally inhaled some smoke from someone else's joint." The pretrial officer, who had a good relationship with Waller, confronted him and said that his story was "nonsense." Waller then broke down in tears and stated: "I'm sorry I lied to you. I did smoke pot two days ago. I just took a couple of hits from a buddy's bong. I don't know why I did it. I ain't used drugs in almost five months. I thought I'd whipped my addiction. I guess I didn't. I'm really sorry." According to the pretrial services officer, Waller showed genuine remorse.

The pretrial services officer reported Waller's failed drug test to the district court and counsel for both the prosecution and defense. At the sentencing hearing, which occurred two days later, the prosecutor asked the district court to deny Waller credit for acceptance of responsibility under USSG § 3E1.1(a) based on his admitted drug use while on bond. Defense counsel, who has the burden of persuasion, urged the court to grant Waller credit for acceptance of responsibility.

Defense Counsel: Argue that Waller should receive credit for acceptance of responsibility.

Prosecutor: Argue that Waller should be denied credit for acceptance of responsibility.

To prepare for this hypothetical exercise, read United States Sentencing Guidelines ("USSG") § 3E1.1(a) and application notes 1 and 3, quoted below,[26] as well

---

26. 18 USSG § 3E1.1 Acceptance of Responsibility

(a) If the defendant clearly demonstrates acceptance of responsibility for his offense, decrease the offense level by 2 levels. . . .

Application Notes:

* * *

1. In determining whether a defendant qualifies under subsection (a), appropriate considerations include, but are not limited to, the following:

as *United States v. Morrison*, 983 F.2d 730, 731, 733–35 (6th Cir. 1993) (court's discussion of USSG § 3E1.1); *id.* at 735–36 (Kennedy, J., dissenting); *United States v. Mara*, 523 F.3d 1036 (9th Cir. 2008).

Hypothetical Two: Sentencing Hearings

United States v. Reed

FBI agents arrested **Eddie Brown** for passing counterfeit $20 bills at a convenience store in Nita City. Brown admitted that he knew the bills were counterfeit and that he'd received them from a man named **George Reed** at Reed's trailer home. Reed was a convicted felon, having been convicted of felony theft. The agents went to Reed's trailer home, knocked on the door, and asked to question Reed about counterfeit money. Reed consented to speak to the agents and also consented to a search of his trailer. Inside the trailer, agents discovered in a trash can a crumpled-up and partially torn $20 bill that appeared to be counterfeit. At that point, the agents obtained a federal search warrant to search the trailer for evidence of counterfeit money. Using the warrant, the agents thoroughly searched the trailer. Although they found no additional evidence of counterfeit money, the agents did find a baggie containing 500 grams of marijuana in a closet. In the same closet, the agents found an unloaded .410 shotgun. A box of .410 shotgun shells with "bird shot"-sized pellets was found in a cabinet in another room of the trailer. Reed admitted that the shotgun belonged to him. He was not asked why he possessed the shotgun and offered no reason for his possession of it.

Reed was arrested and subsequently charged with being a felon in possession of a firearm in violation of 18 U.S.C. § 922(g)(1); he was not charged with possessing the marijuana. He pleaded guilty to the charge in the indictment. At the sentencing

---

(a) truthfully admitting the conduct comprising the offense(s) of conviction . . . ;
(b) voluntary termination or withdrawal from criminal conduct or associations;

* * *

(g) post-offense rehabilitative efforts (e.g., counseling or drug treatment); and
(h) the timeliness of the defendant's conduct in manifesting the acceptance of responsibility.

* * *

3. Entry of a guilty plea prior to the commencement of trial combined with truthfully admitting the conduct comprising the offense of conviction . . . will constitute significant evidence of acceptance of responsibility for purposes of subsection (a). However, this evidence may be outweighed by conduct of the defendant that is inconsistent with such acceptance of responsibility. A defendant who enters a guilty plea is not entitled to an adjustment under this section as a matter of right.

* * *

hearing, the only disputed issue was whether Reed's base offense level should be increased by four levels under USSG § 2K2.1(b)(6), based on a supposed connection between the firearm and Reed's alleged drug-trafficking activities. In addition to offering proof of the foregoing facts, the prosecution put DEA Agent **Stanley Woods** on the witness stand. Agent Woods testified that 500 grams of marijuana is "consistent" with drug-trafficking (as opposed to personal use) and also that "guns are tools of the trade of drug dealers."

When asked by defense counsel, "Isn't it true that a .410 shotgun is the smallest common caliber of shotguns and that such guns are commonly used to hunt small game," Agent Woods responded, "That is true." Defense counsel also asked him, "Isn't it true that bird shot pellets are not designed to kill large game—or human beings, for that matter?" Agent Woods responded: "That's true. But dope dealers have been known to protect their dope and drug money with small caliber weapons—even unloaded ones—whatever can deter someone from stealing the dope or drug money." When asked whether he had ever specifically seen or heard of a drug dealer protecting his drugs or drug money with an unloaded .410 shotgun, the agent responded: "No, I can't say that I have. I guess the closest thing I've seen is a .22 rifle, which roughly is equivalent to a .410 in terms of being a small-game weapon. One's a rifle, the other a shotgun." Defense counsel presented no evidence at sentencing.

Prosecutor: Argue that Reed's offense level should be increased under USSG § 2K2.1(b)(6).

Defense Counsel: Argue that Reed's offense level should not be increased under USSG § 2K2.1(b)(6).

To prepare for this hypothetical exercise, read United States Sentencing Guidelines ("USSG") § 2K2.1(b)(6)(B), quoted below,[27] and *United States v. Mitchell*, 166

---

27. USSG § 2K2.1 Unlawful Receipt, Possession, or Transportation of Firearms or Ammunition; Prohibited Transactions Involving Firearms or Ammunition

* * *

(b) Specific Offense Characteristics

* * *

> (6)(B) If the defendant used or possessed any firearm or ammunition in connection with another felony offense; or possessed or transferred any firearm or ammunition with knowledge, intent, or reason to believe that it would be used or possessed in connection with another felony offense, increase by 4 levels. If the resulting offense level is less than level 18, increase to level 18.

* * *

[Note: In United States v. Booker, 543 U.S. 220 (2005), the U.S. Supreme Court held that the United States Sentencing Guidelines are merely "advisory" rather than "mandatory" in nature. Because the federal Sentencing Guidelines are advisory, aggravating facts that increase a defendant's "points" under the Guidelines may be found to exist (or not to exist) by the

F.3d 748, 749–51, 753–57 (5th Cir. 1999) (discussing USSG § 2K2.1(b)(5), which was subsequently recodified as USSG § 2K2.1(b)(6)(B)).

Hypothetical Three: Sentencing Hearings

United States v. Iverson

A federal grand jury in Nita City returned an indictment charging sixty-six-year-old defendant **George Iverson** with possessing a firearm as a convicted felon, in violation of 18 U.S.C. § 922(g)(1). Although the maximum prison sentence for a violation of § 922(g)(1) is ordinarily ten years, Iverson's indictment also alleged that he had been convicted of three prior "violent" felonies that allegedly occurred "on occasions different from one another," which, if true, would trigger a mandatory minimum prison sentence of fifteen years without parole. *See* 18 U.S.C. § 924(e) (providing for such a prison sentence if a defendant possessed a firearm after being convicted of three or more violent felonies committed on occasions different from one another).

The evidence that Iverson possessed a firearm was overwhelming. A federal park ranger discovered Iverson and his grandson hunting for squirrels with .410 shotguns in a forest near Iverson's rural home that was just across the border between Iverson's land and protected federal parkland (where hunting is prohibited by federal law). The park ranger issued a misdemeanor citation to Iverson for hunting on federal property and only later, when processing the citation, discovered that Iverson was a convicted felon who was prohibited from possessing a firearm. The park ranger notified the ATF and United States Attorney's office, which proceeded to prosecute Iverson under 18 U.S.C. §§ 922(g)(1) and 924(e).

The evidence that Iverson had three prior convictions for violent felonies was beyond dispute. He had a 1986 conviction for armed robbery of a gas station and two 1994 convictions for armed robberies of individuals that occurred during burglaries of their respective residences.[28] The facts concerning the 1994 armed robbery convictions are as follows: At 1:30 a.m. on December 1, 1994, Iverson and his brother burglarized 1211-A Main Street in Nita City—one-half of a duplex—and demanded money and jewelry from its occupants. According to a prearranged plan, at 1:39 a.m., while Iverson still held the occupants of 1211-A Main Street at gunpoint, Iverson's brother entered the other half of the duplex, 1211-B Main Street, and proceeded to demand money and jewelry from its occupants. After Iverson's brother succeeded in robbing the adjacent unit of the duplex, the two brothers then fled from the scene.

---

trial court applying the preponderance-of-the-evidence standard and need not be submitted to the jury or found beyond a reasonable doubt. See USSG § 6A1.3.]

28. Even decades-old felony convictions may support convictions and sentences under 18 U.S.C. §§ 922(g)(1) or 924(e).

Police apprehended both Iverson and his brother the next day when they tried to pawn the stolen jewelry. Iverson (and his brother) pleaded guilty to two counts of armed robbery: one count for the robbery of the occupants of 1211-A Main Street and the second for the robbery of the occupants of 1211-B Main Street.[29]

The trial court sentenced Iverson to serve ten years in state prison on each count and ordered the prison sentences to run concurrently. Iverson served five years in state prison before being paroled in 1999. He successfully discharged his parole in 2009 and had not been convicted of any other crime since that time.

Although Iverson pleaded guilty to violating § 922(g)(1) by possessing a .410 shotgun as a convicted felon, his defense counsel has contested the sentencing "enhancement" allegation in the indictment that Iverson has three prior convictions for "violent" felonies that occurred "on occasions different from one another." In particular, defense counsel has contended that the two 1994 robberies did not occur on "occasions different from one another" and, thus, Iverson has only two "strikes" rather than three "strikes" for purposes of § 924(e).

Prosecutor: Argue that the two 1994 robberies occurred on "occasions different from one another."

Defense Counsel: Argue that the two 1994 robbery convictions occurred on the same "occasion."

To prepare for this exercise, read *Wooden v. United States*, 142 S. Ct. 1063 (2022) (majority opinion and concurring opinion of Justice Gorsuch, joined by Justice Sotomayor), and *United States v. Brady*, 988 F.2d 664 (6th Cir. 1993) (en banc) (majority and dissenting opinions).

Hypothetical Four: Sentencing Hearings

State v. Wilson

Charles Wilson, a thirty-three-year-old man, was convicted in Nita state court of capital murder for a murder that occurred in the course of a liquor store robbery. A jury convicted Wilson of fatally shooting two store clerks, **Tina Howell** and **Myra Bird**. The prosecution seeks the death penalty (which Nita administers by lethal injection). During the capital sentencing phase in front of a jury, the prosecutor introduced "victim impact" evidence concerning the positive character traits of

29. Although he played no direct role in robbing the occupants of 1211-B, Iverson pleaded guilty to "aiding and abetting" his brother in the robbery of 1211-B after admitting that he and his brother had planned on Iverson's holding the occupants of 1211-A at gunpoint to facilitate his brother's robbery of 1211-B.

the two murder victims as well as testimony from their surviving family members about how their murders have negatively impacted them.[30]

After the prosecution rested its case during the capital sentencing phase, Wilson's defense counsel called his mother, **Sharon Wilson**, to testify on her son's behalf. After eliciting information about certain positive character traits of her son (he was a hard worker who provided for his wife and child), defense counsel specifically asked questions about what impact the potential execution of her son would have on her and Charles Wilson's six-year-old daughter, **Brianna**. The prosecutor immediately objected to the latter line of questioning. Before Mrs. Wilson could answer, the trial court asked the lawyers to approach the bench in order to discuss the prosecutor's objection.

Prosecutor: Argue in support of your objection.

Defense Counsel: Argue that the trial court should overrule the objection and permit Mrs. Wilson to answer the question. Make a proffer that if permitted to answer, Mrs. Wilson would inform jurors: 1) that her son's execution would "devastate" his young daughter, and 2) that her son's execution would be "especially hard" on Mrs. Wilson since her only other child, Charles Wilson's younger brother Mike, died of cancer two years ago.

To prepare for this exercise, read *State v. Stevens*, 879 P.2d 162 (Ore. 1994) (majority and dissenting opinions); *State v. Loftin*, 680 A.2d 677, 712–13 (N.J. 1996); *id.* at 744–46 (dissenting opinion), as well as *Payne v. Tennessee*, 501 U.S. 808 (1991).

Hypothetical Five: Sentencing Hearings

United States v. Richardson

A federal grand jury returned an indictment charging the fifty-two-year-old defendant, **Shane Richardson**, with capital murder in violation of 18 U.S.C. § 1111. The indictment alleged that Richardson, who worked as a janitor at a Veteran's Administration Hospital in Nita City, raped and then intentionally killed **Linda Leigh**, a nurse at the hospital.[31] The assistant U.S. attorney handling the case announced the prosecution's intent to seek the death penalty against Richardson pursuant to 18 U.S.C. §§ 3591–3594.

The evidence that Richardson had raped and murdered Leigh was overwhelming: DNA evidence conclusively linked him to the rape; an eyewitness saw Richardson

30. In Payne v. Tennessee, 501 U.S. 808 (1991), the Supreme Court held that admission of such "victim impact" evidence during a capital sentencing hearing does not violate the Constitution.
31. Because the capital murder occurred on federal property, it is being prosecuted in federal court rather than state court.

exiting the basement area where Leigh's dead body was found shortly after the time of death; video surveillance showed Richardson following Leigh to the basement in an elevator; and Richardson confessed on a video-recording. As a result of this overwhelming evidence, Richardson's court-appointed defense counsel strongly advised him to plead guilty and focus on presenting mitigating evidence—including Richardson's long history of mental illness, his honorable discharge from the Army after serving in combat in Vietnam, and his remorse for the crime (as expressed during his video-recorded confession)—at the capital sentencing hearing. Following his attorney's advice, Richardson pleaded guilty to capital murder and hoped for a life sentence.

Under federal law, a jury is the sentencer in capital cases unless waived by the defendant. Although he pleaded guilty to the trial judge, Richardson requested a sentencing jury. Anticipating the capital sentencing phase, the prosecution gave pretrial notice of aggravating factors that it intended to offer in support of its request for the death penalty (in addition to the aggravating factor that Leigh's murder occurred during a rape). Evidence of those additional factors were: 1) certified copies of Richardson's two prior felony convictions (a 1996 conviction for aggravated assault of a neighbor whom Richardson had stabbed during a fight and a 2001 conviction for assault of a police officer, in which Richardson broke the officer's nose with his fist); and 2) the allegation that Richardson had engaged in two other sexual assaults, including one of a six-year-old girl (neither resulted in the death of the victim).[32] Neither alleged rape ever had been prosecuted; by the time of Richardson's capital murder case, both were outside the five-year statute of limitations period. The prosecution gave notice of these two unadjudicated rapes as part of its claim that Richardson posed a "continuing threat to society," an aggravating factor upheld by the Supreme Court of the United States over three decades ago.[33] To establish that aggravating factor under federal law, the prosecution had to prove beyond a reasonable doubt that Richardson was a continuing threat to society.

In response to the prosecution's notice of its intent to offer proof of the two unadjudicated rapes as evidence relevant to the continuing threat aggravating factor, defense counsel filed a motion requesting the trial court to do two things. First, make a preliminary ruling outside of the presence of the jurors that there was clear and convincing evidence of each alleged rape before permitting the prosecution to introduce such evidence to the capital sentencing jury, and second, assuming the trial court made such a finding, instruct the capital sentencing jurors that they could not consider the alleged rapes unless they found that the prosecution had proven them by clear and convincing evidence. The defense also asked the trial

32. The prosecution intended to offer the testimony of both rape victims. One was Richardson's ex-wife's niece, who was six years old at the time of the alleged rape. The second alleged victim was Richardson's former coworker at his prior job. The prosecution had no physical evidence linking Richardson to either alleged sexual assault.
33. Jurek v. Texas, 428 U.S. 262 (1976).

court to define clear and convincing evidence in jury instructions according to its traditional definition (meaning something beyond a preponderance of the evidence although less than proof beyond a reasonable doubt). The prosecution opposed the motion.

Defense Counsel: Argue in support of your motion.

Prosecutor: Argue against defense counsel's motion.

To prepare for this hypothetical exercise, read *State v. Cohen*, 634 A.2d 380, 385–91 (Del. Super. Ct. 1992), and *United States v. Beckford*, 964 F. Supp. 993 (E.D. Va. 1997), in addition to 18 U.S.C. § 3592(c).

Class Thirteen

Post-Conviction Challenges to a Conviction or Sentence

13.1 Motions for New Trial Generally

Every jurisdiction in the United States provides that within a certain amount of time after conviction,[1] a defendant may file a motion for new trial that seeks to set aside their conviction or sentence based on some error (usually constitutional error) having occurred during the prior proceedings. Often such claims are not discovered until long after trial (and well past the due date for a motion for a new trial) and thus are raised for the first time in a post-conviction habeas corpus petition.[2] Typically, the types of constitutional claims raised in a motion for new trial or habeas corpus petition are what are referred to as "extra-record" claims—meaning such claims rely at least in part on facts that are not apparent in the record of the prior proceedings.[3] Thus, such claims usually require factual development, typically at an evidentiary hearing conducted by the trial court or by submission of affidavits or by depositions.[4]

The three most common types of extra-record, post-conviction constitutional claims allege 1) prosecutorial or police misconduct that occurred before or during the trial, 2) jury misconduct that occurred during the trial or during jury deliberations, and 3) ineffective assistance of counsel by a defendant's prior attorney.[5]

---

1. *See, e.g.*, Fed. R. Crim. P. 33(b)(1), (2) (motion for new trial based on newly discovered evidence may be filed within three years of guilty verdict; all other motions for new trial must be filed within fourteen days of verdict); Tex. R. App. P. 21.4(a) (motion for new trial must be filed within thirty days of sentence being imposed); *see also* Herrera v. Collins, 506 U.S. 390, 410–11 & n. 8–11 (1993) (collecting state statutes and procedural rules concerning time limits for motions for new trial).
2. *See, e.g.*, 28 U.S.C. §§ 2241–2255 (federal habeas corpus remedies).
3. *See, e.g.*, Morales v. Calderon, 85 F.3d 1387, 1388 (9th Cir. 1996); Commonwealth v. Grant, 813 A.2d 726, 736–37 (Pa. 2002).
4. *See, e.g.*, Massaro v. United States, 538 U.S. 500, 505–06 (2003).
5. Under the rules of ethics, a defense lawyer cannot challenge his own conduct as ineffective. *See, e.g.*, Holmes v. Norris, 32 F.3d 1240, 1241 (8th Cir. 1994). Therefore, unless new counsel is appointed or retained by the due date for a motion for new trial, an ineffectiveness claim may not be raised until a habeas corpus petition is filed by new counsel.

13.2 Claims of Misconduct by a Member of the Prosecution Team

There are two main types of extra-record claims of prosecutorial misconduct that are commonly litigated in motions for new trials as well as in habeas corpus petitions: 1) the prosecution's failure to disclose evidence favorable to the defense (*Brady* claims),[6] and 2) the prosecution's knowing presentation of perjured testimony or knowing failure to correct such perjured testimony (perjury claims). Both types of claims are rooted in the Due Process Clause.

13.2.1 Brady *Claims*

The first type of claim alleges that some member of the prosecution team—including prosecutors as well as law enforcement officers who worked on a case[7]—failed to timely disclose evidence to the defense that was exculpatory (i.e., was probative of the defendant's innocence or would refute the prosecution's evidence of guilt), that could have been used to impeach a prosecution witness, or that was "mitigating" for sentencing purposes.[8] To prevail on such a claim, a defendant must show that the nondisclosed evidence not only was favorable to the defendant, but also was material.[9] "Materiality" under *Brady* places the burden on the defendant to show a reasonable probability that if timely disclosure of the evidence in question had been made, the result of the proceeding would have been different.[10] Materiality in the *Brady* context does not require a showing of a different outcome by a preponderance of the evidence; rather, it requires a lesser showing, although one that undermines a court's confidence in the verdict.[11]

To prevail under *Brady*, the defendant does not need to show that the evidence was intentionally or recklessly suppressed. Indeed, the good faith (or bad faith) of the prosecutor or other member of the prosecution team in failing to disclose the evidence is irrelevant.[12] Furthermore, the defense need not have requested the nondisclosed evidence from the prosecution before or during trial. The prosecution's duty to disclose favorable material evidence in the possession of any member of

6. Brady v. Maryland, 373 U.S. 83 (1963).
7. United States v. Morris, 80 F.3d 1151, 1169–70 (7th Cir. 1996).
8. *See* United States v. Bagley, 473 U.S. 667, 676–84 (1985) (refining *Brady*'s constitutional standard related to prosecution's failure to disclose favorable evidence to the defense prior to trial).
9. "Materiality" is synonymous here with "harm" or "prejudice." *See* Strickler v. Greene, 527 U.S. 263, 280–82 (1999).
10. Kyles v. Whitley, 514 U.S. 419, 433–34 (1995) (noting that the *Brady* "materiality" standard is similar to the "prejudice" standard applicable to claims of ineffective assistance of counsel); *see also* Banks v. Dretke, 540 U.S. 668 (2004). Ineffective assistance of counsel claims are discussed in the following chapter.
11. *Kyles*, 514 U.S. at 433–34.
12. *Id.* at 437–38.

the prosecution team is *automatic*.[13] However, a defendant cannot complain of nondisclosure when the same evidence could have been obtained before or during trial from a third-party source through the exercise of reasonable diligence by the defense.[14]

13.2.2 Perjury Claims

The Supreme Court has long held that it violates due process for the prosecution to knowingly or recklessly[15] present false testimony or evidence or knowingly or recklessly fail to correct false testimony from a prosecution witness during the course of the trial, even if the trial prosecutor did not elicit it.[16] However, a "mere recantation" by a prosecution witness after a conviction is obtained does not necessarily violate the defendant's constitutional rights if no member of the prosecution team knew of the perjury at the time of trial.[17] Unlike its decisions in the *Brady* context, the Supreme Court in the perjury context has not yet imputed to a trial prosecutor the knowledge possessed by all other members of the prosecution team.[18]

The lower courts have taken divergent approaches concerning the imputation of the knowledge of a member of the prosecution team to the trial prosecutor.[19]

Unlike the type of materiality that must be shown to prevail on a *Brady* claim, the type of materiality required to prevail on a perjury claim is considerably more

---

13. *Bagley*, 473 U.S. at 682.
14. *See, e.g.*, United States v. Fallon, 348 F.3d 248, 252–53 (7th Cir. 2003); United States v. Prior, 546 F.2d 1254, 1259 (5th Cir. 1977); Stewart v. State, 801 So. 2d 59, 70 (Fla. 2001).
15. Virtually all courts treat the prosecution's reckless presentation of false testimony or evidence as tantamount to the knowing presentation of perjury. *See, e.g.*, Smith v. Massey, 235 F.3d 1259, 1271 n. 6 (10th Cir. 2000). A minority of courts have held that the negligent presentation of false testimony or evidence—*i.e.*, the prosecutor subjectively was unaware of the false nature of the testimony of evidence but "should have known" of it—violates due process. *See, e.g.*, United States v. Duke, 50 F.3d 571, 577–78 (8th Cir. 1995); United States v. Biberfeld, 957 F.2d 98, 102–03 (3d Cir. 1992).
16. *See, e.g.*, Napue v. Illinois, 360 U.S. 264 (1959); Alcorta v. Texas, 355 U.S. 28 (1957); Pyle v. Kansas, 317 U.S. 213 (1942); Mooney v. Holohan, 294 U.S. 103 (1935).
17. Hysler v. Florida, 315 U.S. 411, 413 (1942).
18. *See* Briscoe v. LaHue, 460 U.S. 325, 326 n. 1 (1983) (noting that the Court had never addressed whether false testimony of police officer at trial would be imputed to the prosecution); *but cf.* Giglio v. United States, 405 U.S. 150 (1972). In *Giglio*, the Court imputed one prosecutor's knowledge that a witness had entered into a plea bargain with the government to another prosecutor in the same office. *Id.* at 151–54. In *Giglio*, the first prosecutor (who struck the plea bargain) did not participate in the trial, and the second prosecutor had been unaware of the deal when he solicited false testimony from the witness that there was no plea bargain. *Id.*
19. *Compare* Ex parte Castellano, 863 S.W.2d 476, 481–86 (Tex. Crim. App. 1993) (imputing knowledge of "any member of the prosecution team" to trial prosecutor with respect to perjury claim), *with* United States v. Diaz, 176 F.3d 52, 106–07 (2d Cir. 1999) (refusing to impute knowledge of a law enforcement officer who was not a significant member of the prosecution team to trial prosecutor).

favorable to a defendant.[20] The perjury materiality standard is equivalent to the *Chapman* harmless error standard applied to constitutional trial errors addressed by appellate courts on direct appeal.[21] That is, it requires the prosecution to prove beyond a reasonable doubt that the false testimony or evidence did not contribute to the verdict.[22] Unlike a *Brady* claim, which places the burden on the defendant to demonstrate materiality, a perjury claim does not require a defendant to show that there is a reasonable probability that the result of the proceeding would have been different but for the perjury. Rather, the prosecution has the burden under a *Chapman*-type standard once a defendant proves a knowing or reckless presentation of perjury occurred.[23]

13.3 Claims of Jury Misconduct

Occasionally, after a jury has returned a guilty verdict,[24] defense counsel will discover that one or more jurors engaged in conduct or were exposed to some type of outside influence during voir dire, the trial, or jury deliberations that calls into question their impartiality. Recurring examples of such alleged juror misconduct include 1) one or more jurors visited the scene of the crime on their own time; 2) one or more jurors consulted law books, dictionaries, the Bible, or the Internet to research some legal or factual issue in the case; 3) jurors discussed the merits of the case with each other prior to deliberations or a juror discussed the merits of the case with an outside party (such as a spouse) before the verdict was returned; 4) one or more jurors engaged in ex parte communication about the case with a witness, one of the attorneys, or the judge in the case; 5) a juror lied about, or failed to disclose, a material matter during voir dire (such as the juror's prior relationship with one of the parties or lawyers); or 6) one or more jurors slept or were intoxicated during trial or jury deliberations.[25]

Under the Sixth Amendment to the Constitution, jurors must be impartial, and a defendant is entitled to a trial and jury deliberations free of prejudicial extraneous influences.[26] A defendant's right to an impartial jury is violated even if a single member of the jury was biased.[27] The Supreme Court has held that ordinarily, if a

20. Kirkpatrick v. Whitley, 992 F.2d 491, 497 (5th Cir. 1993).

21. *See* United States v. Bagley, 473 U.S. 667, 679 & n. 9 (*citing* Chapman v. California, 386 U.S. 18 (1967)).

22. *Id.*

23. *Id.*

24. Sometimes information concerning juror bias or a prejudicial outside influence on the jury may surface either during the voir dire process or during the trial itself. If that occurs, the issue is initially litigated at that juncture rather than for the first time in a post-conviction motion or petition.

25. *See, e.g.*, Rushen v. Spain, 464 U.S. 114 (1983) (per curiam); Smith v. Phillips, 455 U.S. 209 (1982); Turner v. Louisiana, 379 U.S. 466 (1965); *see generally* Nancy J. King, *Juror Delinquency in Criminal Trials in America*, 1796–1996, 94 MICH. L. REV. 2673, 2708–51 (1996).

26. *See* Irvin v. Dowd, 366 U.S. 717 (1961).

27. Dyer v. Calderon, 151 F.3d 970, 973 (9th Cir. 1998) (en banc).

trial court conducts a full and fair evidentiary hearing on the issue of juror bias and concludes that a juror was not biased—typically based on the juror's claim not to have been biased—the procedural protection afforded by such a hearing is constitutionally sufficient to protect a defendant's right to an impartial jury.[28]

A juror may be either biased in fact or, instead, conclusively presumed to be biased as a matter of law.[29] The former is referred to as "actual bias;" the latter is referred to as "implied bias."[30] A juror with actual bias is one who is found to have been actually biased against a party in a litigation to the extent that the bias affected the juror's ability to be fair and impartial. Such bias ordinarily may be determined to exist—or not to exist—as a factual matter during an evidentiary hearing where the parties are permitted to question the juror and the trial court is permitted to hear the jurors' answers and observe their demeanor.[31] Conversely, in certain extreme or exceptional cases of jurors with implied bias, such bias is established where there are specific facts showing a close connection to the circumstances of the defendant's case.[32] In the latter situation, irrespective of whether the juror claims to have been unbiased and irrespective of whether the trial court found that the juror was actually unbiased, the extreme circumstances of the case require a reviewing court to imply bias "as a matter of law."[33]

Proving juror misconduct can be difficult for the defense. The rules of evidence in almost all jurisdictions prohibit jurors from impeaching their verdict or testifying about what went on during jury deliberations.[34] An important exception to this general rule is that jurors may testify about extraneous influences.[35] Often there is a dispute about what qualifies as an extraneous—as opposed to an internal—influence. For example, in *Tanner v. United States*, a closely divided

28. *See* Smith, 455 U.S. at 215–18.
29. *Id.* at 221–24 (O'Connor, J., concurring).
30. *Id.* at 222 (O'Connor, J., concurring) (recognizing the "implied bias" doctrine in exceptional situations); *see also* McDonough Power Equip., Inc. v. Greenwood, 464 U.S. 548, 558 (1984) (Brennan, J., concurring in the judgment, joined by Marshall, J.) (following Justice O'Connor's concurring opinion in Smith); *Id.* at 556–57 (Blackmun, J., concurring, joined by Stevens & O'Connor, JJ.) (same). As is apparent, Justice O'Connor's concurring opinion in *Smith* later garnered a majority of the Supreme Court in *McDonough Power Equip.*
31. Smith v. Phillips, 455 U.S. 209, 222 (1982) (O'Connor, J., concurring); *see also* Solis v. Cockrell, 342 F.3d 392, 397 (5th Cir. 2003); Hunley v. Godinez, 975 F.2d 316, 318–20 (7th Cir. 1992); Burton v. Johnson, 948 F.2d 1150, 1158–59 (10th Cir. 1991); Tinsley v. Borg, 895 F.2d 520, 528–30 (9th Cir. 1990).
32. United States v. Scott, 854 F.2d 697, 699 (5th Cir. 1988) (citation and internal quotation marks omitted); Gonzales v. Thomas, 99 F.3d 978, 987 (10th Cir. 1996); State v. Faucher, 596 N.W.2d 770 (Wis. 1999).
33. *Smith,* 455 U.S. at 222 (O'Connor, J., concurring); *see also* United States v. Bishop, 264 F.3d 535, 554 (5th Cir. 2001).
34. *See, e.g.*, Fed. R. Evid. 606(b); Tex. Evid. R. 606(b).
35. Tanner v. United States, 483 U.S. 107, 121 (1987); United States v. Rutherford, 371 F.3d 634 (9th Cir. 2004) (permitting judicial inquiry into extraneous influence, but refusing inquiry into internal influence on jurors).

Supreme Court concluded that testimony from jurors that they were intoxicated and sleeping during deliberations as a result of drug and alcohol use was inadmissible because it concerned an internal rather than an extraneous matter.[36]

Even if the defense is able to prove that some extraneous factor was introduced to jurors, courts will not reverse the defendant's conviction or sentence unless the extraneous matter actually or (in extreme cases) presumptively prejudiced the defendant in some manner.[37] In deciding whether to presume prejudice under these circumstances, most courts apply an objective test—namely, how the extraneous factor would have influenced a "hypothetical average juror" rather than rely on a juror's subjective claim not to have been unduly influenced.[38]

In cases in which there has been an extraneous influence on jurors, the lower courts are divided over which party—the defendant or the prosecution—has the burden of persuasion to show prejudice or a lack thereof. Some courts place the burden on the defense to prove prejudice, and other courts place the burden on the prosecution to disprove presumptive prejudice.[39] The Supreme Court of the United States has spoken inconsistently on this issue (without resolving the conflict).[40] Furthermore, those lower courts that place the burden on the defense are divided over what type of showing must be made by a defendant; some courts require a showing of a reasonable *probability* that the extraneous factor affected the jurors' ability to render a fair verdict, while other courts only require a showing of a reasonable *possibility*.[41]

Hypothetical One: Motions for New Trial (Prosecutorial Misconduct)

State v. Nguyen

Evidence Adduced at Trial

A grand jury charged **Harold Nguyen** with murder. The charges arose out of a shooting that occurred at a pool hall in the Chinatown area of Nita City. At Nguyen's murder trial, **Roger Lee** testified that he entered the pool hall on January

---

36. *Compare* Tanner, 483 U.S. at 122–23 (majority), with *id.* at 140–41 (dissent).
37. *See, e.g.*, United States v. DiSalvo, 34 F.3d 1204, 1223 (3d Cir. 1994); United States v. Boylan, 898 F.2d 230, 262 (1st Cir. 1990); United States v. Calbas, 821 F.2d 887, 896–97 (2d Cir. 1987); State v. Faucher, 596 N.W.2d 770, 786 (Wis. 1999); State v. Hartley, 656 A.2d 954, 962 (R.I. 1995).
38. *See, e.g.*, Calbas, 821 F.2d at 896 & n. 9.
39. *Compare, e.g.*, United States v. Pennell, 737 F.2d 521, 532 (6th Cir. 1984) (burden on defense), *with* State v. King, 460 N.E.2d 1383, 1388 (Ohio Ct. App. 1983) (burden on prosecution).
40. *Compare* Remmer v. United States, 347 U.S. 227, 229–30 (1954) (placing burden on the prosecution in a case involving alleged jury tampering), *with* Smith v. Phillips, 455 U.S. 209, 215 (1982) (placing the burden on the defense in the case of a juror who had applied to work for the prosecutor's office at the time of trial). *See* United States v. Gartmon, 146 F.3d 1015, 1028 (D.C. Cir. 1998) (noting that some but not all lower courts have concluded that Smith overruled *Remmer*).
41. *See* Hartley, 656 A.2d at 962 (discussing the division among the lower courts).

4 and, together with two individuals he said were fellow members of a street gang known as the Green Dragons, sat down near the entrance. Lee further testified that there were "close to thirty" other people there at the time. He added that shortly thereafter, three men and one woman came from the back of the establishment toward the entrance to pay for a pool table. The table was near where Lee and his companions were sitting. Lee testified that he knew two of the four by name: Harold Nguyen, who was allegedly wearing a sling on his right arm, and a man Lee called "**Jimmy**." Lee stated that the four were members of a rival gang, known as the White Tigers, which frequented the pool hall.

Lee added that the Dragons and the Tigers had not previously engaged in violence against each other. They had been hostile, but the manifestation of this rivalry had been "[j]ust basically words said back and forth." Consistent with this, when Nguyen and his companions approached the counter to pay for a pool table, there were "hostile stares going back and forth" between the gangs. The staring lasted less than a minute.

According to Lee, however, after the White Tigers had paid for their table, he heard Nguyen say to Jimmy, "When I leave, shoot them." Lee reiterated a slight variation—"Shoot them when I leave"—on cross-examination by defense counsel and added that he remembered the statement distinctly because Nguyen had said it loudly.

Lee further testified that Nguyen, having made the statement, walked out of the pool hall. At that point, the man whom Lee knew as Jimmy allegedly removed his jacket, revealing a gun. Lee then ducked, heard shots fired, and, a minute later, got up to find one of his companions with a gunshot wound. Lee testified that he quickly ran outside and saw Nguyen and the other White Tigers "halfway down the block already running." Lee did not explain what he and his companions did on hearing Nguyen's "loud" order to shoot them or while Nguyen was walking out of the pool hall.

Johnny On, one of Lee's two companions at the pool hall that night, similarly testified that Nguyen had said, "Shoot them," in the pool hall. But the other companion, **Danny Ho**, while testifying that the person who had given the order to shoot was wearing a sling, could not identify Nguyen as the person who made the statement. The prosecution also introduced medical records from a local emergency room showing that Nguyen had been cut on the arm several days before the shooting at the pool hall.[42]

At trial, the defense offered the testimony of **Matt Sacoll**, who ran the pool hall and stated that he had known Harold Nguyen for several months. Sacoll testified that he did not recall seeing Nguyen at the pool hall on the night in question. Sacoll

42. None of the other thirty or so people in the pool hall at the time of the shooting were called on by the prosecution to confirm the allegedly "loud" order or that Nguyen had given such an order.

said that while putting away tools behind the counter, he heard gunshots. Looking up, he saw a woman and two men, one of whom had a gun; the three then fled the scene. Nguyen, he asserted, was not one of the three. The defense also called **Donna Wan**, the proprietor of a hair salon, who testified that Nguyen had been in her shop in the days immediately before January 1 to have his hair cut. Although she noticed stitches and a "nasty wound" on Nguyen's upper arm, she testified that Nguyen was not then wearing a sling and appeared to be able to move his wounded arm.

Evidence Adduced after Trial

After the jury convicted Nguyen of murder, his defense counsel received access to a portion of the prosecution's file of which defense counsel had been unaware previously.[43] That portion of the file concerned a plea bargain with Lee concerning an unrelated charge. At the trial, Lee had testified about his arrest for grand larceny and the ensuing plea and sentencing agreement that he had made with the prosecution. About one month after Nguyen's arrest for the pool hall shooting, Lee was charged with attempted grand larceny. Several months before Nguyen's murder trial, Lee had pleaded guilty to the charge. In chambers, before Lee's judge (a different judge from the one who presided in Nguyen's murder case), Lee's prosecutor (who was not involved in Nguyen's murder prosecution, but who was with the same district attorney's office) gave his understanding of the condition of the plea that Lee was making:[44]

> Condition of the plea[,] the terms and conditions of the plea, as I understand them, Judge, is that the defendant will plead to the charge in the indictment and be offered a promise of probation and, in particular, deferred adjudication probation.[[45]] It is further conditioned upon his continued cooperation in *State v. Harold Nguyen*, including offering testimony . . . truthful testimony in that homicide case with which he's been cooperating. A different prosecutor is handling that case.

During the in-chambers conference, Lee's defense counsel and Lee himself confirmed that this was the agreement. His counsel said, "My client has testified in the grand jury and is prepared to continue with whatever is needed, including viewing

---

43. The portion of the file was disclosed to the defense by a supervisory prosecutor who had not directly participated in Nguyen's trial.

44. The proceedings in Lee's case, both in chambers and in open court, were recorded by a court reporter. The transcript of the proceedings was disclosed to Nguyen's counsel following the jury's guilty verdict in the murder case.

45. Under applicable law in this case, there are two types of probation—"straight" probation (which means that even if the defendant successfully completes the probationary period, the conviction will still remain on his record) and "deferred adjudication" probation (which means that if the defendant successfully completes his probation, then the charges will be dropped at that point and the defendant will have no criminal record for most purposes).

lineups, giving testimony, etc." These discussions were sealed by the district court in Lee's case, and Lee entered his guilty plea. In so doing, Lee specifically answered in the affirmative the judge's question whether Lee had attempted to steal money from a restaurant owner "by means of extortion, in that [Lee] attempted to steal that money by instilling in [the owner] a fear [that] if she did not turn over the money to [Lee], that [he would] cause her injury."

Subsequently, at Lee's sentencing (which occurred months after his guilty plea and on the same day as his testimony at Nguyen's murder trial), Lee's judge indicated that Lee had pleaded guilty and "was promised five years' probation, which will be deferred adjudication." The assistant district attorney then said, "Your Honor, I ask you to honor the negotiated plea, and I also want to reiterate the fact that this defendant [Lee], as part of his plea and as part of the promised sentence, was to give truthful testimony as he did in the grand jury and also at the trial." After Lee's defense counsel also asked the judge to honor the plea agreement, the judge stated, "Consistent with the promise made, the sentence of the Court is five years of probation, deferred adjudication."

The day before the start of Nguyen's trial, the prosecutor in Nguyen's murder case disclosed that Lee had pleaded guilty and was awaiting sentence in the unrelated larceny prosecution. But while the prosecutor went on to say that Lee's judge "basically told the defendant that if he pled to the indictment, he likely would get probation," Nguyen's prosecutor also stated that while "there might have been some talk about deferred adjudication," "[t]here was technically no plea agreement" as far as the prosecutor knew.

On direct examination of Lee at Nguyen's murder trial, which occurred two hours after Lee's sentencing in his own case, the prosecutor elicited the following testimony from Lee:

> Q: Can you tell us whether or not you have been sentenced on that case?
>
> A: Yes, I have.
>
> Q: Did the district attorney's office make any promise to you with regard to what your sentence would be?
>
> A: No.
>
> Q: Would you please tell us what, if anything, the district attorney's office, either me or another assistant district attorney, promised you with regard to a sentencing on that case?
>
> A: Nothing at all.
>
> Q: We had contacted you and wanted you to continue to be a witness on this case?
>
> A: Yes.

Q: Did the judge that you stood in front of make any recommendation about what your sentence should be? That is, did the judge in the courtroom where you were sentenced—what, if anything, did that judge do with regard to your sentence?

A: He didn't promise me anything.

Q: Did he in fact sentence you?

A: Yes.

Q: And he sentenced you prior to your coming to court to testify here?

A: Yes.

Q: What was the sentence of the court?

A: He gave me five years' probation.

Q: Did the judge give you deferred adjudication probation or straight probation?

A: Deferred.

On cross-examination, Nguyen's counsel did not make any further inquiry into Lee's plea agreement. Lee was asked, however, about the nature of the offense to which he had pleaded guilty, to which he responded: "Well, maybe a month before [my arrest] I went in and I asked the owner for money." Nguyen's counsel then asked, "You just asked him politely for money, is that it?" Lee answered, "Yes." When questioned about whether he had made any threat, Lee replied that he had not. Asked further if this is what he told the judge when he pleaded guilty, Lee said that he told the judge that he and his friend had gone into the store and asked for money.

Out of the hearing of the jury, defense counsel argued to the judge and the prosecutor that Lee had lied about the circumstances of the attempted larceny. Counsel said to the prosecutor, "He's lying right there—he extorted money out of that guy based on a threat." The prosecutor did not, however, make any attempt to correct Lee's manifestly false statement. Indeed, when defense counsel mentioned the implausibility of Lee's testimony on this point in summation, the prosecutor, unsuccessfully, objected. And in the prosecutor's closing argument, the prosecutor made a generalized effort to bolster Lee's credibility. "The other two witnesses [one of whom was Lee] were honest with you. [Defense counsel] would want you to believe . . . first of all, that they were evasive. I submit they were not. . . . Ladies and gentlemen of the jury, I submit to you that what they told you was truthful and honest."

Based on the foregoing information made available only after the jury convicted Nguyen, defense counsel filed a motion for a new trial. Nguyen's trial prosecutor was recused and another assistant district attorney was assigned to represent the prosecutor at the hearing on the motion for a new trial. At the hearing, the foregoing facts were undisputed. In addition, the trial prosecutor in Nguyen's case testified that at the time of Lee's trial testimony, she was unaware that there had been a "specific plea agreement per se" between Lee and the other assistant DA: "I believed it was more of an expectation type of thing, as opposed to a formal agreement." She testified that she had only had "a couple of passing" conversations with the assistant DA who prosecuted Lee in the larceny case.

For purposes of hypothetical exercise one, assume that the trial court has made a threshold factual finding that the trial prosecutor in Nguyen's case, at the time of Lee's testimony, was aware of the specifics of the plea bargain struck between Lee's counsel and the other assistant DA who prosecuted Lee (including the deferred adjudication agreement) and that her testimony at the hearing on the motion for a new trial was "incredible."

Defense Counsel 1: Argue in support of your motion for a new trial.

Prosecutor 1: Argue against the motion for a new trial by contending that Lee's perjury and any suppression of evidence by the trial prosecutor was immaterial.

To prepare for this hypothetical exercise, read *Morris v. Ylst*, 447 F.3d 735 (9th Cir. 2006), and *Kirkpatrick v. Whitley*, 992 F.2d 491, 496–98 (5th Cir. 1993) (portion of court's decision addressing *Brady* and perjury claims).

* * *

For purposes of hypothetical exercise two, assume that Lee's larceny charges were filed by the DA's office in a neighboring county (as opposed to the DA's office that prosecuted Nguyen) and, thus, that the prosecutor who struck the plea bargain with Lee in his larceny case worked for a different prosecutor's office than the one that prosecuted Nguyen. Furthermore, assume that the other prosecutor had no role in the murder case (other than to require Lee to cooperate with the Nita City prosecutor in the murder prosecution). Also assume that the trial court in the murder case has made a threshold factual finding that the trial prosecutor in Nguyen's case, at the time of Lee's testimony, was unaware that a specific plea bargain had been struck between Lee and the neighboring county's prosecutor concerning deferred adjudication probation. Therefore, Nguyen's trial prosecutor's representations concerning the circumstances of Lee's guilty plea made to Nguyen's defense counsel before trial were honestly mistaken. Finally, assume that Lee's prosecutor mailed a copy of the court reporter's transcription of Lee's guilty plea to Nguyen's trial prosecutor many weeks before Nguyen's trial, but that Nguyen's prosecutor never got around to reading it because she was too busy preparing for the murder trial; her supervisor in the DA's office read it only after the jury had convicted Nguyen and, at that point, turned it over to defense counsel.

Defense Counsel 2: Argue in support of your motion for a new trial.

Prosecutor 2: Argue against the motion for a new trial.

To prepare for this hypothetical exercise, read *Morris v. Ylst*, 447 F.3d 735 (9th Cir. 2006), and *Kirkpatrick v. Whitley*, 992 F.2d 491, 496–98 (5th Cir. 1993) (portion of court's decision addressing *Brady* and perjury claims).

Hypothetical Two: Motions for New Trial (Prosecutorial Misconduct)

State v. Braxton

Evidence Adduced at Trial

On February 10, the defendant, **Gary Michael Braxton**, called the Nita City police department from the home of his half-brother, **Jack Duggan**, and reported finding his half-brother's body as well as the body of his half-brother's friend, **Michael Nelson**. Officer **Peter Junge** arrived at the scene six minutes later and observed the bodies of the two victims on the floor in the living room. Both men had been shot once in the chest—with the bullets exiting their bodies—and once in the back of the head. He checked them for vital signs and found none. The bodies were still warm and bleeding, suggesting that both men had been killed recently.

A bullet hole in the couch in the living room was consistent with someone having been shot while on the couch. Bloodstains matching Duggan's blood type were found on both the couch itself and on a newspaper laying on it. At the subsequent jury trial, the medical examiner testified that Duggan was shot in the chest while on the couch because only the chest wound would have allowed him to move around and end up on the floor where the police found him.

A .45 caliber handgun lay on the floor between the two bodies and a baseball bat next to Duggan's body. Duggan's head rested next to a gun cabinet, and the glass face of the cabinet, which had a shotgun in it, had been broken. Police found a boot print that matched Braxton's boot on a piece of broken glass next to Duggan's elbow. A blood-spatter expert with the crime scene investigation (CSI) unit of the NCPD testified to finding blood on Braxton's clothes with spatter patterns "fully consistent" with Braxton's having shot Nelson in the head while standing next to his body.

Braxton was charged with two counts of capital murder and was given notice of the state's intention to seek the death penalty. The defense conceded at trial that Braxton had shot both Duggan and Nelson but claimed the shootings were in self-defense after a spontaneous argument between Braxton and Duggan. The prosecution, however, contended that Braxton had planned the killings primarily to cover up his participation with the victims in an arson insurance fraud scheme. At trial, the prosecution relied heavily on various inculpatory statements Braxton allegedly had made to **Roy Patrick**, a jailhouse informant ("snitch") who was in

Braxton's cell block while Braxton awaited trial, as well as on circumstantial evidence relating to the alleged arson.

The prosecution's evidence at trial showed that on the day of the shootings, Braxton had been at **Larry Kilen**'s barbershop before he went to Duggan's house. While at the barbershop, Braxton spoke to Duggan on a cell phone, and Kilen heard him say: "What the hell is going on? I will be right back—I will be right there. What's the matter? What is that?" According to Kilen's testimony at trial, Braxton told Kilen that Duggan was drunk and wanted him to come over because he had fallen down. Multiple witnesses at trial testified that Duggan was an alcoholic, and his autopsy revealed that he had a blood alcohol content of 0.08 (the legal limit) at the time of his death. Similarly, Nelson's autopsy revealed that he had a blood alcohol content of 0.11.

In his post-arrest, post-*Miranda* statement to the police, Braxton denied that he went to Duggan's house with the intention of harming either him or Nelson. A police search of Braxton's car revealed that he had a .22 caliber pistol in the car that he had not taken inside the house with him. Braxton did not testify at the trial, and much of his version of the events was presented through statements he made to the police and also admissions made to his brother, **Monte Braxton**. The prosecution called Monte to testify at trial.

Monte testified that Braxton had described the following series of events to him. When Braxton went into Duggan's house on the day of the shootings, he found a piece of paper on the kitchen counter with **Gail Fisk**'s phone number on it. Fisk was Braxton's ex-girlfriend with whom he had been trying to reconcile. Braxton thought that Duggan and Nelson were harassing Fisk because he had seen Nelson's car at Fisk's house on occasion. Braxton had questioned Duggan about Fisk previously, but Duggan had denied harassing her. After Braxton discovered the note with Fisk's phone number on it, he took the note into the living room and confronted Duggan. In response, Duggan said, "Well, Braxton, you got me," and reached for the .45 caliber gun that he routinely kept on his living room coffee table. Braxton then grabbed the gun and shot Duggan in self-defense. After being shot, Duggan moved toward the gun cabinet. Nelson then got up and threw a beer can at Braxton. Braxton, an Iraq War veteran with diagnosed post-traumatic stress disorder (PTSD), remembered shooting Nelson, but did not remember much else.

On cross-examination by defense counsel, Monte testified that he "got the impression" that the shooting was in self-defense. He also told the jury that Duggan had a reputation for violence in the community. Other evidence presented at the trial corroborated parts of Braxton's story. A medical examiner testified that the path of the bullet that struck Duggan's chest and then entered the back of the couch was consistent with Duggan being in the act of rising from the couch at the time he was first shot. Moreover, Officer **James Jones** testified that Duggan probably broke the glass face of the gun cabinet "as he fell . . . after being wounded" or while he was "trying to get a weapon." The defense theory was that Braxton shot Duggan a second time because Duggan was trying to get another gun. During the investigation, the police also found an empty beer can underneath Nelson's right knee. This was consistent with Braxton's claim that Nelson threw a beer can at him while he was standing next to the living room table near where the bodies were found.

Roy Patrick, the jailhouse informant who shared a cell with Braxton when Braxton was awaiting trial, testified on behalf of the prosecution. According to Patrick's testimony, Braxton confessed to him and asked Patrick to help him find someone "on the outside" who would be willing to take the blame for the murders. Patrick testified that Braxton drew diagrams of the murder scene and gave him details about the murder to relay to the person he found so that the person's statements would be believable. No such "fall guy" was ever located, according to Patrick.

The prosecution's theory was that the shootings were part of a premeditated scheme. Patrick's testimony provided critical support for that theory. Specifically, he testified that Braxton told him about his involvement in a conspiracy with Duggan and Nelson to perpetrate an insurance fraud. According to Patrick's testimony, Braxton, Duggan, and Nelson staged a burglary of Braxton's trailer and collected the insurance. Then, a few months later, they burned down the trailer and collected insurance again. Both times, however, Braxton refused to share the proceeds with Duggan and Nelson. Nelson and Duggan then threatened to disclose the crimes to the police, and, according to Braxton's alleged jailhouse confession to Patrick, Braxton "had to kill them" to keep them from doing so.

Police records introduced at trial showed that Braxton had in fact previously reported a burglary of his trailer and collected insurance proceeds, but the only evidence of an insurance fraud with respect to that burglary (aside from Patrick's testimony) was the fact that Braxton reported that ivory carvings were taken in the burglary and the police recovered some ivory figures from Duggan's bedroom closet after he was killed. After the trial, however, a friend of the family stated that the half-brothers both owned ivory figures from Alaska. Similarly, there was evidence introduced about a fire at Braxton's trailer, but there was no evidence, aside from Patrick's testimony, that the fire was an act of arson.

At trial, the defense attempted to prevent the arson-insurance-fraud theory from being mentioned at trial by arguing in a motion in limine that there was no evidence of arson. In ruling that the information was admissible, the trial court said, "This is probably the key decision in this case." The trial judge went on to state:

> So far as the probative value is concerned, it goes to the very heart of the murder case. It is the kind of evidence that the prosecution needs to prove if it's going to prove premeditation as opposed to a spur-of-the-moment shooting. But I find that Roy Patrick's testimony is sufficient to let the matter go to the jury.

In addition to testifying about Braxton's burglary-arson-insurance-fraud motive, Patrick also testified that Braxton had told Patrick that Braxton wanted to kill Duggan because Duggan had removed Braxton from his will and had given Braxton's portion of his estate to his homosexual lover, **William Hastings**. Hastings testified that he was listed as a beneficiary in Duggan's will, although there was nothing in the estate because Duggan was so much in debt. Hastings did, however, get $40,000 from a separate life insurance policy that Duggan had carried. Patrick did not say anything about a life insurance policy.

Finally, Patrick testified that Braxton told him that he had tried to hire someone named "Pete" to kill Duggan for $500, but then changed his mind. Braxton told Patrick that he wanted whoever took the rap for the murders to kill Pete. The prosecution emphasized this point in closing arguments, noting that Braxton tried to "reach out" and kill someone from prison.

At trial, the defense sought to impeach Patrick on cross-examination by establishing that Patrick was in jail with Braxton because he had pled guilty to and was awaiting sentencing for burglary of a vehicle. There was a zero- to two-year sentencing range for this offense, and the prosecution had originally offered a plea bargain of a nine-month sentence (prior to Patrick's cooperation in Braxton's prosecution). Following Patrick's cooperation, he received a plea offer of six months rather than nine (which he took). In closing arguments, the prosecutor downplayed the importance of the sentence reduction by sarcastically stating, "The reward that he got was that he got six months instead of nine months. Big reward."

The defense also sought to impeach Patrick by eliciting testimony that as part of his plea bargain, Patrick had been ordered to pay costs and restitution for his burglary-of-a-vehicle conviction and had failed to do so; that he had previous convictions for credit card fraud, burglary, and drug possession; that he had been paid $2,000 by Crime Stoppers for his testimony as an informant (in addition to the plea bargain); and that the prosecution was paying for his food and hotel expenses while he was testifying.

At the trial, **Walter "Pete" Hartman**, a convicted felon with a long history of violence, testified on behalf of the prosecution and said that Braxton offered to pay him to kill Duggan. Hartman said that he initially thought it was just talk and that he never took Braxton up on his offer. **Denver Carter**, a former roommate of Braxton, testified for the prosecution as well and said that Braxton admitted to him that he had shot Duggan and Nelson. At one point, Carter said that Braxton told him that a man named Pete owed him a favor and that Braxton had a job for him, but that Braxton never mentioned what the job was. Braxton told Carter that when Braxton called Duggan's house on the day of the murder, no one was supposed to answer the phone, but Braxton never explained what that meant. Defense counsel impeached Carter with proof that he had nine prior felony convictions, including a perjury conviction (based on a false report of a crime allegedly committed by his ex-wife).

After deliberating for approximately seven and a half hours, the jury returned a verdict of guilty on both counts of capital murder. After a separate sentencing hearing, the jury sentenced Braxton to death.

Evidence Adduced after Trial

During post-trial proceedings, the following facts were established (which led to the filing of a motion for a new trial).

Even though the prosecuting attorneys had taken their first statements from Patrick over a year before the trial, Patrick's identity was not disclosed to the defense until the day before trial, when he was added to the witness list. The lead trial prosecutor admittedly lied to the defense and stated that Patrick's identity could not be disclosed beforehand because he was in a witness protection program. It was later determined that he was never in such a program.

The day that Braxton's trial was scheduled to begin, the defense brought to the court's attention the fact that *Brady* material relating to Patrick had not been provided. The defense noted specifically that it did not have information about Patrick's prior contacts with the police, including whether Patrick had made statements in the past that had turned out to be incorrect. The trial court agreed and ordered the prosecution to turn over any written material relating to Patrick's contacts with law enforcement in the year prior to the murders. No such material was ever produced. The court also stated that "the prosecutor would have an obligation to tell the defense if there are prior situations where the informant had not been truthful." The lead trial prosecutor acknowledged this obligation and stated that they "ha[d] been notified of no such situations, Your Honor."

The prosecution never turned over any information that Patrick had engaged in improper conduct while acting as an informant. It was later discovered that the prosecution did not attempt to obtain this information from any of the police detectives working on the case. Additionally, the defense later discovered that detectives **Ronald Lewis** and **Thomas Padukiewicz**, both of whom supervised Patrick while he was assisting in law enforcement investigations, knew that Patrick had stolen both drugs and money during drug busts and that he had lied to the police about it. The defense was never told about this. Detective Padukiewicz had even gone so far as to write up a "deactivation memo" stating that Patrick could no longer work as an informant because he would not abide by department rules. The defense was never told about Patrick's deactivation.

The defense was also not informed that Patrick had broken into the evidence room of the police department while working as an informant and had stolen drugs that the police had previously seized. Nor was the defense told that as a result of this offense, Patrick was charged with burglary and numerous counts of obstruction of justice and ultimately pled guilty only to burglary.

The prosecution did not inform defense counsel that Patrick had admitted to making false charges while in prison on a fraud conviction in the early 1990s. Patrick had believed that he could get his time reduced if he reported the presence of firearms within the prison. He therefore had shotguns smuggled into the prison and then told the officials that he had found them. The prison officials discovered the scheme, and Patrick's prison sentence was extended.

The prosecution failed to disclose that Patrick was given $150 during Braxton's trial as an advance payment for a video that Patrick said he had in his possession, which, he claimed, showed a prostitute being murdered by Braxton and several other men. Patrick said that the video concerned an unrelated, high-profile serial murder investigation in Nita City. Patrick never produced the video, and the detectives working on the case said that they thought Patrick was lying about its existence and that his story about Braxton being involved in the serial murders was "trash." The detectives also stated that they had spoken with the prosecutors in Braxton's case about the video and the money that was paid to Patrick. The prosecution, however, never told the defense about either the false story concerning the alleged "murder tape" or the payment that Patrick had received for his false claim.

When Patrick was awaiting his testimony at Braxton's trial, he was stopped for a traffic offense and arrested because of some outstanding warrants. He called the lead trial prosecutor from jail, and the trial prosecutor ensured that he was released without being charged. The defense was never told about the arrest or the trial prosecutor's actions.

During Braxton's trial, the Nita City police department submitted police reports to the lead trial prosecutor requesting that Patrick be charged with burglary. The prosecutor's office entered an "NCF" (no charges filed) the same day that closing arguments ended in the penalty phase of Braxton's trial. These facts were never disclosed to defense counsel until after Braxton was sentenced to death.

During Braxton's trial, the prosecution arranged to postpone the filing of a warrant against Patrick for violating the conditions of his probation. Prosecutors told Patrick's probation officer not to do anything with the violation report or the order to issue a bench warrant. The warrant did not issue until two weeks after Braxton's verdict. The prosecution never told the defense that it had prevented the issuance of the warrant.

Testimony at the hearing on Braxton's motion for a new trial revealed that Patrick had acted as an informant in another murder case before Braxton's trial, although at the trial he denied ever having done so previously. The defense was never told that Patrick had been an informant in a prior murder case and that in that case also he had claimed that the defendant had confessed to him while in jail.

At trial, Patrick denied that he used drugs while acting as an informant; however, testimony at the hearing on Braxton's motion for new trial revealed that he continuously used drugs during his time as an informant and that the police knew about it. This information was not disclosed to the defense.

The day after Braxton's death sentence was imposed, an anonymous third party told defense counsel that the police had executed a warrant to search Patrick's hotel room during the trial proceedings based on a confidential informant's tip that Patrick was dealing drugs from the room. His room had been searched, and crack pipes, a bong, rolling paper, a razor blade, and a copper Brillo pad (all of which are used to prepare and smoke crack and marijuana) were recovered, but no arrests were made. The prosecution knew about this search and failed to disclose information about it to the defense.

The defense later learned **Melvin Stevens** was the confidential informant who had provided the information for the warrant. Stevens later testified that Patrick was doing drugs while he was awaiting his testimony at Braxton's trial. Stevens also said that Patrick told him that Braxton did not commit the murder, but that Patrick "knew enough to convict him" and needed the Crime Stoppers money.

Finally, after Braxton's trial was over, the prosecution turned over a fire marshal's report concerning the fire at Braxton's trailer. This report concluded that the fire was an accident. It was prepared by deputy fire marshal Ted Thompson and electrical inspector Walter Erickson. According to Erickson, the Coleman furnace in Braxton's trailer was the same make and model as the one that he owned, and this particular make and model had been recalled by the manufacturer due to a flaw that causes fires. Moreover, Deputy Fire Marshal Thompson concluded that the fire was accidental because:

> First, it is not uncommon for electrical heaters in older mobile homes to accidentally malfunction and cause fires. Second, there were no accelerants, such as gasoline, in the trailer. Third, it is not uncommon for electrical heaters to malfunction in the winter. Fourth, I opened up the front of the electrical heater and everything appeared to be in place; I observed nothing suspicious. My fifth reason for determining the fire was accidental, not arson, was that I observed only one locale where the fire originated (the furnace), not multiple locales. Sixth, I saw no signs of forced entry, which are indicative of arson.

After this initial report, a second and more detailed report was prepared. The second report, which was turned over to the defense before trial, was misleading. Its only reference to the conclusions of deputy fire marshal Thompson and electrical inspector Erickson was in a section stating that there was "no fault or failure" of the lead electrical wire and no evidence of tampering with the fuse panel. The second report did not state that both the fire inspector and deputy marshal had concluded that the fire was accidental and could not have resulted from arson.

Rather, it offered no definitive conclusion regarding the cause of the fire. It did not state that there had been a manufacturer's recall of this type of furnace and that it was the same type of furnace that Erickson had in his own home. To the contrary, it suggested that Coleman furnaces did not cause fires. Specifically, the second report stated that **Al Pearson**, the furnace technician, said that "he could find and think of no situation in which a furnace [such as a Coleman] had caused a fire in a mobile home." Finally, the report did not relate the six reasons deputy fire marshal Thompson gave for concluding that the fire was accidental.

The foregoing facts were established at a hearing on Braxton's motion for a new trial. A new prosecutor—one from the state's attorney general's office—was assigned to the case because the district attorney recused himself and all his assistants from Braxton's case based on the allegations of prosecutorial misconduct made in the motion for a new trial.

Defense Counsel: Argue that your motion for new trial should be granted.

Prosecutor: Argue that the motion for a new trial should be denied.

To prepare for this hypothetical exercise, read *Morris v. Ylst*, 447 F.3d 735 (9th Cir. 2006), and *Kirkpatrick v. Whitley*, 992 F.2d 491, 496–98 (5th Cir. 1993) (portion of court's decision addressing *Brady* and perjury claims).

Hypothetical Three: Motions for New Trial (Jury Misconduct)

State v. Sanchez

Martin Sanchez was charged with committing burglary of **Gloria Martinez**'s garage in Nita City. During jury selection, the judge stated to the members of the venire:

> Now, this defendant, Martin Sanchez . . . stand up, Martin, so they can get a good look. You'll look at him. Martin Sanchez is the defendant. Thank you. You can have a seat. We want you to look at him because, obviously, if you're related to him or you know something about him, it would be inappropriate for you to be a juror in this case. These lawyers will be asking you about it.

The prosecutor then stated: "This case originates out of the West Side neighborhood in Nita City. Are any of you from that neighborhood?" At that point, two prospective jurors, **Rogelio Cantu** and **Porfirio Rodriguez**, raised their hands and stated that they were from that neighborhood, which is predominately occupied by Mexican-Americans. The prosecutor asked each of them—in the presence of the other members of the venire—whether they knew or ever had seen Sanchez. The prosecutor also asked the members of the venire, "If there's anything that you'd rather not answer out loud in front of the whole panel, just let us know and we'll talk to you individually with the court." During voir dire, **Juan Tellez**, who ultimately was selected as a juror, did not make any statements or otherwise communicate with either the trial judge or the attorneys for the parties.

During trial, the prosecutor introduced evidence that Sanchez took some carpenter's tools from the garage of Gloria Martinez, whose house was located in the West Side neighborhood. Sanchez had worked for Mrs. Martinez's husband, who was a carpenter, earlier in the same week. The day after Mr. Sanchez took the tools, his father and brother returned the tools to Mrs. Martinez. Mrs. Martinez testified that her husband typically did not lend his tools to anyone, but that her husband and Mr. Sanchez had a conversation outside of her hearing before Mr. Sanchez took the tools. Mr. Martinez, the owner of the tools, did not testify for the prosecution or the defense at the trial.

During jury deliberations, the jury foreperson, **Cynthia Jones**, sent out a note to the trial judge, which read: "Judge, one of the jury members lives close to the accused. We need your advice." In response, the trial court sent back a note that read: "You are referred to the fifth paragraph on page 5 of the jury instructions. Reread that paragraph." That portion of the jury instructions read: "During your deliberations in this case, you must not consider, discuss, or relate any matters not in evidence before you. You should not consider or mention any personal knowledge or information you may have about any fact or person connected with this case which is not shown by the evidence." Thereafter, the jury returned a guilty verdict. Sanchez, who had two prior felony convictions for auto theft and drug possession, was sentenced as a "habitual offender" to sixty-five years in prison.

Sanchez thereafter filed a motion for a new trial. At the hearing on Sanchez's motion for a new trial, juror Tellez testified that he was the juror who had preexisting knowledge about Sanchez. He testified that he lived "[n]ot more than two blocks" from Sanchez in the West Side neighborhood. Juror Tellez had known of Sanchez and his family for "more than twenty years because [he] used to work with his dad in the construction business." Juror Tellez testified that he did not remember being asked during voir dire whether he knew Sanchez or whether he (Tellez) lived in the West Side neighborhood.

Tellez admitted that, during jury deliberations, he had informed the other jurors that Sanchez and his brothers lived near him and that it was common knowledge that they "break into people's homes." Tellez also testified that he was "scared" of Martin Sanchez and his brothers. In response to a leading question from the prosecutor, Juror Tellez agreed that despite such prior knowledge of Sanchez, Tellez nevertheless "based his decision to convict on the evidence in this case."

The foreperson of the jury, Cynthia Jones, also testified at the hearing. She stated that the jury deliberated for approximately twenty minutes before jurors took a poll. She did not remember whether Sanchez said anything during those twenty minutes of discussions. After the polling of the jurors revealed a 12–0 vote to convict Sanchez, she asked: "Is there anyone [who] has anything to say before we turn in [the guilty verdict] to the judge?" At that point, Tellez responded that he felt "bad" because he lived only two or three blocks away from Sanchez, and "I know Sanchez and his brothers and they all have committed burglaries before." The other jurors told Tellez to stop talking about his prior knowledge because it was irrelevant to the case. Foreperson Jones then sent the note to the trial judge, which stated that one of the jurors lived close to Sanchez. The note failed to mention that Tellez also had informed the other jurors about Sanchez and his family's reputation for committing burglaries.

Defense Counsel: Argue in support of your motion for a new trial.

Prosecutor: Argue against defense counsel's motion for a new trial.

To prepare for this hypothetical exercise, read *Dyer v. Calderon*, 151 F.3d 970 (9th Cir. 1998) (en banc) (majority opinion only), and *Lawson v. Borg*, 60 F.3d 608 (9th Cir. 1995) (majority and dissenting opinions).

Hypothetical Four: Motions for New Trial (Jury Misconduct)

State v. Fullwood

The following facts were established at **John Fullwood**'s capital murder trial. Fullwood and **Deidre Waters** were romantically involved for three years, although they never married or lived together. In March 1998, the relationship between Fullwood and Waters became strained, and Fullwood, who had a history of mental problems and violent acts, eventually began threatening to kill her. Ultimately, he broke into her apartment and killed her by repeatedly stabbing her and nearly decapitating her with a butcher knife. After he was arrested, he confessed to the police and was charged with capital murder. The jury convicted him of capital murder in early 1999. Fullwood's trial then proceeded to the sentencing phase, where the jury voted to impose the death penalty.

Subsequently, after nearly fifteen years of direct and collateral appeals in the state and federal court systems, a federal appeals court on habeas corpus review finally reversed Fullwood's death sentence based on a jury instruction error (although Fullwood's capital murder conviction was not reversed). A resentencing was then held. The prosecution, which again sought the death penalty, not only introduced evidence of the 1998 murder but also introduced evidence of Fullwood's prior criminal record from the early 1990s, including two armed robbery convictions. The resentencing hearing lasted three days. After two days (a total of fifteen hours) of deliberation, the second jury also imposed the death penalty after initially sending out a note saying that jurors were "deadlocked" and unable to reach a verdict (which was followed by an instruction by the trial court that jurors should continue deliberating).

During the resentencing hearing, at the request of the defense, the trial court intentionally withheld from the jury the fact that Fullwood originally had been sentenced to death by another jury over a decade before and that he had successfully appealed the first death sentence. The jurors thus were not given any explanation about why the sentencing hearing was occurring over a decade after the murder. Jurors did learn that Fullwood was arrested and taken into custody in 1998, shortly after the murder occurred.

After the second death sentence was imposed, defense counsel interviewed each member of the second jury. Juror **Joyce Austin** told defense counsel that when she went home each night during the proceedings, her husband "was constantly telling me that I should sentence [Fullwood] to death." Austin admitted that by discussing the case with her husband, she had violated the trial court's instruction (given at the outset of the resentencing hearing) not to discuss the case with anyone, including spouses, until after jury deliberations were over. Austin stated to defense counsel, however, that "I am an independent woman and make up my own mind. I listened to my husband, of course, but I voted my own conscience, not his."

Defense counsel also discovered from **Sam Johnson**, the second jury's foreperson, that at the very outset of the jury deliberations jurors briefly discussed whether Fullwood would be eligible for parole if the jury imposed a life sentence. During the trial proceedings, one of the members of the jury, **Theresa Brown**, became aware from a family member who worked as a legal assistant in a criminal defense law firm that life imprisonment did not mean the duration of a defendant's life under the 1998 parole statute applicable to Fullwood. According to Brown's family member, who actually misunderstood the law,[46] a life sentence meant that Fuller "would be paroled in twenty years." Brown shared that information with the other jurors at the outset of the deliberations. Foreperson Johnson informed defense counsel that "we briefly discussed—maybe for a minute—how Mr. Fullwood must have been in jail since 1998 and that given credit for the time he already had been in jail, he would be paroled on a life sentence in just a few more years. That did not seem fair to us. One juror, I forget who, said that 'I bet [Fullwood] was sentenced to death by another jury a while ago and won an appeal.' That's what I assumed, too."

Johnson informed defense counsel that after the jurors engaged in such brief discussion based on Brown's mentioning her family member's comment about the parole law, Johnson told the rest of jurors that "we're not really supposed to be considering anything other than the evidence offered by the lawyers, so let's move on to a different topic." The other jurors shook their heads affirmatively, and they never mentioned parole again during the remainder of their deliberations.

---

46. Under the applicable state statute, a capital defendant sentenced to "life" imprisonment was eligible for parole in as little as twenty calendar years. The parole board, of course, would not be required to release the defendant even after twenty years had passed. Under the law applicable to Fullwood's case, the trial court and lawyers in capital cases were prohibited from informing jurors when a capital defendant would be eligible for parole in the event that the jury sentenced him to a "life" sentence.

When asked whether he would have voted for a death sentence if he had been unaware that a life sentence was not truly life without parole, Johnson stated: "It's hard to say for sure, of course, but I very likely would have voted for a death sentence even if I thought the alternative was life without parole. It was a very brutal murder, and Fullwood had a long criminal record. He deserved the ultimate punishment for what he did to that poor girl." In response to the same question, Juror Austin said that she "absolutely" would have voted for a death sentence under those circumstances. In response to the same question, Juror Brown testified:

> I honestly don't know. I was affected by the thought that Fullwood would be paroled in a few years if we didn't give him the death penalty. I originally voted for a life sentence, along with another member of the jury. We were split 10–2 originally. The thought of him getting paroled soon was one thing that led me to change my mind and vote with the other jurors for death.

In a response to a follow-up question from the prosecutor, Brown further testified: "There were other reasons I changed my mind, too. I kept thinking of those gruesome autopsy pictures; the murder was so brutal. And also that Fullwood had a prior criminal record. All of the jurors focused on that fact."

Under state law, in order for a death sentence to be imposed, all twelve members of a capital sentencing jury must vote for a death sentence. In order for a life sentence to be imposed, at least ten members of the jury must vote for a life sentence. Failure for the requisite number of jurors to agree one way or the other results in a mistrial and resentencing.

Defense counsel filed a motion for a new trial, alleging jury misconduct. The trial court held an evidentiary hearing on the motion, at which the foregoing facts were established through the testimony of Jurors Austin, Johnson, and Brown.

Defense Counsel: Argue in support of your motion for a new trial.

Prosecutor: Argue against defense counsel's motion for a new trial.

To prepare for this hypothetical exercise, read *Lawson v. Borg*, 60 F.3d 608 (9th Cir. 1995) (majority opinion only), and *Drew v. Collins*, 964 F.2d 411, 415–17 (5th Cir. 1992) (portion of decision discussing the jury misconduct claim).

Class Fourteen

Post-Conviction Challenges Continued

14.1 Ineffective Assistance of Counsel Claims

The Sixth Amendment to the United States Constitution guarantees criminal defendants who are charged with all felonies and certain misdemeanors in state or federal court the right to the "assistance of counsel"—including appointed counsel when a defendant cannot afford privately retained counsel.[1] The Supreme Court has interpreted this Sixth Amendment guarantee to include the "effective" assistance of counsel.[2]

There are three main types of ineffective assistance of counsel ("IAC") claims:

> 1) a claim that defense counsel performed in an incompetent manner in some respect that actually prejudiced the defendant (a "*Strickland* claim"[3]); 2) a claim that there was a "constructive denial" of the assistance of counsel or that counsel's acts or omissions caused a "breakdown in the adversary system," thus requiring an irrebuttable presumption of prejudice to the defendant ("a *Cronic* claim"[4]); and 3) a claim that defense counsel labored under an impermissible conflict of interest without the defendant's valid waiver of the right to conflict-free counsel (a "conflict claim"). Each claim is analyzed under a different legal standard.

14.1.1 Strickland *Claims*

The first type of IAC claim—alleging defense counsel's incompetence—encompasses the vast majority of IAC scenarios and requires a defendant to establish two things in order to prevail: 1) that defense counsel performed "deficiently" in some respect, i.e., their performance was incompetent when judged by an objective standard of competence generally applicable to criminal defense attorneys; and

1. Gideon v. Wainwright, 372 U.S. 335 (1963) (felonies); Alabama v. Shelton, 535 U.S. 654 (2002) (misdemeanors, when the sentence is a suspended jail sentence or any amount of time actually served in jail; no right to counsel if there is a fine-only sentence).
2. McMann v. Richardson, 397 U.S. 759 (1970).
3. Strickland v. Washington, 466 U.S. 668 (1984).
4. United States v. Cronic, 466 U.S. 648 (1984).

2) that such deficient performance "prejudiced" the defendant.[5] Even if a defendant makes a strong showing concerning one of the two prongs, a court cannot grant relief unless both requirements are met.[6]

The first prong of the *Strickland* standard does not require "good lawyering." Rather, it measures the acts or omissions of the defense attorney in question against what courts would expect of an attorney of *average* competence[7] or, in the apt words of the Supreme Judicial Court of Massachusetts, "an ordinary fallible lawyer."[8] The first prong is "highly deferential" to the challenged attorney and requires reviewing courts to afford a "strong presumption" that the lawyer was reasonably competent—thus erecting a relatively "high hurdle" for most defendants challenging their attorneys' competence under *Strickland*.[9] Especially strong deference is given to legitimate "strategic" decisions made by defense counsel. If an attorney made an informed decision after a reasonable investigation to pursue one available option over another (e.g., the attorney opted not to call a potential defense witness after interviewing them because it reasonably appeared that they hurt the defense's case as much as or more than they would help it), the attorney's decision is "virtually unchallengeable" under the Sixth Amendment.[10] This strong deference to strategic or tactical decision-making recognizes that defense attorneys often are required to "make difficult choices among a number of legitimate options" and that reasonable legal minds can disagree about the best choice to pursue.[11]

Merely because a challenged attorney describes his acts or omissions in a case as strategic, however, does not insulate the acts or omissions of the attorney from scrutiny under *Strickland*; the attorney's conduct in fact must have been a reasonably informed choice based on more than one reasonable alternative after a reasonable investigation.[12] An attorney's decision not to investigate a particular matter will pass muster under *Strickland* only when the attorney's prior investigation or research made the decision to forego further investigation a reasonable conclusion.[13]

The second prong of the *Strickland* standard places the burden on the defendant to show a "reasonable probability" that "but for" the attorney's deficient performance,

5. Strickland, 466 U.S. at 687–94; *see also* Wiggins v. Smith, 539 U.S. 510, 534–38 (2003) (discussing the *Strickland* standard).
6. Strickland, 466 U.S. at 687.
7. Riles v. McCotter, 799 F.2d 947, 954 (5th Cir. 1986) (Rubin, J., concurring, joined by Johnson, J.).
8. Commonwealth v. White, 565 N.E.2d 1185, 1189–90 (Mass. 1991) (internal citation and quotation marks omitted).
9. Strickland, 466 U.S. at 689–91; *see also* United States ex rel. McCall v. O'Grady, 908 F.2d 170, 173 (7th Cir. 1990) (Strickland's first prong poses a "high hurdle").
10. Strickland, 466 U.S. at 690–91.
11. Lewis v. Lane, 832 F.2d 1446, 1461 (7th Cir. 1987).
12. Paine v. Massie, 339 F.3d 1194, 1200 (10th Cir. 2003); *accord* Hardwick v. Crosby, 320 F.3d 1127, 1182 (11th Cir. 2003); Silva v. Woodford, 279 F.3d 825, 846 (9th Cir. 2002); White v. McAninch, 235 F.3d 988, 995 (6th Cir. 2000); *see also* Wiggins v. Smith, 539 U.S. 510, 521–38 (2003).
13. *See* Wiggins, 539 U.S. at 521–22; Strickland, 466 U.S. at 690–91.

the result of the proceeding would have been different.[14] This standard is somewhat of an "outcome-determinative" test[15] and makes it more difficult for a defendant to prevail than under the traditional harmless error standard[16] applied to other types of constitutional violations.[17] Quantitatively speaking, the *Strickland* "reasonable probability" standard requires a defendant to show that a different outcome would have occurred by a quantum of proof less than by a preponderance of the evidence; qualitatively speaking, a reviewing court's "confidence in the verdict" must be "undermined."[18]

Strickland's two-pronged standard applies to a defense attorney's alleged incompetence during all critical stages of a prosecution—including in pretrial motion practice;[19] an attorney's pretrial advice (or lack thereof) to a defendant concerning which plea to enter (including whether to accept a plea offer from the prosecutor);[20] an attorney's acts or omissions during the guilt-innocence phase of a trial;[21] and a defense attorney's representation of a defendant during sentencing.[22]

14.1.2 Cronic *Claims*

The second type of IAC claim involves acts or omissions by defense counsel that, because of exceptionally bad lawyering or because of interference with the attorney-client relationship by the prosecution or the court, resulted in a "breakdown of the adversarial process" or in a "constructive denial of the assistance of counsel."[23] In such a case, which rarely is established by defendants claiming ineffective assistance of counsel, there is an irrebuttable presumption that the defendant was prejudiced and a new trial is required.[24] In other words, if an attorney's acts or omissions rise to the level of "*Cronic* IAC," then the defendant need not show "actual prejudice" under *Strickland*.[25]

---

14. Strickland, 466 U.S. at 694–95.
15. *Id.* The Court has held that *Strickland* prejudice is not solely an "outcome-determinative" test; a defendant must also show that an attorney's deficiency caused the result of the proceeding to be "unreliable" or "unfair." Lockhart v. Fretwell, 506 U.S. 364 (1993).
16. Chapman v. California, 386 U.S. 18 (1967).
17. *See, e.g.*, United States v. Lott, 310 F.3d 1231, 1251–52 (10th Cir. 2002) (contrasting *Strickland* prejudice standard with *Chapman* harmless-error standard).
18. Strickland, 466 U.S. at 694–95.
19. Kimmelman v. Morrison, 477 U.S. 365 (1986).
20. Hill v. Lockhart, 474 U.S. 52 (1985).
21. Strickland, 466 U.S. at 686–87.
22. Glover v. United States, 531 U.S. 198 (2001).
23. United States v. Cronic, 466 U.S. 648 (1984); *see also* Bell v. Cone, 535 U.S. 685, 695–96 (2002) (discussing the *Cronic* standard); Florida v. Nixon, 543 U.S. 175 (2004) (same).
24. *See* Restrepo v. Kelly, 178 F.3d 634, 641 (2d Cir. 1999). For a thorough collection of lower cases applying (or refusing to apply) *Cronic*'s irrebuttable presumption of prejudice in a wide variety of scenarios, *see* Keith Cunningham-Parmeter, *Dreaming of Effective Assistance: The Awakening of* Cronic*'s Call to Presume Prejudice from Representational Absence*, 76 TEMP. L. REV. 827 (2003).
25. Cronic, 466 U.S. at 659.

The types of *Cronic* claims that courts have found meritorious involved:

i) defense counsel's sleeping or physical absence from the courtroom during an appreciable portion of the trial or other "critical stage" of the court proceeding;[26]

ii) a trial court's refusal to allow defense counsel to communicate with his client during a significant period of time during the trial or a recess in the proceedings;[27]

iii) defense counsel's racism or other bigotry toward the defendant that interfered with the attorney-client relationship;[28]

iv) defense counsel's total failure to perform as an advocate during one or more critical stages of the proceeding;[29] and

v) an attorney whose law license had been permanently revoked or suspended at the time of his representation of a defendant or an "imposter attorney" (i.e., a person who had never passed a bar examination).[30]

Conversely, lower courts have refused to apply *Cronic*'s irrebuttable presumption of prejudice—and, instead, have applied the *Strickland* "actual prejudice" standard—to claims of:

i) a defense lawyer who was intoxicated on drugs or alcohol during a critical stage of the court proceedings (so long as he remained conscious);[31]

---

26. *See, e.g.*, French v. Jones, 332 F.3d 430 (6th Cir. 2003) (temporarily absent lawyer); Siverson v. O'Leary, 764 F.2d 1208 (7th Cir. 1985) (same); Burdine v. Johnson, 262 F.3d 336 (5th Cir. 2001) (en banc) (lawyer who dozed off repeatedly during trial); Tippins v. Walker, 77 F.3d 682 (2d Cir. 1996) (same).

27. *See* Geders v. United States, 425 U.S. 80 (1976) (trial court violated right to counsel by prohibiting defense counsel from communicating with defendant during overnight recess of trial); *but cf.* Perry v. Leeke, 488 U.S. 272 (1989) (no Sixth Amendment violation when trial court prohibited defense counsel from communicating with client during fifteen-minute recess of trial).

28. *See, e.g.*, Frazer v. United States, 18 F.3d 778 (9th Cir. 1994).

29. *See, e.g.*, Quintero v. Bell, 368 F.3d 892 (6th Cir. 2004) (attorney's total failure to act as a meaningful advocate for defendant during voir dire); Rickman v. Bell, 131 F.3d 1150 (6th Cir. 1997) (defense counsel was openly hostile towards client in front of jury and did not act as an advocate); Childress v. Johnson, 103 F.3d 1221 (5th Cir. 1997) (defense attorney was a "potted plant" at defendant's guilty plea proceeding, having entirely failed to consult with client at or before plea).

30. *See* United States v. Novak, 903 F.2d 883 (2d Cir. 1990) (citing decisions of various lower courts); *see generally* Bruce A. Green, *Lethal Fiction: The Meaning of "Counsel" in the Sixth Amendment*, 78 Iowa L. Rev. 433 (1993); Jay M. Zitter, *Criminal Defendant's Representation by Person Not Licensed to Practice Law as Violation of Right to Counsel*, 19 A.L.R.5th 351 (1994 and annual updates).

31. *See, e.g.*, Berry v. King, 765 F.2d 451 (5th Cir. 1985); People v. Garrison, 765 P.2d 419 (Cal. 1989).

ii) a defense lawyer who suffered from mental illness or other type of brain disorder during a critical stage of the proceedings;[32]

iii) a defense lawyer who provided unusually "bad" or "maladroit" assistance of counsel, but who did not *entirely* fail to act as an advocate for his client;[33] and

iv) an attorney whose law license had been temporarily suspended at the time of the representation, but who otherwise was eligible to practice law (e.g., an attorney whose license was temporarily suspended for failure to pay bar dues).[34]

14.2 Conflict-of-Interest Claims

The third type of IAC claim alleges that defense counsel labored under an impermissible conflict of interest vis-à-vis the defendant. The Supreme Court's 2002 decision in *Mickens v. Taylor*[35]—both its holding and dicta—altered the conflict-of-interest jurisprudence followed by most lower courts before *Mickens*.[36]

The Court in *Mickens* discussed three types of conflicts—"multiple representation" conflicts, "successive representation" conflicts, and other types of conflicts (usually based on an attorney's personal interests that conflict with a client's interests).[37] A "multiple representation" conflict stems from an attorney's *concurrent* representation of two or more codefendants charged with the same offense (whether in a joint trial or in separate trials). A "successive representation" conflict stems from an attorney's representation of a defendant in a case in which a *former* client is an actual or potential witness in the case. The final class includes all other types of conflicts, but usually involves an attorney's personal or financial interests that conflict with the defendant's interests (e.g., an attorney should withdraw as the defendant's counsel and become a defense witness).[38] For purposes of determining

---

32. *See, e.g.*, Dows v. Wood, 211 F.3d 480 (9th Cir. 2000); Johnson v. Norris, 207 F.3d 515 (8th Cir. 2000).
33. *See* Scarpa v. DuBois, 38 F.3d 1, 13 (1st Cir. 1994) (citing cases).
34. *See, e.g.*, Reese v. Peters, 926 F.2d 668 (7th Cir. 1991) (citing decisions from various jurisdictions); State v. Green, 643 A.2d 18 (N.J. Super. Ct. App. Div. 1994).
35. Mickens v. Taylor, 535 U.S. 162 (2002).
36. *See* Mark W. Shiner, *Conflicts of Interest Challenges Post* Mickens v. Taylor: *Redefining the Defendant's Burden in Concurrent, Successive, and Personal Interest Conflicts*, 60 WASH. & LEE L. REV. 965 (2003). The Court's specific holdings in *Mickens* were: 1) the "automatic reversal" rule announced in Holloway v. Arkansas, 435 U.S. 475 (1978), only applies to "multiple representation" conflicts; and 2) even in "multiple representation" situations, *Holloway* only applies if the defense objected in a timely manner to the conflict and the trial court failed to take appropriate corrective action. The Court also suggested in dicta that its decision in Cuyler v. Sullivan, 446 U.S. 335 (1980), may not apply to any type of conflict except a "multiple representation" conflict (but reserved that question for resolution in a future case). *See Mickens*, 535 U.S. at 166–76.
37. *Mickens*, 535 U.S. at 167–75.
38. *See id.*

whether a conflict of interest exists, most courts have imputed a conflict by one member of a law firm to another member of the same law firm.[39]

14.2.1 Multiple Representation Conflicts

In multiple representation scenarios, the applicable legal standard depends on whether the defendant or defense counsel raised a timely objection to the alleged conflict and whether the trial court adequately dealt with the alleged conflict. If there was an objection to the conflict at the time that it first was apparent and the trial court did not take appropriate corrective action (i.e., appoint new counsel or secure a valid waiver[40] of the right to conflict-free counsel from the defendant), then a reversal of the defendant's conviction is automatic without a showing of any prejudice to the defendant.[41]

Conversely, if an objection to the conflict was voiced only after a defendant was convicted—even if the defendant was unaware of the conflict until then (which is usually the case)—the defendant's conviction will be reversed only if he shows:

> 1) an "actual" (as opposed to a "hypothetical") conflict of interest, and 2) such an actual conflict had an "adverse effect" on counsel's representation of the defendant.[42]

Under *Cuyler*, an "actual" conflict is one that results from an attorney who "actively represented [the] competing interests" of multiple clients at the same time, as opposed to a hypothetical conflict where a court must speculate about whether an attorney had divided loyalties.[43] A classic example of an actual conflict of interest

39. *See* Austin v. State, 609 A.2d 728, 731–33 & n. 2–3 (Md. 1992) (citing cases from various jurisdictions). In Burger v. Kemp, 483 U.S. 776 (1987), the Supreme Court assumed without deciding that the conflict of one member of a law firm should be imputed to another member. *Id.* at 783. A more difficult question, which has divided the lower courts, is whether the conflict of one member of a large public defender's office should be imputed to another member of the same office when the conflicted attorney has not assisted in any manner in the defense of the client. *See* Austin, 609 A.2d at 732 n. 3 (citing cases).

40. For a discussion of what is required for a valid waiver of the right to conflict-free counsel, see, *e.g.*, Belmontes v. Woodford, 350 F.3d 861, 884–85 (9th Cir. 2003); Tyson v. District Court, 891 P.2d 984, 990–92 & n. 1–2 (Colo. 1995). Essentially, for a waiver to be valid, it must be knowing, voluntary, and intelligent, meaning that the defendant must be informed of the specific nature of the conflict and fully understand how it could adversely affect representation by the conflicted attorney. *Belmontes*, 350 F.3d at 884–85.

41. *See* Holloway v. Arkansas, 435 U.S. 475 (1978); *see also* Atley v. Ault, 191 F.3d 865 (8th Cir. 1999) (*explaining Holloway*). The scenario in which a timely objection is made almost always involves a court-appointed lawyer who is assigned to represent codefendants who are unwilling to waive an actual or potential conflict.

42. Cuyler v. Sullivan, 446 U.S. 335 (1980).

43. *Burger*, 483 U.S. 776, 783–84 (internal citations and quotation marks omitted); *see also* United States v. Johnson, 569 F.2d 269, 270–71 (5th Cir. 1978) (an actual conflict exists "whenever one defendant stands to gain significantly by counsel adducing probative evidence or advancing plausible arguments that are damaging to a codefendant whom counsel is also representing") (citation and

that adversely affects a defendant involves a single attorney who represents both a husband and wife at a joint trial at which a plausible defense for one or both spouses was to shift blame to the other.[44] Not all multiple representation situations pose actual conflicts that adversely affect one or more of the codefendants represented by a single attorney.[45]

An "adverse effect" under *Cuyler* is not the same as "prejudice" under *Strickland.* Rather, the defendant only needs to show a "plausible" or "reasonable" "alternative strategy" that was not pursued by the conflicted defense attorney because of the conflict of interest—even if there is not a "reasonable probability" that the alternative strategy would have resulted in a different outcome.[46]

14.2.2 Successive Representation Conflicts

In *Mickens v. Taylor,* the Supreme Court overruled a large number of lower court decisions by holding that "multiple representation" conflicts are only subject to *Holloway*'s[47] automatic reversal rule when there was a timely objection by the defense and no corrective action by the trial court.[48] The Court held that it is an "open question" concerning which standard should apply to "successive representation" conflicts—*Cuyler* or *Strickland.*[49] Since *Mickens,* the lower courts have split over which standard to apply when a defendant or defense counsel lodges a timely objection based on a "successive representation" conflict and the trial court fails to inquire into the conflict or secure an adequate waiver of the right to conflict-free counsel. Some courts have applied the *Cuyler* "adverse effect" standard, while others have applied the more rigorous *Strickland* "prejudice" standard.[50] The lower courts are also divided over which standard applies when there was not a timely objection to a successive representation conflict.[51]

---

internal quotation marks omitted). For an "actual" conflict to exist, the attorney in question must be aware of the circumstances giving rise to the alleged conflict. United States v. Hopkins, 43 F.3d 1116, 1118–19 (6th Cir. 1995).

44. *See, e.g.*, United States v. Pinc, 452 F.2d 507 (5th Cir. 1971).

45. Burger v. Kemp, 483 U.S. 776 (1987) (single lawyer who represents two codefendants does not possess a per se conflict of interest).

46. *See, e.g.*, United States v. Feyrer, 333 F.3d 110, 116 (2d Cir. 2003); Reynolds v. Chapman, 253 F.3d 1337, 1343 (11th Cir. 2001); Perillo v. Johnson, 205 F.3d 775, 806 (5th Cir. 2000); State v. Martinez-Serna, 803 P.2d 416, 418 (Ariz. 1990).

47. United States v. Holloway, 781 F.2d 124, 125 (8th Cir. 1986).

48. Mickens v. Taylor, 535 U.S. 162, 167–68; *see also* McFarland, 356 F.3d at 700–01.

49. Mickens, 535 U.S. at 174–75.

50. *Compare, e.g.*, Koste v. Dormire, 345 F.3d 974, 981–82 (8th Cir. 2003) (applying *Cuyler*), *with* Thompson v. State, 94 S.W.3d 11, 17–18 n. 1 (Tex. App. 2002) (applying *Strickland*).

51. *Compare, e.g.*, Lewis v. Mayle, 391 F.3d 989 (9th Cir. 2004) (applying *Cuyler*), *and* Tueros v. Greiner, 343 F.3d 587, 593–94 (2d Cir. 2003) (same), *with* Sparks v. State, 92 P.3d 542 (Idaho App. 2004) (applying *Strickland*).

14.2.3 Other Types of Conflicts

As noted, *Mickens* limited *Holloway*'s automatic reversal rule to "multiple representation" conflicts, even when a timely objection was made to another type of conflict, such as one between an attorney's personal interests and the interests of the defendant. Prior to *Mickens*, the lower courts were divided over whether the *Cuyler* standard applied to conflicts other than "multiple" or "successive" representation conflicts, even when a timely objection was made.[52] Since *Mickens*, the lower courts remain divided on this issue, with a majority apparently applying Strickland rather than *Cuyler*.[53]

Hypothetical One: Motions for New Trial (Ineffective Assistance of Counsel)

State v. Haverford

Paul Haverford met and began dating **Cynthia Janecka**. Janecka had two children from a prior relationship. Their relationship was physically violent on two occasions, and Haverford threatened to "beat up" Janecka on several occasions and once threatened to kill her. Janecka eventually broke off the relationship. Thereafter, Janecka began dating Haverford's friend, **Bill Stremlow**. Janecka eventually moved in with Stremlow. Before moving in with Stremlow, Janecka confided in a friend, **Doris Jenner**, that Haverford had previously threatened to kill her if she ever lived with another man.

Janecka confided in Jenner that she wanted to see Haverford one last time to "make peace with him." Shortly thereafter, Janecka dropped Stremlow off at work and borrowed his truck for the rest of the day. Janecka picked up her daughter, Tonya, at school that afternoon. At that time, Tonya's teacher saw Tonya get into Stremlow's truck next to an unidentified white man who was not Stremlow. Janecka failed to pick up Stremlow from work that evening as planned. Later that night, Stremlow's truck was found burning in a field in a rural area of Nita City. The truck's windows were broken out. An accelerant had been used to set the truck on fire.

A few days later, a farmer discovered the bodies of Janecka and her two children buried in a shallow grave in another field. At the grave site, Nita City police found broken glass, tire tracks, a footprint, shell casings, a child's bloody sock, and a pool of

52. *Compare, e.g.*, Spreitzer v. Peters, 114 F.3d 1435, 1451 n. 7 (7th Cir. 1997) (applying *Cuyler* to all types of conflicts), *with* Beets v. Collins, 65 F.3d 1258 (5th Cir. 1995) (en banc) (applying *Strickland* to conflicts other than multiple or successive representation conflicts).

53. *Compare, e.g.*, Rubin v. Gee, 292 F.3d 396, 402 & n. 2 (4th Cir. 2002) (applying *Cuyler*) *and id.* at 407–08 (Motz, J., dissenting) (same), with Echols v. State, 127 S.W.3d 486, 493–94 (Ark. 2003) (applying *Strickland*); *see generally* Mark W. Shiner, Note, *Conflicts of Interest Challenges Post Mickens v. Taylor: Redefining the Defendant's Burden in Concurrent, Successive, and Personal Interest Conflicts*, 60 Wash. & Lee L. Rev. 965 (2003).

blood near a tree with a freshly broken branch. On top of the grave, police found a tree branch in which a nine-millimeter bullet was embedded. The bullet pinned white fibers to the branch. The fibers were consistent with the white fibers in Tonya Janecka's jacket. The jacket had a charred hole in the hood. The branch appeared to have been broken off a tree near the pool of blood. Each victim had suffered two gunshot wounds to the face or head. Although investigators never recovered the bullets, the wounds were consistent with nine-millimeter ammunition, according to a medical expert.

After obtaining warrants to do so, police arrested Haverford and searched his parents' home (where he was living at the time). After being arrested and charged with capital murder, the trial court appointed a local defense lawyer, **Randy Burgess**, to represent Haverford.

During their search of Haverford's parents' home, the police recovered a nine-millimeter weapon that Haverford had purchased several months before the murders.

Police also recovered two shovels with soil that was consistent with soil from the grave site (according to an expert witness for the prosecution), two gas cans, and broken glass that was consistent with glass found in Tonya's coat and near the gate at the field. Police officers also seized Haverford's tennis shoes. The shoes made prints similar to those found at the murder scene, and DNA tests revealed the presence of blood consistent with Tonya Janecka's blood on the shoes. At trial, a ballistics expert testified that shell casings from the crime scene matched casings fired from Haverford's weapon. Haverford's former wife testified that Haverford was familiar with the field where the bodies were found and that he previously had visited the field with her on several occasions.

Based on this evidence, the jury convicted Haverford of three counts of capital murder. At a separate capital sentencing proceeding, which commenced the following day, the prosecution sought the death penalty. During the sentencing hearing, the prosecution argued that many aggravating factors existed that justified the death penalty, including that Haverford had murdered multiple persons, among them innocent children, and also that Haverford was a continuing threat to society and a sociopath, and, finally, that life imprisonment would not prevent him from posing such a danger.[54] The jury sentenced Haverford to death.

Dissatisfied with the jury's decision, Haverford's family hired a new defense counsel for Haverford the day following the jury's verdict sentencing him to death. New counsel discovered that prior to the Janecka murders, Haverford had received counseling from a psychologist, **Dr. Ralph Adams, PhD**, to address Haverford's anger and depression. After six months of counseling, Dr. Adams also had given Haverford

54. The prosecution introduced evidence that on two prior occasions when he was in custody, Haverford had gotten into fights with jail guards. On another occasion, he had threatened to kill a fellow inmate who had stolen some of his personal items in the jail cell.

several neuropsychological tests to diagnose possible learning disabilities and help him make career and educational plans. According to Dr. Adams's report, Haverford's cognitive functioning was "largely adequate" and his intelligence average, but his difficulty spelling might be evidence of a learning disability. The tests also indicated that Haverford had some emotional and psychological problems and that he had difficulty controlling his anger and coping with everyday problems. Dr. Adams's report had been submitted to former defense counsel, Burgess, prior to the trial.

New defense counsel also discovered that prior to trial, former counsel Burgess had retained a psychologist who specialized in capital sentencing mitigation, **Dr. Randolph Murphy, PhD**, to review Dr. Adams's report. Based solely on Dr. Adams's findings, Dr. Murphy prepared a one-page summary report. In his report, Dr. Murphy indicated there was evidence of "mild but probable brain damage" that could increase the likelihood of violence, especially if Haverford was under the influence of alcohol or other substances. In addition, Dr. Murphy noted that Haverford might suffer from a "serious psychiatric thought disorder." Haverford had a psychological "profile often . . . associated with psychotic behavior . . . [and] definite difficulties with interpersonal relationships." Dr. Murphy qualified his impressions by noting that both "possible disorders require further diagnostic investigation to confirm." He also "recommend[ed] that [he] personally interview Mr. Haverford."

New defense counsel learned that former counsel Burgess had telephoned Dr. Murphy during the time between the jury's guilty verdict and the capital sentencing hearing.[55] Burgess requested that Dr. Murphy testify at the capital sentencing proceeding that was scheduled to start the following day. Dr. Murphy informed Burgess he "ethically could not testify because I have never personally evaluated" Haverford. Dr. Murphy also informed Burgess that what he could say about Haverford would be "as aggravating as mitigating based on the limited amount of information that I know about the guy." On the phone, Burgess agreed that Dr. Murphy would not testify. Nonetheless, later that day, Burgess subpoenaed him to testify the following morning. Surprised by the subpoena, Dr. Murphy expressed anger at Burgess, but showed up the following morning.

During a court hearing outside of the presence of the jury, Burgess explained that he wanted Dr. Murphy to authenticate his report so they could admit into evidence both his report and the report of Dr. Adams, on which Dr. Murphy's report relied. Defense counsel requested permission to treat Dr. Murphy as a hostile witness in light of the hostility Dr. Murphy directed toward Burgess.

During the capital sentencing proceeding, Dr. Murphy was called as a witness by Burgess.[56] In response to Burgess's questions, Dr. Murphy identified both

55. Burgess had not spoken with either Dr. Murphy or Dr. Adams about their reports before the jury's guilty verdict.
56. Dr. Murphy was the only defense witness called during the capital sentencing proceeding.

reports, and the trial judge admitted each into evidence. Burgess then passed the witness to the prosecutor. On cross-examination of Dr. Murphy by the prosecutor, Dr. Murphy admitted to jurors that he did not put enormous stock in his conclusions because he did not personally evaluate Haverford. He admitted that Dr. Adams, having evaluated Haverford in person, would be in the best position to address whether Haverford had brain damage.

The prosecution then called Dr. Adams as a rebuttal witness. Contrary to Dr. Murphy's limited assertions, Dr. Adams testified Haverford had a mild learning disability, but no brain damage. In addition, Dr. Adams asserted that, although Haverford had some psychological problems, he opined that Haverford "had many of the characteristics of a 'sociopath,' that is, a person with an antisocial personality disorder."

In his closing arguments at the sentencing hearing, Burgess argued to the jurors that they should impose a life sentence because "there is some evidence that he has brain damage, which caused him to commit the murders." In the prosecutor's rebuttal, the prosecutor responded that "there is no evidence of brain damage, as we know from Dr. Adams, the only doctor who actually examined Haverford." The prosecutor also repeatedly referred to Haverford as a "sociopath, . . . as his own doctor said!"

After learning the foregoing facts about Burgess's representation of Haverford, new defense counsel filed a motion for a new trial alleging that Burgess had provided Haverford with ineffective assistance of counsel with respect to the capital sentencing phase. New defense counsel's motion asked the trial court to vacate the death sentence and order a new capital sentencing hearing, at which the new defense attorney would represent Haverford. The prosecution filed a response in opposition to the motion for a new trial.

The trial court conducted an evidentiary hearing at which the foregoing facts were established. In addition to offering proof of the foregoing facts, new defense counsel also introduced testimony from Haverford's aunt and uncle about the harsh child abuse (including severe beatings, which resulted in visible bruises) and neglect (including no parental supervision during most of Haverford's youth) that Haverford had suffered as a young child at the hands of his mother and stepfather. The aunt and uncle testified that Burgess had never contacted them and never had asked them to be defense witnesses during the punishment phase. Burgess, who was called as a witness at the hearing by the prosecution, testified that he was unaware of Haverford's history of child abuse and neglect because "Mr. Haverford never told me about it." Burgess admitted that he never had asked Haverford or anyone else whether Haverford had been abused or neglected as a child.

The defense called Dr. Murphy as a witness at the hearing on the motion for a new trial. He testified that if he had been able to examine Haverford (which he did at the request of new defense counsel after Haverford had been sentenced to death) and to speak to his relatives about the child abuse and neglect that Haverford suffered, he would have testified at the sentencing phase that Haverford was not a sociopath and that his violent tendencies as an adult were the product of his abusive upbringing, which mental health therapy could help overcome. Such mental health therapy was available in prison, Dr. Murphy added.

At the hearing, Burgess also testified that in his view, he had made a "strategic" decision about introducing Dr. Murphy's report and calling him as a witness during the sentencing phase even though he had not examined Haverford at that point. "I knew that it was risky calling Dr. Murphy to the stand to authenticate his report. I had to call him for the limited purpose of authenticating his report. I hoped that the prosecutor wouldn't cross-examine him in the manner that the prosecutor ended up doing. I felt like I had no choice. As far as I knew at that point, the possible brain damage was the only thing that I believed that we had going for us. It was a sure death sentence without some mitigating evidence being offered to cause at least one juror to vote for life. I didn't know anything about the child abuse evidence because Mr. Haverford never told me about it. Based on what I knew then, I think I made the right decision."[57] When asked by new defense counsel why he waited until the day before the sentencing hearing to contact Dr. Murphy regarding his initial, cursory report, and why he didn't have Dr. Murphy examine Haverford prior to the sentencing phase, Burgess replied: "In an ideal world I would have contacted him before then and had him examine Mr. Haverford. But I was spending my time preparing for other parts of the trial."

Defense Counsel: Argue in support of your new trial motion seeking a new capital sentencing hearing.

Prosecutor: Argue against new defense counsel's new trial motion seeking a new capital sentencing hearing.

To prepare for this hypothetical exercise, read *Hamblin v. Mitchell*, 354 F.3d 482 (6th Cir. 2003) (majority and dissenting opinions).

Hypothetical Two: Motions for New Trial (Ineffective Assistance of Counsel)

State v. Monroe

Charlie Lee Monroe was arrested and charged with first-degree (premeditated) murder for the shooting death of **Raymond Harlin**, who was killed after a fight broke out in Monroe's kitchen. Attorney **Gerald Erickson** was appointed counsel for Monroe. Erickson represented Monroe at a preliminary examination, during

57. Under applicable state law, if even a single juror refused to vote for the death penalty, the trial court automatically was required to impose a life sentence.

which he called one witness (Monroe's mother) and argued (unsuccessfully) that bail should be granted.[58]

Erickson next represented Monroe, close to four months later, at a pretrial conference; at that hearing, which lasted only four minutes, the trial judge simply reset the trial date at the joint request of the lawyers. Three months later, Erickson was suspended from practicing law by the state supreme court in Nita based on his failure to pay bar dues. His license was reinstated on the following month (after he had paid his delinquent dues and a penalty), the day before jury selection began for Monroe's trial.

According to the evidence offered at trial by the prosecution, Monroe was the leader of a drug-trafficking ring and his apartment served as a wholesale warehouse for several street-level sellers who sold drugs in the lobby of the building. Harlin, the deceased, allegedly worked for Monroe as a drug seller. The prosecution's theory was that Monroe directed the events that took place in his apartment surrounding Harlin's murder. On the night in question, Monroe, Harlin, codefendant **Lamont Mason**, and several others were present in Monroe's apartment around 10:00 p.m. According to trial testimony, a fight broke out between Mason and Harlin in Monroe's kitchen. The only reason offered at trial for the start of the fight was that Mason did not like the way Harlin was looking at him. After the fight began, **Tyrone Thompson** arrived. Thompson, who was the prosecution's principal witness, testified that when he arrived at the apartment, he saw a gun in plain view on the windowsill. Thompson also testified that Monroe said, "shoot a hole in his [Harlin's] heart" and thereby ordered the killing. According to Thompson, at that point Lamont Mason then picked up the gun and shot Harlin in the neck and back.

Monroe and Mason were charged with first-degree murder. Separate juries heard Monroe's and Mason's cases. Mason, the alleged shooter, was acquitted at his trial, which occurred before Monroe's trial.

Before his trial, Monroe had written six separate letters to the presiding trial judge, the chief judge of the district, and others in the court system requesting new counsel. Monroe alleged that Erickson had not visited him once in jail nor had Monroe had the opportunity to speak with Erickson in court.[59] A week before

---

58. The trial court detained Monroe without bond. He remained in custody during the pretrial and trial proceedings.

59. His letters stated in pertinent part:

> I have been locked up for five months and not once have my lawyer took time out to talk to me. . . . Three times after I went to court my lawyer has told me that he would be over to talk to me, but never did. . . . Ever since my second month of being incarcerated I have had my mother go over to his office concerning an evidentiary hearing, she have been at his office many times, she has wrote many letters but he has never replied to her. . . . I know I'm charged for something I haven't done, but I know that if I can't express to Gerald Erickson what happen on the night this incident occurred he will not know the best strategy of what and how to fight this case. . . . For five months I have waited patiently, I have tried every

jury selection was to begin, the trial court held an ex parte hearing on Monroe's pro se Motion for Withdrawal of Counsel, at which Monroe appeared on his own behalf. Erickson did not appear for the hearing, although he had notice of it. At the hearing, Monroe informed the court that he had received a letter from his counsel informing him that he was suspended from the practice of law for a month. He also asked for a new lawyer and a postponement of the trial to afford a new lawyer the chance to review his case. Because Erickson was not present, the trial court held the motion under advisement.

On the morning of the day of jury selection, Monroe again renewed his pro se motion for new counsel. At that point, Erickson, whose law license had been reinstated the day before, informed the court that Monroe wanted him removed because he had failed to visit him the night before in jail as promised. The trial court conducted another ex parte hearing on Monroe's motion. At the hearing, Monroe told the court:

> Well, from the very beginning, you know, Mr. Erickson promised to talk with me. He has failed to talk with me on every occasion that he promised. He has failed to make any motions for me, and he's failed to talk with my mother, which she has written many letters and calls, and went to his office, also, left word with his secretary. And he also showed up an hour late on my final pretrial conference and by him letting me know yesterday that he was going to come over and talk with me and by him failing to do that, I just, I just feel it's just incompetent.

When the court asked, "Now, in those letters, it was a question of his not keeping appointments, or seeing you as many times as you'd like to be seen in the jail; is that right?" Monroe then replied: "Yes. Never seeing me at all." He further asserted that "[t]he only time I meet him is in the courtroom, or brief discussion in the courtroom holding cell with plenty of other people in the same cell. I just don't see how courts can say that that's true fairness." Monroe, who is hard of hearing, also claimed that because he was not wearing his hearing aid in the holding cell, he could not hear much of what his lawyer was saying to him. At one point, Monroe asked, "How can I make it all the way to trial when Mr. Erickson has never heard my true side of the story?"

Erickson testified at length during this hearing. While he argued that he had delivered discovery materials to Monroe and was in the process of working out a deal with the prosecutor to suppress certain evidence on the eve of trial, he never disputed the substance of Monroe's allegations concerning Erickson's failure to meet with his client prior to trial. The trial court denied Monroe's motion without

---

way I can to get him to talk to me, I am tired of being in the dark and knowing he's in the dark. . . . So, your honor, please take him off my case because he's not representing me at all.

prejudice. "Let's see what happens with the verdict and go from there," the judge commented. The trial then commenced after the jury was selected.

At Monroe's trial, which lasted six hours, defense counsel Erickson did not present an opening statement, but did cross-examine each of the prosecution's witnesses. Monroe did not testify, nor did Erickson present any witnesses or evidence on Monroe's behalf. At the close of the prosecution's case, Erickson moved for a judgment of acquittal. The court partially granted the motion by reducing the charge to second-degree murder[60] and permitting that lesser charge to be submitted to the jurors. During closing arguments, Erickson argued at some length that Thompson's testimony was incredible and that the prosecution had not carried its burden of proof. The jury convicted Monroe of second-degree murder after deliberating less than two hours. Monroe was sentenced by the trial judge to fifteen years' imprisonment.

After Monroe was convicted and sentenced, his family hired a new defense counsel to review the case. New counsel filed a motion for a new trial, alleging that former counsel Erickson had provided ineffective assistance of counsel. The prosecution filed a response in opposition to the motion. A new trial judge was assigned to conduct an evidentiary hearing on the motion.

At the hearing, Monroe and Monroe's mother testified. Attorney Erickson was not called as a witness. Mrs. Monroe's testimony was offered to establish her numerous efforts to contact Erickson and have him meet with her son prior to trial.

Monroe also testified to his efforts to contact Erickson and discuss his case with his lawyer prior to trial.[61]

---

60. Unlike first-degree murder, second-degree murder does not require premeditation under applicable state law.

61. Monroe's testimony included the following:

Q: Who was your attorney for this case?
A: Gerald Erickson.
Q: Do you recall when you saw this person in relation to the preliminary examination?
A: I recall seeing him sitting in the courtroom, the first time I met him.
Q: At the preliminary examination?
A: Yes.
Q: And how much contact with him did you have before the preliminary examination?
A: None.

* * *

Q: When did you next see your attorney?
A: Well, I would see him in the holding cell behind the courtroom, maybe about three times—three different proceedings.
Q: And, roughly, would you say how much contact did you have with him before the court proceedings?
A: One or two minutes.

* * *

Defense Counsel: Argue in support of your motion for a new trial.

Prosecutor: Argue against defense counsel's motion for a new trial.

For purposes of this hypothetical, assume that the trial court already has ruled that Monroe cannot prevail under the "prejudice" prong of *Strickland v. Washington*, 466 U.S. 668 (1984), because Monroe failed to offer any evidence that the result of the proceeding would have been different with competent counsel, and that the only theory of ineffectiveness that the court will entertain is whether Erickson's alleged ineffective assistance rises to the level of presumed prejudice under *United States v. Cronic*, 466 U.S. 648 (1984). Thus, defense counsel and the prosecutor are limited to arguing whether a new trial is required under *Cronic*.

To prepare for the hypothetical exercises, read *Burdine v. Johnson*, 262 F.3d 336 (5th Cir. 2001) (en banc) (majority and dissenting opinions), and *Bell v. Cone*, 535 U.S. 685 (2002).

Hypothetical Three: Motions for New Trial (Ineffective Assistance of Counsel)

United States v. Haney

Robert Haney was charged in federal court with possession with intent to distribute thirty grams of crack cocaine, in violation of 21 U.S.C. § 841(a) and (b), a felony offense carrying a mandatory minimum offense of five years in prison. He pleaded not guilty and had a jury trial.

The prosecution's evidence at trial showed that a police officer pulled over Haney for speeding. Haney was driving a rental car that his girlfriend had rented in her name. She was not in the car with him. Another police officer, Officer **Sharon McCord**, arrived with a drug dog while the first officer was processing Haney's driver's license and vehicle registration on the patrol car's computer. When the drug dog ran around the rental car, it alerted to the presence of cocaine inside the car. Based on the probable cause provided by the drug dog's alert, Officer McCord searched Haney's car, finding a plastic sandwich bag containing thirty grams of crack cocaine in the form of a single "cookie" (as opposed to broken up

---

Q: Did you see Mr. Erickson at the county jail before your trial in this case?
A: No, I never did.
Q: When was the first time you saw him in the jail, if at all?
A: The second date —I mean the first day of picking the jury.

* * *

Q: Before your trial started, in the weeks or months leading up to it, did you contact, or attempt to contact your attorney?
A: Yes, I did. I wrote him letters. His office wouldn't accept my collect telephone calls.

into "rocks"). The bag was located under the driver's seat. Immediately next the bag was a second sandwich bag contained $600 (in $5, $10, and $20 bills) and a fake driver's license bearing Haney's photo and his middle and last name (but lacking his first name). The officers seized both sandwich bags and arrested Haney, who was eventually charged with violating § 841.

At trial, Officer McCord testified about the above events. The prosecutor asked her whether thirty grams of crack cocaine was consistent with "personal use as well as with consistent with a quantity that a drug dealer would possess." Officer McCord responded that, "usually that amount is possessed with the intent to distribute it to others, but I've once in a while seen a crack addict with sufficient resources possess that much just for himself." McCord followed up by testifying that she believed Haney had possessed with intent to distribute based on the $600 in cash found in the second bag (also containing Haney's fake driver's license). "That much cash, in those denominations, indicates that he was a dealer," she told jurors. The defense called no witnesses at trial. Haney exercised his right to be silent and did not testify.

Before trial, Haney had told his defense counsel, **Aaron Mersino**, that Haney was "innocent" and that he had been unaware that there was a bag of crack cocaine underneath the passenger seat next to the other bag. Mersino never discussed with Haney the option of pursuing a lesser-included offense instruction and conceding that Haney was guilty only of simple possession of crack cocaine (without the intent to distribute), a misdemeanor offense carrying a maximum penalty of one year in prison under 21 U.S.C. § 844.

Shortly before closing arguments, the trial judge announced that she was going to give the jury an option of convicting Haney of the lesser-included offense of simple possession based on Officer McCord's testimony, even though neither defense counsel nor the prosecutor had asked for it. Mersino did not discuss the judge's decision with Haney. During Mersino's closing argument, he initially argued that the prosecution had failed to prove the "knowing possession" element of 21 U.S.C. § 841(a) beyond a reasonable doubt, but abruptly concluded his closing argument as follows:

> But, you know, considering that the other bag with his fake ID was located next to the baggie with the crack, I can see how you may think that Mr. Haney knew the crack cocaine was in the car and thus possessed it. You know what? That's fine. I get it. So, I'm going to pivot and ask you to convict him of the lesser-included offense of simple possession. You heard the officer tell you that thirty grams is consistent with personal use. Her testimony created a reasonable doubt about the "intent to distribute" element. So, simple possession. Thank you, ladies and gentlemen.

Haney, who was sitting at the defense table, was confused by what Mersino had just said. Haney did not understand that Mersino had asked jurors to convict him the lesser-included offense rather than acquit him outright.

After deliberating for ten minutes, the jury convicted Haney of the greater offense of possession of thirty grams with intent to distribute. Haney retained a new attorney, who filed a motion for a new trial contending that Mersino had constructively deprived Haney of the assistance of counsel by conceding that Haney was guilty of simple possession of the crack cocaine.

Defense Counsel: Argue in support of your motion for a new trial.

Prosecutor: Argue against defense counsel's motion for a new trial.

To prepare for this hypothetical exercise, read *McCoy v. Louisiana*, 138 S. Ct. 1500 (2018); *Haynes v. Cain*, 298 F.3d 375 (5th Cir. 2002) (majority and dissenting opinions); *Elmore v. Shoop*, 2019 WL 3423200, at *9 (S.D. Ohio July 30, 2019), adopted by *Elmore v. Shoop*, 2020 WL 3410764 (S.D. Ohio June 22, 2020).

Hypothetical Four: Motions for New Trial (Ineffective Assistance of Counsel)

State v. Wren

Willie Wren and **Antonio Brown** were jointly charged with the murder of **Brian Palmer**, who was shot to death in Nita City on Father's Day. Wren and Brown, who were denied release on bail, pooled their resources and hired a single lawyer, **Robert Charlton**, to represent them both at a joint trial. Both men consistently told Charlton that they were in Florida at the time of the murder. After consulting with Charlton, Wren and Brown agreed that their joint defense at trial would be an alibi defense—namely, that they were in Florida on the date and time of the murder.

At no time before or during the trial did Charlton, Wren, or Brown object to the trial court that Charlton's joint representation of both men created an impermissible conflict of interest. The trial judge never asked Wren or Brown whether they wanted a separate lawyer.

Before trial, after extensive plea bargain negotiations, the prosecutor's best and final plea offer was seven years of prison for Brown and fifteen years of prison for Wren. With respect to Wren, who had two prior felony convictions for drug possession, the prosecutor stated that he would "enhance" Wren as a habitual offender (based on his two prior felony convictions) and seek a life sentence if he were convicted of the murder charge after a trial. Charlton advised both Wren and Brown to reject that plea offer because, in Charlton's opinion, they had a "good shot" at beating the charges if the case went to trial. Charlton further stated: "The best chance we have of getting a deal we all could live with would be if we counteroffer with time-served[62] for both of you. In other words, a package deal for both of you. All or nothing." The prosecutor rejected the package deal proposed by Charlton, and the case proceeded to trial.

At trial, the prosecution's theory of the case was that Wren intended to kill Palmer because Palmer previously had snitched to police about an armed robbery that he and Wren had committed. The prosecution's star witness at trial was **Damon Dawson**. He testified that Wren and Palmer separately came to Nita City in the week leading up to Father's Day and that Palmer contacted Wren. Wren and Palmer agreed to join Brown and his friend, Dawson, in committing an armed robbery in Nita City. Dawson testified that the robbery plan was a ruse to enable Wren to murder Palmer. According to Dawson, he and Brown conspired with Wren to help him set up Palmer and have him murdered.

Dawson further testified that on Father's Day, around 10:00 p.m., he guided Wren, Brown, and Palmer to the apartment complex where the armed robbery was supposed to occur. As Wren and Palmer were walking ahead of Dawson and Brown, Wren (who was armed) suddenly shot Palmer in the head, then shot him again in the back when he was on the ground. Palmer was fatally wounded by the multiple gunshots. Wren, Brown, and Dawson then ran away to Dawson's house. According to Dawson, Brown later buried the murder weapon in the backyard of Dawson's house. The following day Wren and Brown left town and went to Florida. Ten days after the shooting, Dawson voluntarily contacted the police and informed them of the foregoing facts. The prosecution agreed not to charge Dawson with any crime in connection with Palmer's murder in exchange for his testimony against Wren and Brown.

Geraldine Harris, Dawson's mother-in-law, also testified for the prosecution at trial. Harris lived with Dawson, her daughter (Sherrie Dawson), and her daughter's three children by Dawson in a house in Nita City. Harris testified that Brown was present at her home on Father's Day, i.e., the day of the murder; that he had asked her to drive him to Florida (but that she had not taken him); that she saw Dawson cleaning "something dirty"[63] in her bathtub; that she saw Dawson and Brown go to her home's backyard repeatedly; and that she overheard Brown tell Dawson that he (Brown) was "sorry for what had went down, and he didn't mean to put him through it." Harris also testified that Brown had called her from jail and told her, "I was with you the whole time on Father's Day," which she interpreted as an attempt

62. "Time-served" means that a defendant is sentenced to the time that he has already served up until the time of sentencing with no more additional time in custody. At the time of trial, Wren and Brown had been in custody a little more than one year.
63. In regard to Brown, Dawson had testified that when the three men returned to the house after the murder, Brown used a large kitchen spoon to bury the murder weapon in the backyard.

to concoct an alibi. When asked whether Harris recognized Wren, she stated that she did not recognize him.

Charlton cross-examined Dawson and Harris only briefly. His questioning of Dawson was limited to his bias resulting from his plea bargain—i.e., that Dawson's testimony was motivated based on the dismissal of the murder charge against him—and his questioning of Harris was limited to her dependence on her son-in-law Dawson's paycheck that supported the entire household, including Harris, her daughter, and her grandchildren.

Wren and Brown each testified on his own behalf at the joint trial. They both testified that Dawson was lying; Brown further testified that Harris was lying. Wren and Brown admitted that they had visited Nita City briefly before the date of the murder, but claimed to have traveled together to Miami, Florida, six days before the murder. They testified they did not return to Nita City until extradited in connection with this case.

In addition to calling Wren and Brown as witnesses, Charlton also called **Suzanne Smith** as a defense witness. She testified that she was Wren's "common-law wife" and mother of his son and that she had lived in Miami, Florida, all of her life and had come to Nita City for the first time for the trial. She testified that Wren and Brown—whom she described as "best friends"—were together with her for Father's Day, which they celebrated with a barbecue at her home. She testified that the barbecue occurred "around 6:00 or 7:00 p.m. It was dinnertime." She also testified that Brown and Wren remained in Miami for the rest of Father's Day.

In closing arguments, Charlton contended that Wren and Brown were in Florida, not Nita City, at the time of the murder and that Dawson and his mother-in-law Harris were lying "to save Dawson's skin and his paycheck." Charlton concluded that "Dawson is the real killer who's trying to shift the blame to two innocent men."

The jury found both Wren and Brown guilty of murder. The trial judge sentenced Wren as a habitual offender to life in prison and Brown to twenty-five years in prison.

After the guilty verdict, Wren's family hired a new lawyer. New defense counsel filed a motion for a new trial, alleging ineffective assistance of counsel on the part of Charlton, i.e., that Charlton possessed a conflict of interest based on his representation of both Brown and Wren at the same trial.

Defense Counsel (for Wren): Argue in support of your motion for a new trial.

Prosecutor: Argue against Wren's motion for a new trial.

To prepare for this hypothetical exercise, read *Perillo v. Johnson*, 205 F.3d 775 (5th Cir. 2000), and *United States v. Feyrer*, 333 F.3d 110 (2d Cir. 2003).

Hypothetical Five: Motions for New Trial (Ineffective Assistance of Counsel)

State v. Rojas

Lisa Rojas, a thirty-two-year-old heir to a large family fortune, was a homemaker and a part-time personal trainer. She was married to **Timothy Baker**, an insurance company executive. Rojas was charged with the premeditated murder of Baker. There is no dispute that Rojas shot and killed Baker with six rounds from a .38 handgun, which he had purchased for her only weeks before. However, Rojas, the only defense witness called at her trial, claimed she was acting in self-defense.

A series of events ultimately led to the shooting. During her marriage to Baker, Rojas had an affair with **William Murphy**. Rojas and Baker ended up bringing a civil suit against Murphy because Murphy physically assaulted Rojas during the affair. In the course of the civil trial, Murphy was poisoned to death when he drank out of a can of cola containing cyanide.

After the civil proceeding against Murphy ended in a mistrial, Rojas and Baker separated. Rojas subsequently hired a private investigator, **Robert Sokolow**, to determine whether Baker was having an affair. Rojas also told Sokolow that Baker had confessed to her that he had poisoned Murphy. Rojas claimed she was afraid of Baker and wanted to tell the police what she knew about the attempt on Murphy's life. Sokolow referred Rojas to **Darrel Ramsey**, an attorney for whom Sokolow frequently worked, so that Ramsey could arrange for Rojas to meet with the police. After Ramsey secured immunity for Rojas, Rojas and Ramsey met with a police officer to tell him about Baker's alleged confession to the murder of Murphy.

Four days after meeting with the police officer, Rojas met Baker at a rural veterinary clinic in Nita City to have one of their horses put to sleep. During a walk with Baker in the woods behind the clinic, after they had said good-bye to their horse, Rojas admitted to Baker that she had gone to the police about his confession to the poisoning. Rojas explained that she had informed the police because she had been angry that Baker had cheated on her; she said she'd try to get the police not to pursue the matter any further. According to Rojas's testimony at trial, Baker became enraged and tried to grab Rojas's purse—which, according to Rojas, Baker knew contained a .38 handgun (which he had given her weeks before). Rojas testified that Baker said, "I'll shoot you, bitch," and reached for her purse. Rojas claimed that she successfully pulled her purse away and knocked Baker down to the ground after kicking him in the groin area. She further testified that she was able to pull the pistol out before Baker got up from the ground and lunged at her. As he lunged, she shot Baker six times—three shots in the head and three shots in the chest. Baker died immediately from the shooting.

After the shooting, Rojas proceeded back into the veterinary clinic and called private investigator Sokolow. Sokolow noted that Rojas sounded "amazingly calm" at that time. Following Sokolow's instructions, Rojas met Sokolow and attorney Ramsey at a nearby gas station. The three of them then returned to the scene of the crime, which had not yet been discovered by anyone (Baker's dead body still lay on the ground). By that time, which was over two hours after the shooting, it became clear that Rojas had taken an excessive amount of her prescription anxiety and sleeping medications. Rojas told Ramsey that she had taken the pills at the gas station shortly before Sokolow arrived. Ramsey told Sokolow to take Rojas to the hospital for a possible drug overdose. However, Ramsey went one step further. In an effort to have Rojas evade detection by the authorities, Ramsey instructed Sokolow to have Rojas admitted to the hospital under a false name.

After Rojas had been checked into the hospital under a false name, Ramsey notified the police that Baker was dead and that "an unnamed client" had informed him of the location of Baker's corpse. Ramsey did not disclose Rojas's identity or whereabouts. Rojas remaining at large allowed Ramsey to direct her actions to ensure himself ample compensation. The day after the shooting, Ramsey checked Rojas out of the hospital and drove her to her bank so she could withdraw $50,000 to cover Ramsey's retainer fee and expenses. Meanwhile, Ramsey took possession of key evidence in the case. Ramsey took Rojas's .38 caliber handgun and kept it at his law offices. Finally—only after Ramsey discovered that a warrant was out for Rojas's arrest for Baker's murder—Ramsey drove Rojas to the police station at 7:00 p.m. on the day after the shooting. With Ramsey present, Rojas gave police a brief voluntary statement in which she admitted that she had shot Baker but claimed self-defense (as recounted above). Her statement did not mention any events after the shooting other than the fact that "I then checked myself into the hospital." The following day Ramsey turned over the .38 pistol to the police.

Ramsey continued to advise Rojas after she turned herself in to the police and was arrested and charged with Baker's murder. He recommended to Rojas another attorney who should serve as her trial counsel. He persuaded her to hire board-certified criminal defense attorney **Barry Gonzalez**. Gonzalez charged Rojas a $100,000 fee to represent her at trial, which she paid in advance. Ramsey remained part of the defense team even after Gonzalez was brought into the case. Ramsey collected another $50,000 fee from Rojas, even though he did not sit at counsel table during her trial. Only Gonzalez sat at counsel's table and questioned witnesses for the defense during the trial. Gonzalez regularly conferred with Ramsey, who helped him prepare for trial. However, as Gonzalez later testified at the hearing on Rojas's new trial motion, Gonzalez—not Ramsey—was the "ultimate decision-maker" when it came to strategic or tactical decisions made prior to and during the trial.

Except for the fact that Rojas had checked into the hospital after the shooting, none of the foregoing facts regarding the events following the shooting were brought out during Rojas's direct examination by defense counsel Gonzalez. Ramsey was not called to testify about his role in directing Rojas's actions in the immediate aftermath of the shooting. However, the prosecutor brought out some of the events immediately following the shooting during the cross-examination of Rojas—i.e., her leaving the crime scene and her checking herself into the hospital under an alias, as well as the fact that she did not immediately call the police and report shooting Baker in self-defense (and only told the police of her version of the shooting after an arrest warrant had been issued the following day). The prosecutor, who was unaware that Ramsey had gone to the crime scene and had his investigator Sokolow check Rojas into the hospital under an alias, did not question Rojas about Ramsey's role in the two days after the shooting. The prosecutor's leading questions to her—"After the shooting, you left the vet clinic and checked yourself into the hospital under a false name?"—did not permit her to mention Ramsey. Defense counsel Gonzalez did not follow up with a redirect examination about Ramsey's involvement with Rojas immediately after the shooting.

In his closing arguments, the prosecutor used Rojas's leaving the crime scene and checking herself into the hospital under a false name to refute Rojas's self-defense claim. contending that her "flight from the crime scene" and her "use of an alias" showed "a consciousness of guilt." The prosecutor also focused on the fact that Rojas had not called the police immediately after the shooting and only gave her "self-defense story" after a warrant had been issued for her arrest the following day. The jury convicted Rojas of murder, and the trial court sentenced her to thirty years in prison.

After the guilty verdict, Rojas hired new defense counsel, who filed a motion for a new trial alleging ineffective assistance of counsel by Gonzalez and Ramsey, i.e., a conflict of interest. At no time before filing this motion had Rojas or either of her former lawyers complained about a conflict of interest to the trial court.

At a hearing on the motion, the foregoing facts were established. In addition, Gonzalez testified at the hearing. When asked why he did not call Ramsey as a defense witness at trial, Gonzalez testified:

> It would have opened up a can of worms by waiving the attorney-client privilege that existed between Mr. Ramsey and Ms. Rojas. Mr. Ramsey would have been subject to testifying that Ms. Rojas had the presence of mind to call Robert Sokolow from the vet clinic after the shooting and then stay around the area for a significant amount of time before going to the hospital. In addition, the prosecution then would have known about Mr. Sokolow's involvement. Mr. Sokolow, in turn, would have been subject to being called as a prosecution witness. He would have been put in the position of testifying that Ms. Rojas sounded "amazingly calm" within minutes of the shooting. Any prosecutor surely would have asked about her mental state immediately after the shooting. That would have undercut our theory of self-defense.

Gonzalez admitted that neither he nor Ramsey ever told Rojas that Ramsey had any type of conflict of interest regarding his representation of her.

Defense Counsel: Argue in support of your motion for a new trial.

Prosecutor: Argue against Rojas's motion for a new trial.

To prepare for this hypothetical exercise, read *Perillo v. Johnson*, 205 F.3d 775 (5th Cir. 2000); *United States v. Feyrer*, 333 F.3d 110 (2d Cir. 2003); and *Mickens v. Taylor*, 535 U.S. 162 (2002) (majority opinion only).